R00004 17231

D1239438

REF
PS
325
.P4

Peters, Robert
Louis, 1924-

The great American
poetry bake-off

DATE			

REF   FORM 125 M

LITERATURE & PHILOSOPHY DIVISION

The Chicago Public Library

Received_____   JUL 9 1980

© THE BAKER & TAYLOR CO.

Books by Robert Peters

Criticism

The Crowns of Apollo: Swinburne's Principles of Literature and Art (Wayne
State) 1965
Pioneers of Modern Poetry, with George Hitchcock (Kayak Press) 1967

Editions

The Letters of John Addington Symonds, with Herbert Schueller (Wayne State)
3 vols., 1967-69
Victorians on Literature and Art (Appleton-Century-Crofts) 1961
Gabriel: A Poem by John Addington Symonds (London: Michael de Harting-
ton) 1974
The Collected Poems of Amnesia Glasscock (John Steinbeck) (Manroot Books)
1977

Poetry

The Little Square Review #2: Fourteen Poems, 1967
Songs for a Son (Norton) 1967
The Sow's Head and Other Poems (Wayne State) 1968
Eighteen Poems, 1971, 1972, 1973
Byron Exhumed (Windless Orchard Press) 1973
Red Midnight Moon (Empty Elevator Shaft Press) 1973
Connections: In the English Lake District (London: Anvil Press) 1973
Holy Cow: Parable Poems (Red Hill Press) 1974
Cool Zebras of Light (Christopher's Books) 1974
Bronchial Tangle, Heart System (Granite Books Press) 1975
The Gift to Be Simple: A Garland for Ann Lee (Liveright) 1975
The Poet as Ice-Skater (Manroot Books) 1975
Gauguin's Chair: Selected Poems (Crossing Press) 1977
Hawthorne (Red Hill and Poet-Skin Presses) 1977
The Drowned Man to the Fish (New Rivers Press) 1978
Ikagnak: The North Wind: With Dr. Kane in the Arctic (Kenmore Press)
1978

the
great american
poetry
bake-off

by

robert peters

1979

the scarecrow press, inc.   metuchen, n.j., & london

ACKNOWLEDGMENTS

For permission to reprint, thanks to:

Viking Penguin Inc., for lines from Leonard Cohen's Energy of Slaves. Copyright © 1973.

Alfred A. Knopf, Inc., for excerpts from William Meredith's Hazard the Painter. Copyright © 1975.

Doubleday & Company, Inc., for random lines from "Early Illusion" which appear in Bratsk Station and Other New Poems by Yevgeny Yevtushenko. Copyright © 1966 by Sun Books Pty. Ltd.; for passim lines from "The Incendiary" translated by Stanley Kunitz, copyright © 1971 by Doubleday & Company, Inc. and "The Old House" translated by Geoffrey Dutton, published by Sun Book Pty. Ltd. in 1968 New Poems both are from Stolen Apples by Yevgeny Yevtushenko; for passim lines from "A Moment Half-Winter, Half-Fall" which appears in

Library of Congress Cataloging in Publication Data

Peters, Robert Louis, 1924-
   The great American poetry bake-off.

   Includes index.
   1. American poetry--20th century--History and criticism--Addresses, essays, lectures. I. Title.
PS325.P4   811'.5'09   79-16090
ISBN 0-8108-1231-2

Drawing on cover and section pages by
Meredith Peters

Copyright © 1979 by Robert Peters

Manufactured in the United States of America

From Desire to Desire by Yevgeny Yevtushenko. Copyright © 1976 by Doubleday & Company, Inc.; and for passim lines from "Cochise," "Sins of the Tongue," "Pulling Weeds," and "Sun Tea" which appear in Cochise by Peter Wild. Copyright © 1969, 1972, 1973 by Peter Wild.

Little, Brown and Company for lines from James Tate's Absences. Copyright © 1970 by James Tate.

Houghton Mifflin Company for lines from The Book of Nightmares by Galway Kinnell. Copyright © 1971 by Galway Kinnell.

City Lights for selections from Fast Speaking Woman by Anne Waldman. Copyright © 1975 by Anne Waldman; for selections from Hotel Nirvana: Selected Poems by Harold Norse. Copyright © 1974 by Harold Norse; and for selections from The Fall of America. Copyright © 1972 by Allen Ginsberg.

Celestial Arts for selections from Will I Think of You? by Leonard Nimoy. Copyright © 1974 by Celestial Arts, Millbrae, California.

New Directions for lines from Eagle or Sun? by Octavio Paz, translated by Eliot Weinberger. Copyright © 1976 by Octavio Paz and Eliot Weinberger.

Charles Scribner's Sons for lines from For Love by Robert Creeley. Copyright © 1962.

Atheneum for lines from poems in Writings to an Unfinished Accompaniment, by W. S. Merwin. Copyright © 1973 by W. S. Merwin.

W. H. Allen & Co. Ltd., for world rights to quote passim lines from Yevgeny Yevtushenko's Stolen Apples; copyright © 1972.

Hanging Loose Press for lines from Katy Akin's Impassioned Cows by Moonlight; copyright © 1974 by Katy Akin.

Cherry Valley Editions for lines from Roxie Powell's Dreams of Straw; copyright © 1974.

Momo's Press for lines from Stephen Vincent's Artie Bremer; © 1974.

The Crossing Press for lines from Howard McCord's Selected Poems; copyright © 1975.

Second Coming Press for lines from William Wantling's 7 on Style; copyright © 1975.

Black Sparrow Press for lines from Charles Bukowski's Burning in Water, Drowning in Flame, copyright © 1977; from Clayton Eshleman's Coils, copyright © 1973; from Diane Wakowski's Smudging, copyright © 1972.

Christopher's Books for lines from John Thomasson's White Hope White Saddhu White Trash; copyright © 1973.

New Rivers Press for lines from Victor Contoski's Broken Treaties; copyright © 1973.

Panjandrum Press for lines from Nanos Valaoritis' Diplomatic Relations: Followed by Birds of Hazard & Prey; copyright © 1972.

Red Hill Press for lines from Paul Vangelisti's Air; copyright © 1973.

Boa Editions for lines from W. D. Snodgrass' The Fuhrer Bunker: A Cycle of Poems in Progress; copyright © 1977.

Big Sky for extracts from Homage to Frank O'Hara; copyright © 1978.

Capra Press for lines from Lyn Sukenick's Houdini; copyright © 1973.

J. D. Reed for lines from his Fatback Odes; copyright © 1972 by Sumac Press.

Dustbooks for lines from William Wantling's The Source, copyright © 1966; from San Quentin's Stranger, copyright © 1976.

Arthur Gregor for lines from his The Past Now; copyright © 1975 by Arthur Gregor.

Michael McClure for lines from several of his books of poetry.

TABLE OF CONTENTS

PART THREE

For

Paul Trachtenberg

"Don't praise my book! Pascal had a nail-studded belt
he used to lean against every time he felt pleasure
at some word of praise. I should have a belt like that.
I ask you, be a friend; either do not write to me
about the book at all, or else write and tell me
everything that is wrong with it. ... Every author
is surrounded by an aura of adulation which he nurses
so assiduously that he cannot begin to judge
his own worth or see when it starts to decline. "

--Leo Tolstoy to the critic Strakhov

Preface:
THE CRITIC AS BIG BAD WOLF

For some readers criticism is a sexual act--the critic either rubs up against poets (virgin and seasoned ones) or ravishes them. Other readers regard such writing as among the least sexual of all cultivated postures--the arbiter of literary taste sponsors careers and moves into power with the abandon of a disinterested savage seated on a pile of freshly-cut scalps.

What I am saying is that any criticism, be it pure or outrageous, moves towards power, whether written by a poet or not. Prestigious critics have cannibalized some poets and canonized others in pursuit of what might be called disinterested truth. Shades of Matthew Arnold! Nearly all critics seem obsessed with their own cerebrations and convolutions. This kind of criticism I call masturbatory as distinct from congressional.

I introduce the term congressional in the sense that the truest critical act requires intense congress with a poet's work. To introduce a metaphor from one of the most original of all poet-critics, D. H. Lawrence, blood flows freely in the urgent channels of a critic's body-psyche, receiving a further excitement from the energy-blood flow of the poet whose work he treats. I agree with Lawrence's assumption that any critical act, privately obsessive or otherwise, is a blood-sexual act. Criticism as congress, therefore, celebrates energy, even where it damns, and particularly where it praises. Good criticism should keep readers awake. Good criticism should be humorous, outrageous, iconoclastic, alive. Good criticism should be insightful and seductive. It should expose the sham and the popular and direct attention to the neglected and the fine. I regard the critical pieces I've written as blood-congress, energy-induced, energy-informed, and energy-celebrating pieces.

Most criticism today, including that appearing in the little magazines, is chokingly entwined with the virginia

creepers of traditional critical prose. Academic moss flour-
ishes fulsomely in the overgrowth. Nevertheless_es vie with
therefore_s and perhaps_es for nest space. There is hardly a
critic who ungirds his (or her) loins and stands upon his or
her hill and delivers judgments fearlessly, as if he really en-
joyed them. Most critical pieces, including most regular
columns appearing in the literary periodicals, are flab.

II

If, as I suggest, the critical act is sexual, cannibalistic, and
parasitic (frustrated, unsuccessful poets and novelists have
made large reputations fastening themselves like mistletoe to
successful poets and novelists), why does a poet take time
from his creative life to write criticism? Is his sex life
either impoverished or so jaded he needs new kicks? Is the
urgency of his blood so strong that he must write in all forms
possible? Like Matthew Arnold, is his creative talent drying
up as he ages? If he exercises his critical muscles now,
perhaps he'll have something to fall back on as he waits for
the stiffening of that final mouth-syllable! THRUST: Poetry
is too important to leave in the hands of pure critics!

        Obviously, if you are a poet and care about your art
and its reception in the world, you'll wish to use whatever
power you possess to oppose and demolish fashion, ignorance,
mutual-perpetrations, etc., as you see certain good but dull
talents pushed to fame, while superior talents languish ig-
nored. I am not sufficiently passive to believe that meritori-
ous work will eventually have its day. I wish it were true!
The woods are full of imitation Red Riding Hoods and Little
Pigs masquerading as poets.

III

My own career as a poet has been and remains dissociated
from any coterie or group. I began writing poetry late (at
age thirty-nine) after a career as a critic of Victorian liter-
ature, as an editor of scholarly editions of letters and jour-
nals, as author of a book on Swinburne's criticism, as a
trustee for the American Society for Aesthetics, and as an
assistant editor for the Journal of Aesthetics and Art Criti-
cism and Criticism. I am currently an associate editor for
the new The American Book Review. I began to write poetry,
jolted into it by the unexpected death of a 4 1/2 year old son.
I wrote without the aid of writing programs, or of friendships

with established poets. I was lucky that my first book was
accepted and eventually published by W. W. Norton, Inc.
As I say, I had no connections, letters of introduction, etc.
And I am grateful. I sincerely hope that my critical efforts
may help other free talents find publishers.

IV

In travelling about the country giving readings and talking
with writers and editors, I sense that the atmosphere for
publishing grows less free all the time. Atheneum restricts
itself to poets who have passed through Iowa. Braziller pub-
lishes few poets. Random House relegates poetry, I am in-
formed, to the newest of its minor editors. My own pub-
lisher told me to "go away and get famous; then come back
and talk to us"--when they promised a contract they reneged
on it. Farrar Straus goes for protégés of Robert Lowell
and products of the eastern establishment. Black Sparrow
limits itself almost entirely to writers with Black Mountain
or New York connections. This drift I've elsewhere called
Poetry-Biz.

V

And I don't think I'm paranoid. If one scrutinizes the history
of American poetry, one finds no time free of coteries. The
unknown poet without connections has always had it rough. If
this is true, that the climate for unknown talent has never
been sufficiently free, there's even more reason for voices,
like Jonathan Williams' and Robert Bly's, to shout their op-
position to the powers, thrones, and dominations commanding
poetry now. We need as free an atmosphere as possible.
One way to help, obviously, is for poets themselves to write
more criticism, eschewing if possible the careers of their
friends.

VI

This country has had a mania for celebrities ever since we
lost King George III. When Robert Frost died (he had be-
come a celebrity), Time-Life Inc. scrambled to find a suc-
cessor. Shortly, Robert Lowell's picture appeared on Time,
and the celebrity-makers had conferred the ermine-touched
tippet, and could breathe easily again. Since Lowell's death
there's been no front-cover poet. I suppose James Dickey

is up for it. Yet Dickey, one of the liveliest ruthless poet-critics we've had since D. H. Lawrence, seems to me to have never quite adjusted to the celebrity role--despite the movie, the novel, the poems for Life, and some of the nasty things he's said about people. He's a sort of anti-celebrity, if that makes sense. Ginsberg, on the other hand, began as an anti-celebrity, a funky enfant terrible, eventually becoming a darling of the TV talk shows and an establishment figure, loved as America's good gay poet, a jot over to the left of Walt Whitman. But there's still a lot to love about Ginsberg, and persons who don't read poetry, or any books, for that matter, flock to his readings. The celebrity syndrome!

I dwell on this because, obviously, it bothers me. I don't see that hype has much to do with real poetry; and the poet who gets caught up in it runs terrible risks. Ginsberg's work has been damaged by his public obligations, I think--and I try to explain how in my essay on his The Fall of America. Lowell, up to the time of his death, was writing up his present life hot from the frying pan as memories, in tour de force revelation volumes of the sort his panting public expects. Gary Snyder, another cult figure, has, so far as I can tell, almost stopped writing fresh poetry. Anne Waldman and Gerard Malanga slink and swirl along the celebrity ramp. James Tate floats off into narcissistic moonscapes on the wings of too much early, florid praise. W. S. Merwin blatantly repeats himself. Charles Bukowski so much loves his role of celebrity as a gross, dirty old man he's taken to flinging spit, ordure, used condoms, and mugs of beer in the public's face--and his poems are becoming imitations of an exciting earlier self. Few poets seem to stay home and do their work--Clayton Eshleman, Robert Duncan, and Diane Wakoski are among the few.

I simplify. Poets with immense early successes frequently do write themselves out in middle-age, and possibly for reasons other than their renown. No attention at all might have similar effects on the poetic psyche. My quarrel is not so much with poets as it is with the public who, enamored and busy licking away, fail to realize that most poets have melting points like that of an Eskimo Bar in the tropics.

VII

If my critical method has a drift, it is towards the informal

and the funky. And no matter how bravura, lovely, and spec-
tacular my essays may appear, I am trying to say a few
things--not simply do cartwheels to amaze my friends.

My models are A. C. Swinburne, D. H. Lawrence,
and Kenneth Rexroth. Swinburne was one of the most icono-
clastic, original, and most readable critics of his day. And
a voluminous critic. He derived his manner and method
largely from Thomas Carlyle, that fearless dyspeptic of
Cheyne Walk, London, who set generations on their ears with
Sartor Resartus and The French Revolution. Nearer our own
time, James Joyce paid Carlyle the ultimate compliment: he
carried Sartor around in his pocket and wrote an imitation
of Carlyle's style in Ulysses. Swinburne also called Carlyle
"the Caledonian coprophile," yet honored him by modelling
his own prose techniques after his. Lawrence, I feel, also
knew his Carlyle well. Few critics are more readable than
Swinburne and Lawrence. The latter's Studies in Classical
American Literature is, of course, for its life and perspi-
cacity, unparalleled in modern criticism. Kenneth Rexroth
in a trenchant few pages can say more about writers and
works than less-gifted critics say in fifty pages of com-
mentary.

VIII

I have tried to reflect my models in my essays. In general,
I have isolated a theme or themes generally overlooked or
misinterpreted in criticisms of the poets I've looked at, and
have sought to explain as fully as possible what some of
their strengths and/or weaknesses are. I have tried for
congress with their works.

Not that all readers will be happy with my conclusions.
I hope not! I want to unsettle poetry-readers, to barb them
into perception. Some readers will run away, denouncing (or
worse) what they find. So be it! The iconoclastic critic is
dead if he strikes no opposition. As D. H. Lawrence said:
"Damn the consequences, we have met." We shall, hope-
fully, have congress.

VERBAL MUSCULATURE AND CONCEALED KINETICS

IN THE EARLY POETRY OF WALT WHITMAN:

A Study in Projective or Open Field Composition*

Critical opinion has tended to link the early American poet Walt Whitman with what has come to be called modern Projective or Open Field verse. While we may agree with Sculley Bradley that readers are not "greatly puzzled" by Whitman's rhythmic line, since they are accustomed today "to a whole new poetry in which the logical rhythm is more important than the strict distribution of syllables in the older conventional feet, " we may nevertheless feel somewhat uncomfortable over our inability to delimit precise technical relationships between Whitman's lines and those in the work of such modern poets as William Carlos Williams, Robert Duncan, Robert Creeley and Denise Levertov, to name only a few. This paper is an attempt to correct this situation by reconstructing certain portions of Whitman's "Song of Myself" (July 4, 1855) along modern principles of breath-structure; I shall hope to supply, in other words, some of the daring that Whitman himself lacked in arranging his lines on the printed page. We can, of course, merely conjecture and speculate as to the degree to which "the good grey poet of Camden" might have hastened American poetry along had he, as early as 1893, say, stimulated the appearance of a William Carlos Williams.

I shall begin with my version of the opening section of "Song of Myself" and shall emphasize what Robert Duncan has brilliantly and lucidly termed "the complex of muscular gains that are included in taking hold and balancing, verbs, but more, the movement of the language, the level of the ear, the hand, and the foot. " Here, then, is the version:

*Reprinted by permission from Kayak, Vol. 8 (1966) pp. 58-63; Copyright © 1966 by Kayak Books.

        I celebrate
                myself
        and what I
                assume
        you shall
                assume

        for:

        every atom
        belonging
                to me
        as good
        belongs
                to you.

        I loaf
        and invite
        my soul.

        I lean
        and loaf
        at my ease

        observing
        a spear of
        summer grass.

It is tempting, following the example of Jack Kerouac's "Mexico City Blues: 183d Chorus," ll. 17-18, to break the first line into even simpler elements for the sake of increased emphasis:

                I
            cele-
                brate
            myself.

On second thought, however, it seems that Whitman, man of fairly simple tastes in things mundane, would have preferred the less baroque unhyphenated arrangement. Whitman would undoubtedly have sympathized with the observation of Kenneth Rexroth that "ornamentation is confabulation in the interstices of the structure." And there is a sufficient suspense, I feel, in the unbroken version as it stands. The reader finds himself on the brink of wonder: "What does the I celebrate?" As his gaze falls to the right he discovers that

it is myself (a neat reinforcement of the I theme and pleas-
ing formlette composed of egoword-verb-egoword). This
triad of words (I, myself, I) reveals the basic structural unit
of the rearranged poem: all parts occur either in threes or
in units divisible by three.

The first unit consists of six lines, three of which
are formed by single end words myself, assume, assume.
Readers of modern poetry will of course welcome the stun-
ning numbness (to borrow a term Yeats favored) of the re-
peated assume, an effect entirely lost in the conventionally
printed poem. These three end words have a force similar
to that of end rhymes in conventional poems; the modern ones
are superior, the reader will certainly agree, particularly
since their numbness reflects today's existential world and
demonstrates a laudably tight rapport of theme and form.
There is also the additional beauty of the relaxed vowel
sound (myself) vs. the tight vowel sound of assume. This
first unit also contains a subtle counterpoint of person: I,
I, you, located like specially variegated bricks throughout
the firm structure of the entire unit. The placing of I at the
beginning of one line and at the close of another--a happy
stroke--may suggest the ominous placing of some monster's
feet, a brilliant contrast with the serenity of the last stanzas.
Certainly, the I's have a distinctive heaviness which suggests
at the very least the straddling of worlds, or of centuries:
a monster stands with one foot in the nineteenth century, the
other in the twenty-first. The cumulative effect here is not
unlike that in Marvell's well-known poem of the chariot and
the threatened lovers.

For, obviously placed in a transitional position (I have
supplied the colon), alone, acquires a considerable strength
and suggests that matters of great moment are about to be
revealed. Also, after the complex involvement he has ex-
perienced so far, the reader has a respite for catching his
breath. The poet, we might observe, is in little danger of
losing his reader here, saved as he is by the r of for, a
floating sound, or a gently soaring one, hinting also at things
to come (the completion of the verse sentence, for one thing).
Atom, released now from hiding, is allowed to take its place
in a vital new structure; the image both receives and lends
strength from to me, a phrase which sounds vaguely like
atom spelled backwards. To me and to you, serving as mod-
ern end-words, are superbly dulled and simple enough to
avoid offending the most careless reader. Their precise
vowel music provides exactly the appropriate support for the

powerful cosmological themes of the poem: self and soul,
the universe as a spear of grass, the mutual ownership of
flesh-atoms.   Not to be overlooked is the subtle use of be-
longs, a truncated but clear variation of belonging.

   The third triad of lines is a relief from the intensity
of the poet's metaphysical revelation.   Nothing could be more
effortlessly stated (and arranged around the interwoven long
i and o sounds); a whole universe of summer relaxation tan-
talizes the preoccupied reader.   While there is nothing overt-
ly mystical here, in the sense that St. Theresa of Avilon,
the seventeenth-century metaphysical poets, or Allen Gins-
berg are mystical, the reader who cares to reflect has the
break between the stanzas for his uses.   The poet would not
be averse to his readers acquiring transcendental experiences
through his work.

   The repetition of the loafing theme in stanza four may
seem gratuitous; but I don't think it is.   The repetition is
important since it firms up the contemplative mood, the ease
and film of reverie characteristic of most of the fifty-two sec-
tions of Whitman's poem.   Also, there are some subtle addi-
tions in this stanza: the new triad of lines is framed by the
long e sound, a fine musical complement to the i and o
sounds of the preceding stanza.   Further, the new lines run
over into the final stanza, itself a superbly wrought variation
on r sounds.   The first two lines of stanza five contain their
own frame: ob completed by of, a rather hare-lipped pair,
to be sure, but nevertheless sound.

   I shall briefly treat two other portions of "Song of
Myself" to reinforce my argument.   The reader will note
that in these added passages Charles Olson's requirement
that the Projective poem must "at all points, be a high en-
ergy-construct and, at all points, an energy-discharge" and
that it must transfer this energy "from where the poet got
it ... to, all the way over to, the reader" is not diminished
but is, rather, greatly heightened.   The first passage, from
section 15, is a Creeleyesque neo-imagist poem complete in
itself, formed around vigorously arranged explosive sounds
culminating in a delicate long-vowelled anapest.   The skep-
tical reader who may feel that the line takes on the effect of
a drill used by students learning to typewrite will come to
see, I think, that the spacing of the passage militates
against the regularized rhythm essential for such unpoetic
activities:

The crew
        of the
                fish-smack
pack
        repeated
layers of
        halibut
in the hold.

The second (section 40) reveals Whitman up to his
eroticism.   If such passages were not so ubiquitous in "Song
of Myself" I would not include any examples in this study.
My aim is not to offend readers whose tastes do not turn
easily to cottonfields and privies, but to release the "energy-
discharge" present, so that it will leap "all the way over to,
the reader. " For the sake of contrast and emphasis I have
assigned roman numerals to the sub-sections:

I

To a drudge
        of the cottonfields
or
        emptier
                of privies
I lean.
                On his right cheek
I put
                the family kiss,
And
        in my own soul
I swear
I will never
        deny him.

II

On women
        fit for conception
I start
        bigger
                and nimbler
        babes,

This day
        I am jetting

```
                              the stuff
                          of
                      far  more
                         arro-
                            gant
                               republics.
```

     I might note briefly the unit formed by the r̄ sounds
of the first six lines, the richly circuitous syllabic͞ music of
e͟m͟p͟t͟i͟e͟r and p͟r͟i͟v͟i͟e͟s, the stark end positions of elemental k͟i͟s͟s͞
a͟n͟d͟ s͟o͟u͟l, the m͞arvellous ambiguity of c͟h͟e͟e͟k, and the bala͞nce
achi͞eved by the relegation of the narciss͞istic I͟ to the left
hand of the stanza--this latter positioning allo͞ws for a meta-
phoric "jetting" of force from one side of the stanza to the
other.

     This modest study demonstrates, I hope, that the step
from Whitman to Williams and Zukovsky, to Creeley, Dun-
can and Levertov is not quite so vast and unbridgeable as it
hitherto seemed. What we require now is an edition of
Whitman, particularly of the more seminal poems, rewritten
according to modern standards of euphony, open-field compo-
sition, and breath-structure. Ideally it should be printed by
a large trade publisher and distributed as widely as possible,
probably even by supermarkets.

FUNKY POETRY:

Allen Ginsberg's The Fall of America*

I

Funky poetry is my invention for a genre of poem best
executed by Allen Ginsberg. Poetry in Salvation Army
clothes hung with rusted medals and pendants culled from the
trash heaps of America and from the headshops of eastern
mysticism. Poetry in Whitman's easiest colloquial, cata-
loguing, suspiring manner, of the Whitman clad in frayed
and soiled Big Mac overalls just in from the barn of the uni-
verse, that Vedantaesque-pseudoBlakean-Keroucian stables.
The poet is to locate nuggets in the animal-magical ordure
of this life--these states.

Yes, a tatty form, a diarrhea (frequently) of phrases
and projective verse breathgroup clusters, a telegraphic mode
intended to speed (no pun intended) the reader along towards
enlightenment, and at its best a Garysnyderesque sufi-zenism
scaling the nearest ponderosa pine tree towards nirvana,
drunk on manzanitaberry tea and the memory of friends'
anuses.

In the most recent issue of the Camels Coming News-
letter (3) Ginsberg produces this cover-page definition of lit-
erary pollution:

> What's literary pollution? Immediate association,
> first thought, is plethora of books mimeo mags
> papers arriving in mail & more in bookstores,
> wherein's reprinted every body & soul's amateur
> celestial ravings & scribblings. More than eye can
> read. Over-load of poetic information. A million

*Reprinted by permission from NEW, No. 22-23 (1973-74)
pp. 68-75; Copyright © 1974 by John Gill.

9

authors can't be read, even by most well-meaning
scholar. Space age proliferation of written paper
& conspicuous consumption of raw language. Tow-
ers of Babel! So I shut up and meditate an hour
a day, silence.

An hour a day suffices for meditation! That leaves
23 hours for verse! There is no more prolific poet (male)
in the nation, yeah, perhaps in the world than Allen Gins-
berg! And it is his glory and his pain that he seems to pub-
lish the faintest of his tape-recorded eructations along with
his powerful, energetic poem-statements-feelings. His pres-
ence on the American (world) literary scene as liberating
poet-figure--great baggy-kneed, balding courage-poet who re-
directed poetry in the 1950's and served to direct, as every-
body knows, the way of living today (via rock and dope) known
as the counter-culture, all this has been sufficiently noted.
He is so popular that people who never open a book flock to
his readings--a true culture love-hero.

So, understandably, whatever he chooses to see in
print is automatically of some interest, simply because of
his position as King not only of May but of every month.
His poems fly into the world like hailstones--or perhaps they
drift like feathers and leaves to the mouths of caves.

What interests me (as a poet whose own poetry has
been influenced by Ginsberg) is what works in Ginsberg's art
and what doesn't seem to. I can't obviously say everything
in the space of this essay about his poetry; I merely want to
describe one quality, Funk, that I discern in his work. My
grapes are sweet, and my nectarines, I hope, will fall mer-
rily to the ground as loving and sharing. I shall focus on
his production The Fall Of America: Poems of These States
1965-1975.

I assume that Funk damages Ginsberg's poetry and at
its worst is literary pollution of the very sort he decries in
Camels Coming. When the mode succeeds, however, there
is a fusty humorous quality, one at times charged with en-
ergy and a melancholy poignancy. The elegiac tone seems
to work for him quite well then.

I realize that when I complain at all of Allen Gins-
berg's poetry I trample on the skirts of motherhood, apple-
pie, and the flag, not to mention Whitman, W. C. Williams,
various Indian gurus, Blake, Gary Snyder, Bob Dylan, and
perhaps Robert Creeley. I mean to be helpful, I think.

II

In The Fall of America telegraphically presented in-
formation is boringly prolix.   Yes, I admit it is crucial if
one hopes to achieve a journalistic sense of a journey across,
around, through and over "these States" to drop the names of
places you traverse.   But after the fifteenth poem mentioning
sites like Oroville, Nespelem, Dry Falls, Lincoln Airforce
Base, Riverside, Ruby, US 80 near Big Blue River, etc., one
begins to feel the juices of triple A strip maps in his veins.
There have to be little Refreshment Gasoline Spirit and Blad-
der-Relief Stations along the way.

Authenticity.   Yes.   That's needed.   A sense of the
literal helps to locate one's peregrinations (or meanderings)
towards transcendental consciousness.   What makes this de-
vice funky is that the peregrinations seldom go anywhere far,
or far out.   They remain dull places on the map.   True,
sometimes there are cows, roadsigns, goats pissing, name-
less persons, colors, and towns.   And sometimes there is
a poetry compressed, visually provocative, and symbolically
alive--viz.

> At Dry Falls 40 Niagaras stand silent & invisible,
> tiny horses graze on the rusty canyon's mesquite
> floor.

I like that.   This next passage, though, I don't like: its at-
tempt to elevate the commonplace is strained.   And the final
disporting of the final line as three staggered phrases mov-
ing across the sky is sleazy.   The cannon image is forced:

> Moss Landing Power Plant
>   shooting its cannon smoke
>   across the highway.   Red taillight
>   speeding the white line & a mile
>   away
>   Orion's muzzle
>   raised up
>   to the center of Heaven.

The example, ecologically relevant, is essentially
static, tacky, and telegraphic.   We've been there so many
times before.   Seldom in these new poems does Ginsberg
transmute the funky, smog-ridden, garbage-strewn, junked
landscape of the present into the anger of Howl and Kaddish
and some of Planet News.

Also, at its worst, Ginsberg's Western Unionman style is monotonous in the extreme. Slabs (globs) of phrase-subjects parallel each other without much syllabic variation. See "Continuation of a Long Poem of these States" and "Reflection in Sleepy Eye, " dedicated to Robert Bly, with its "much land, new folk. " When the method works, Ginsberg allows time for developing an object in its landscape:

> At the end of a long chain, Billy makes
> a circle in grass
> by the fence, I approach
> he stands still with long red stick
> stretched throbbing between hind
> legs
> Spurts water a minute, turns his
> head down
> to look & lick his thin pee
> squirt--
> That's why he smells goat like.

Ginsberg's culture-figures are for the most part funky people, or heroes of counter-culture movements: Bob Dylan, Timothy Leary, Buffy St. Marie, Barry McGuire, The Rolling Stones, Jack Ruby (this one puzzles me). And these figures he treats with a too-frequent sentimentality. One of the funkiest passages of pure funk is this one where the association of the fieldgrass called timothy leads (You've guessed it!) to Timothy Leary and a bleeding-heartfelt piece of emotion:

> Timothy turned brown, covered with
> new spread manure
> sweet smelt in strong breeze,
> it'll be covered in snow couple
> months.
> & Leary covered in snow in San Luis
> Obispo jail?

On the other hand, this device works in "Memory Gardens, " in a passage relating Kerouac's burial. The passage is a fine use of the funky telegram style:

> ...Jack drank
> rot gut & made haikus of birds
> tweetling on his porch rail at dawn--
> Fell down and saw Death's golden lite
> in Florida garden a decade ago.
> Now taken utterly, soul upward,

> & body down in wood coffin
> & concrete slab-box.
> I threw a kissed handful of damp earth
> down on the stone lid
> & sighed....

A comment on another device central to funky poetry:
the numerous elisions where articles are omitted ("in Florida
garden a decade ago"; "bending his knuckle to Cinema ma-
chine").   There is a useful analogy here between mothholes
in the fabric of your Salvation Army cast-offs and the fabric
of your verse.   Tattered Whitman too, perhaps.   Each miss-
ing article is a moth-hole, each dangling phrase another
spray of claybeads or South American ritual seedpod attached
to your sleeve.

Language at times takes the form of Zap Comix lan-
guage, tatty--as the English say, transparently untutored, un-
conventionally lettered, hokey:

> Kesey's in Oregon writing novel language
> family farm alone

The first line above tosses out its key words creating
a little Kesey world where the speaker maintains his breath
and provides latchpoints in an otherwise miasmatic fog-con-
sciousness.   Here we don't need the connectives: "Man, it's
like, well, you know, man, outasight, it's like words ain't
that needed, like, just get what needs said laid out, each
word a slap of paste slapp'd down with a trowel.   Know what
I mean?"   This kind of writing, I suggest, is speed-writing,
an equivalent for speed-reading.   Perhaps most of these
poems should be read down the middle of the page.

Too frequently Ginsberg can't allow an easy idea to
drift off after a breath or two; the motif becomes a series
of funky gulps, predictable, commonplace.   Here he is in
Riverside ruminating on an automobile graveyard.   "Palm-
trees on valleyfloor/stick up toothpick hairheads. "   This
metaphor points up the inadequacy of words to compete with
paintings.   Ginsberg's metaphor is a schoolgirl's attempt at
haiku.   I know he is capable of better; to opt for the easy
effect is in itself a camp act.   Note how hanging becomes
the latch for the superficial matter to follow:

> Toy automobiles piled crushed and
> mangled

                    topped by a hanging crane,
            The planet hanging,
                    the air hanging,
                        Trees hang their branches,
            A dirt truck hanging on the
                                highway--

"Hanging crane" is interesting; it's the crane that
hangs the crushed automobiles. An immense leap to "planet
hanging," then down to the pallid "air hanging," losing the
sense of the death-doom and pathos of the car image (this
followed the news of Ginsberg's uncle's death); then to a
Robertlouistevensonian "trees hang their branches." The
"dirt truck" eludes me. Is the truck "hanging" around wait-
ing to haul dirt? Is it hanging in the sense that it is sus-
pended? The motif becomes irresponsibly conglomerated: a
hanging-word stew boiled up in a Maxwell House coffeecan
over a vagrant's open fire. Yeah! Walt's open road! Let's
free-associate, much as the undisciplined mind, or the mind
rejecting logic and reason associates, cultivating the obvious
hoping that in the refuse (garbage) filling the corner where
we lie, the ecstatic moment may seize us and enable us to
soar aloft amidst the Blakean cockspaces of the transcenden-
tal universe, the Neo-K(C)untian Nirvana-Consciousness.

G-d knows, I'm not one to demand that poems be well-
scrubbed or sanitized! I like poems that are gross, wild,
expectorative, glandular, spuming. I insist however that the
writer's mind interest me and engage me; let him sort
through his dirty laundry on his own. Yes, what should ap-
pear in our poems, I'm saying, is the fraction (small) of the
iceberg above the water; the rest of it, its bulk, beneath,
represents the commonplace, the trite, the adventitious we
deal with as we move towards insight. To present it all
bare-assed is a campy prostitution of the long-poem as a
form. To imply epic dimensions, as The Fall Of America
does, assumes the writer's responsibility for freshness, in-
ventiveness, originality. There is mica in the rock; but
there is not enough mica; or to wrench the image, the jock-
strap is tattered, useful only to voyeurs.

                              III

After Gary Snyder, Ginsberg better than any other
American poet (Whalen fits in here too) has earned his brown-
ie points and badges for the sincerity of his quest after truth.

His peregrinations throughout South America and the Far
East have been well-documented, as have his prostrations be-
fore the seats of various gurus and visionaries dead and alive.
One has the impression from The Fall Of America of a vast
mellowing out.   The overwhelming Hebraic-Jeremiah tones
so searing in Howl and Kaddish have devolved into:

> Louder wind! there'll be electric to play the
> Beatles!
>
> O wind! spin the generator wheel, make
> Power Juice
> To run the New Exquisite Noise Recorder, &
> I'll sing
> praise of your tree music.
>
> Sir Spirit, an' I drift alone:
> O deep sign.
>
> Cigarettes burned my tastebuds' youth,
> I smelled my lover's behind.

In fairness, I should say that shreds of the old anger
occurs in some of the poems about Viet Nam, once he moves
away from sentimental Dos Passos-type camera eye passages.
"Returning North of Vortex" and "War Profit Litany" are good
examples.

Yes, what finally fails is Ginsberg's power to trans-
form the wisdom of the east into any fresh vision for the
west.   Perhaps I expect too much; since, in general, gurus
depend for their success on pointing towards grand abstrac-
tions without very specific definitions attendant; hypnotic fire
in the eyes, a sense of presence imagined as trembling in
the trees within a mile or so of the guru's cell, these do not
invite precise definition, and, like signs along the road, can
merely be read and felt.   My own experience with these
quests has not been entirely negligible; in other words, I am
not simplifying for the purpose of denying value to Ginsberg's
quests.   I do respect them.   I say, though, that his handling
of the meditational-chant moment in The Fall Of America in-
vites the funky responses of the dope-religion freak who is
essentially mindless and inexact about his faith, and who ig-
nores the role of intense discipline as the only means to-
wards any worthwhile faith.   And if such people don't buy
and read books, those of us who do expect more than an
adolescent religiosity.

Here are some examples. This first one is campy-
humorous and is in its way refreshing. Ginsberg is lying in
the grass on Independence day:

> Independence Day! the Cow's deep moo's
> an Aum!

In "Guru Om" he presents his own discomfort over
"boys and girls in jail for their bodies poems and bitter
thoughts." He interlards Oms and Gurus throughout. "Guru
Guru Guru Guru Guru Guru Guru Citaram Omkar Das Thakur
...." His own physical discomfort contrasts with a meta-
physical discomfort he experiences as Guru and as a receiver
of Guru wisdom: "Guru is equal to the Om of the Seeker."
There are references to Dehorahava Baba and Nityananda and
Babaji and Blake. To the initiated these all would probably
mean something; but little makes their relevance clear. Per-
haps the names are meant to be Cabbalistic ... say the name
and some talismanic power ensues. I will grant that pos-
sibility, especially because of Ginsberg's fondness through-
out all of his work for the prophetic voice. The moment of
metaphysical surrender almost works; but the fact that it re-
mains statement finally intrudes, making it difficult for the
reader to share Ginsberg's illumination.

In its third part, the poem moves into a campy al-
most hysterical collage, incorporating allusions to Leary,
Errol Flynn, the stock exchange, Hilton hotel faucets, gaso-
line fumes smothering trees in Ganeshpuri. The world of
rubber, glass, neon, and aluminum have cheapened Maya,
Samsara, and Illusion. Thoughts of his mother move Gins-
berg again to his own body where "all beings" are "at war."

In general, though, mysticism flickers through Gins-
berg's mind as of little more consequence than the funky
trappings of the day's news flashed over the radio, scenes
out the window of his volkswagen, memories of persons, etc.
There is rarely any illumination, or vision; Hindu motifs are
patchouli moments, part of the aromatic trappings of a coun-
ter-culture way of life in which the Urantia is displayed and
not read, in which Hesse's novels are carried around unread,
in which thonged medallions are hung with bells around necks
and waists, in which ubiquitous canines of no certainly de-
finable breed romp freely among the smog-infested trees,
and in which almost every devotee can maintain with ease
the lotus position for an hour, particularly after a few tokes.

IV

I hunger in The Fall of America for more. The ele-
gies on Neal Cassady are the best parts of the book. And
"Please Master" is a brilliant incantatory homosexual poem
uniquely moving. Technically, I find "Bixby Canyon Ocean
Path Word Breeze" the most consistently fine in its use of
funky techniques. This is a funky poem that transcends its
methods. It is beautifully imaged (the butterfly, lupine field,
morning glory, etc.), tender in its celebration of a benign
nature, clean in its formed short line, quietly passionate.
It closes with one of the happiest of Ginsberg's inspirations
from Walt Whitman: the image of the sea, "grandmother,"
provides a close. Also, in the earlier "Bixby Canyon" the
lines improvising on a memory of Cassady's body as a sea
plant, is poetry of a high order.

In conclusion I wish to stress that funky poetry suits
only one aspect of Ginsberg's work. I see excesses in the
mode--as I have explained; and, since Ginsberg is our most
accomplished practitioner of this kind of poetry, it is im-
portant to define the genre. My attempt has been towards
a definition rather than a complete definition. Despite Gins-
berg's disclaimer of literary pollution, I sincerely hope that
he continues to write and to publish. He is capable of tre-
mendous power and beauty; selfishly, I do not want to see
him settle for less than his best.

FEMINISMO:

Diane Wakoski's Smudging*

Diane Wakoski's province is utterly female, frequently
self-parading, and full of little bushes quivering with cunts
craving cocks. Wakoski is the Boadicea of modern poetry.
Her country behaves according to her rules and obsessions.
By comparing her to that legendary British queen I am not
hinting that she should experience Boadicea's fate: weren't
the queen's limbs tied separately to different horses and then
the horses beaten so that they ran madly off in all directions?

What I'm saying is that Wakoski is a marvellously im-
perious poet! To use another analogy, she presides over the
distaff side of contemporary poetry like the Queen of Swords,
smiling, yes, and with charm and, I hope she'll forgive the
crudity, balls.

To be less cumbersome: Wakoski's energy is terrific,
and her personality, as it emerges from the poems, is unique,
despite the sometimes vast and frequently annoying indul-
gences that mar the poetry. Wakoski understands well the
correlation between being a character and finding readers for
her work; and it is because her achievement and her talent
are so vast that I am writing these things about her new
book.

An irritation I felt much less slightly in her earlier
work here erupts for me. I'll invent a word to explain the
cause: feminismo. In "Ladies, Listen to Me," a poem with
a Carrie Nationesque title, Wakoski tells "ladies" how to be-
have, to cultivate and employ their feminismo with a ven-
geance: she begins the poem by splitting herself apart in a
sort of Ovidian (Ovarian?) way: she "snaked up" on herself

*Reprinted by permission from NEW, No. 20 (Jan. 1973) pp.
50-57; Copyright © 1973 by John Gill.

18

(which is actually an atrocious pun; these things do sneak up
in Wakoski's poems) and saw herself as a cottonmouth snake
(ho, shades of D. H. Lawrence, that feminine sensibility
obsessed with his own maleness and the maleness in the world
around him) looking at a woman--herself. Right, folks, we
must be in the Garden of Eden and Diane-Eve invents her
own snake in order to achieve self-awareness as a woman
bent on finding the knowledge to lord it over man, that loathed
but essential creature.

Then appears another of her myths about herself: her
plain ugly-duckling appearance. In a poem memorable for
these two lines: "... I have the spirit of Gertrude Stein /
but the personality of Alice B. Toklas, " Wakoski concludes
by confessing her inadequacy at not having "very much to
say. " Poets are supposed to be brilliant and scintillating.
She feels just the opposite. She's "usually taken for / some-
body's / secretary. " Far out, Diane! In "Ladies, Listen to
Me, " she moves into an apparently self-deprecating ugly-
duckling theme: Just see me, people: "a plain ordinary wom-
an" who wears glasses, lets her hair grow long "to change
the shape of her face, " is neither fat nor thin, is equally
shy and aggressive, "self-righteous and self-effacing. "

This theme appears in various places in this book, and
in other poems in other books. "Nobody Loves Me, not even
the Voles, Hyraxes, or Elephants" is a particularly memor-
able handling of the theme. In general, though, after being
an inveterate Wakoski fan for some years, I am beginning to
feel like the good Gestaltist who knows that a person who
continually sends out the same self-message (no matter how
true or self-deprecating) is, in fact, inviting, nay, demand-
ing that the world provide statements the exact opposite of
those he makes about himself. In other words, if his lament
is "I don't love myself, " the world is to respond, "We love
you; you're beautiful. " There is a point where self-objectivity
breaks down and narcissism rears its head. If a poet con-
tinually stares into the orchid (or pitcher plant) of the self,
he (or she) risks alienating his readers. And, what poet
doesn't feel like an ugly duckling? Isn't that why poetry, in
the first place?

In "Ladies, Listen to Me, " Wakoski explains that her
secret--and she hasn't yet made clear exactly what it is--is
a secret "only a few men have / and all women, if they were
not soft and spoiled and foolish / could have. " Eve's wisdom

has to do with prisons and "iron gates against the body" which
turn body, "or its counterpart / the mind" into "a coiling
spring. " I'm not sure the image is good: it seems to as-
semble too much around it.   One is reminded first of a
coiled-spring bed, automobile, teeter-babe.   Next, because
of the cottonmouth image, a snake readies to spring on its
victim.   Finally, one thinks of Robert Frost's springs being
cleared up or returning to their sources.   Wakoski says,
though, that this spring is "no source of water then, / but
the crystal container, / the cup which holds / everything. "
I am confused, unless this is a new kind of image which be-
gins simply for gluing other objects to it, a piece of assem-
blage art.   Try gluing a "crystal container" to a spring
(metal? water?).   The passage needs revision, and, to con-
tinue the Frostian motif, unmuddying.

Wakoski delights in her "tough" image: Diane, not of
the moon, but of motorcycles, symbolic Leather Jacket
Queen.   She partially rejects the image here, but she also
relishes it: poets these days can hardly be successful with-
out cultivating an eccentricity or two of personal manner or
dress.   Wakoski's self-image is of the eternal woman delud-
ing the man near her who feels he is "the firm enclosing the
soft" when in actuality the woman is "the soft encasing iron. "
Who is duped? I don't really think that this is news: even
the Marlboro Man senses that in the midst of a good lay the
vagina is rough and that the mons veneris rises over hard
bone.   And most men know that the lashings, and the will,
of even the weakest-seeming woman are Boadicean.   I ad-
mire Wakoski's attempt to deal with male-female relation-
ships freshly, and despite my reservations about this poem,
it moves to one of those insights frequent in Smudges:

> Life is a serious question
> of when to love
> and when to pass unfalteringly on.

Wakoski's feminismo takes yet another form: what I shall
call Gossip-Poetry.   The poems that suffer most from Gos-
sip-Poetry are "Greed: Parts 3 & 4. " Moments are em-
barrassingly private and ephemeral: "Robert Kelly is over-
weight. " Diane "the wife of the Hawks' Well Head ... told
me she'd never pay $30 for a dress.... " Carol Berge:
"that beautiful black orchid of the Chelsea" who sent a poison
pen letter so angers Diane she finds it "necessary to say nice
things about her / even when no one else wants to. "

I do feel that these mucho-in vogue, across-the-back-fence-to-the-horny-neighbor moments have little to do with poetry and would be better in journals or letters published during the senile years of the principals. It's a matter of taste, and I am offended by the preciosity of such material Gossip-Poetry. Wakoski knows that she commands enough respect in the commercial and small press worlds that any eructations she desires to see in print will see print. The regrettable fact is that there are tremendous things in Greed, viz., "The Turtle."

Other poems suffer, I think, from the impulse to write Gossip-Poetry: they go on too long and are too obvious. A sort of verbal Dianarrhea results. One such poem--and its basic metaphor is fine--is "Being a Landlord of the Emotions."

Another side of Wakoski's feminismo strikes me as regressive in these days of supposed advanced sexuality. The woman intent upon her own feminismo feels enormously threatened by homosexuality (each homosexual is one male less for her pleasure and domination) and protects herself (and womankind) by name-calling and by advertising her own immense skill in the sack. Wakoski's love poems, particularly "Anger at the Weather, " "The Moon Explodes in Autumn as a Milkweed Pod, " and "To bed, " are powerfully erotic love-struggle poems. In a curious way, Wakoski feels compelled to translate her female sexual energy into violence-tenderness-hate-love comparable to the physical energy of the male. "To Bed, " one of her best love poems, contains many images of violence: a cut-off finger, blood--and, later, bleeding on the sheets, a nose nipped off, a sharp beak kissing a human mouth, a bleeding face. Wakoski is always beautifully aware of tight, deep moments of touch, taste, and hurt passing between men and women. In "Water under the Bridge" her lover is watching the light on the river

> you watch it
> with the sun sparkling on it
> as only your eyes are when you first wake up
> and I am kissing the soft parts of your body....

Tender, intricate, simple, beautiful: loving is pain. Wakoski is, I think, a major love poet.

Her statement regarding homosexuals is in her lengthy "Poem for Judy Garland Which is A Field Guide to Butter-

flies. " The butterflies are clichéd gays who lament Gar-
land's death--weak-handed amorites of "Over the Rainbow. "
Because of the stereotype, Wakoski's effort to expand the
image of the butterflies to include "we--craftsmen and ad-
mirers of accomplishment" (by which I assume she means
poets) fails.   The concluding pathos is false: the young men,
again, "with weak hands" (gratuitous information), clutching
their sheet music wait for a "dispersal of energy" from Judy's
spirit.

Beneath almost all of these poems I feel a tremendous
female persona obsessed with keeping a (the) penis close and,
preferably, erect.   If through her sheer strength she drives
the man away, her own feminism is sufficiently potent to
give her life meaning, and she pities herself.   Sisters are
not enough!   A penis present, with attendant bitterness and
rage, induces more life in the woman than a cockless placid
life.   This, I would say--this sense of immense struggle in
the presence of men to control them and to keep them at-
tached (feminismo) is what makes for a good deal of Wakos-
ki's originality as a love poet.   When men are absent she
feels entirely useless: see "Handbook of Marriage & Wealth"
--truly fine Wakoski.   The moving "The Joyful Black Demon
of Sister Clara Flies through the Midnight Woods on her
Snowmobile, " one of my favorites of all Wakoski's poems,
concludes with a potent prophecy-curse against the man who
betrayed the nun:

> The man who betrayed you
> opened his book to the wrong place.
> When he turns the page
> he will find your name spoken,
> his hands will turn black and his beads crumble like
> dust in them.

I have concentrated on these aspects of Wakoski's
book simply because I have read no other reviewers who have
seen them as I think they are.   What I have called feminis-
mo is, I think, a very real dimension to the current woman's
movement in this country; and, as I have tried to demon-
strate, there are enormous contradictions which no female
poet writing now reflects so powerfully as Wakoski does.
The male is antagonist, he must be dominated (short, of
course, of having his penis cut off), he must be enticed and
coerced by the woman's apparent softness (which is actually
iron), he must be encouraged to maintain his entire virility.
Without him woman is sterile and miserable.   Perhaps the

cynic might recommend masturbation as a way out. But, the
carrot and/or dildo has/have no voice, nor have they a heart;
and it is here in a total human engagement male-female,
spiritual-physical that life finds its crazy meaning. It comes
down simply to this:

> All the earth
> rushes
> with water
>   but
> I am the moon,
> Diane, dry
> waiting to be taken care of.
>
> Price: quoted on inquiry.

ON CLIMBING THE MATTERHORN: MONODNOCK

Galway Kinnell's The Book of Nightmares*

Finding flaws in a poet as impressive as Galway Kinnell is about as presumptuous as fussing about the Matterhorn--the fact of a magnificent presence should be enough to satisfy all confronters. Few poets have been as well-dined and admired on the Poetry and Visiting Writer Circuits as Kinnell--the fact of his craggy presence and his memorized recitals of his work provide the chemistry of unforgettable appearances. He is so impressive that one is carried away, as if in the preliminary soundings of a Föhn wind, by his excellence. His books sell, and fresh young poets, particularly those attached to the more prestigious writing programs around the country, carry his books with the covers exposed to passersby, garnering Brownie points for their intelligence and perspicacity, and, meanwhile, inspiring the uncritical reverence one reserves for natural wonders.

My sense of Kinnell's work, after several years of reading it with admiration, is that it has become repetitious and flawed; his self-critical sense seems diminished--or, perhaps the truth is that since he has become a star, no editor dares give him the criticism he needs. He overstates, here, is sentimental there, overuses certain words until they become tags--Kinnell-words setting off easy Existentialisms. (The fact that Kinnell apparently knew Albert Camus is not entirely beside the point.) The Book of Nightmares has been almost universally praised since its appearance; and I make the complaints I am about to, realizing that there is still the energy, originality, and power in Kinnell to nurture several lesser poets.

*Reprinted by permission from Northeast Rising Sun, Vol. 1 (Jan. 1976) pp. 21-22, 25; Copyright © 1976 by Cherry Valley Editions.

Nevertheless, Kinnell seems to have reached the bottom of his bag of tricks. He presents too many of the same old devices. They don't explode the way they used to. Consider his diction, for example: certain words appear with the inevitability of Cher Bono's navel. Here is a sampling of Kinnell's navel-words: darkness, light, bone/bones, haunted, existence, dying, graves, scars, rot. The most cursory reading of Nightmares reveals these overworked tags. Consider darkness. Not only is the word sentimental; its vagueness belies precise meaning. The reader is lulled. A flag with darkness written on it goes up, and we are excused from any potent engagement with the poem. We experience a general gloom, a hissing bleakness. The poet spreads soft black butter (tar?) over our minds.

As a philosophical concept, of course, darkness had meaning in the forties and fifties when French Existentialism was in vogue at the better American colleges and universities. Darkness then was what roses were to the 1890's, and what fuck became to the sixties. A dark world, void and black, with God absent.... There's no use rerunning the Sisyphean tape. Kinnell lays his black slabs out there much as he laid them out during his earlier books.

Obviously, it is pigheaded to fault a poet for maintaining a life/world view throughout his career. Why should we expect a poet to change as he ages, to transmogrify his wisdom, so to speak, as living accumulates around him, as the barnacles and weeds adhere to his toughening hide? Thomas Hardy kept a knucklehold on similar views all his life, and barely changed them. Hardy called his stance meliorism--a sort of cop-out. And Hardy was frequently bad-- repetitious, obvious, selfpitying. Most of the time, though, Hardy employed humor and irony to make his grim view somewhat more palatable. And he was, of course, a superb craftsman.

Kinnell generally lacks Hardy's saving irony. He wears a choirboy's seriousness. His interior bleeding is exactly that--unadulterated interior bleeding. The ease of his thinking, and the predictability, maintain a bright undergraduate's addiction to fairly slick philosophical concepts. His pain appears with an undergraduate's pride that he hurts so deeply. Passive and predictable, his sufferings now maintain themselves without a real, communicating pain.

But, to return to Hardy. I accept Hardy because of

his irony, lyric skill, and wit, and I begin now to laugh at
Kinnell as he presents me with further duplicate-images of
himself as Existential Ur-mensch standing there facing me,
holding his guts in his hands, his underwear sweat-fetid,
seedy, his body scarred in various stages of healing, as he
prepares to tuck his guts back into the cavity so as to free
his hands for pushing that rock back up that interminable
Monodnockian mountain.

Perhaps Kinnell is growing tired.   Perhaps he is too
famous, and merely repeats what fawning readers expect.
His suffering is supposed to give us strength.   His pain-pos-
tures make our own somehow easier to undergo.   Or, they
used to.   I once thought his poems the nearest modern
equivalents for those defiant Oedipean moments in Greek
tragedy.   I still respect his early work--and his personal
courage on his trips to the South with freedom riders.   There
are original moments in Nightmares.   The central sections of
"Under the Maud Moon" are the best passages on birth I have
read; the early portions of "The Hen Flower" exude much of
Kinnell's earlier brilliance; and "Dear Stranger" is tellingly
inventive.

To be more specific: his fancy writing frequently as-
sumes the delayed periodicity of old-fashioned poeticized
writing.   Here is a so-so, elaborate, periodic slab reminis-
cent of the Homeric delay Matthew Arnold loved so well.   I
guess that by using it Kinnell means to add to the momen-
tousness of his theme--a momentousness he has already
earned via the superb birth passage.   But he doesn't sense
that he might have intensified his power if he had been will-
ing to edit out the excessive and the pretentious.   Kinnell
learns his "only song" during those first glimmerings of
"the Maud Moon, " when the Archer lay "sucking the icy
beistings of the cosmos, / in his crib of stars. "   The poet
creeps down to riverbanks, with "their long rustle / of being
and perishing, " reaches the marshes and the oozing earth,
touches "the underglimmer" of the world's beginning.

Too often, however, Kinnell seems increasingly to
lack what the 19th century poets called tact--that poetic sense
allowing the poet to know when he has violated formal de-
mands of a work by pushing emotion too far (sentimentality),
or by settling for mannered, dull writing when the poem re-
quires his best work, or by his overwriting and straining.
Obviously, the problems Kinnell has with his diction, already
discussed, are failures of tact.

Here is another of his devices--incorporating prepositional phrases into a line, seeking a portentousness which strikes me as simple pomposity: "he who crushed with his heel the brain out of the snake...." " This is hokey Swinburne or William Morris.   "In the Hotel of Lost Lights, " periodicity winds down to a facile moment of almost absurd writing. Listen to the post, postcards, posterity word-play worthy of that lesser Victorian Stephen Phillips: Using "this anguished alphabet of worms, " he writes for him his final words, and posts for him "his final postcards to posterity. "

More egregious than these lapses of tact within small areas of specific poems (a fine perfectly-shaped blue santa rosa plum with rot festering beneath the skin) is Kinnell's sentimentality.   I realize that his poems to his children are much praised--and they are telling whenever Kinnell recites them.   It is difficult to fault a man who writes of his kids. Who he is comes through, usually in the identifications of his own fate with his children's fate.   "Little Sleep's-Head Sprouting Hair in the Moonlight, " with its mythic overtones (the name sounds like a papoose-name), coming fairly well on in the book, will illustrate.   The experience of the poet's taking his child out of her bed during one of her nightmares (after a few lines) turns sentimental.   Kinnell hasn't earned, at least so far in this poem, the right to his pity.   How does he know that little Maud feels lost?   Isn't this merely a version of that old pathetic fallacy ... a poet's imposing human gut-feelings on inanimate things in nature?   A child, in a sense, especially a sleeping one, is an inanimate man (Wordsworth notwithstanding).   It's as if Kinnell stains his child's veins with needles full of his own spleen.   The image of his "broken arms" doesn't work for me.   He forces the image into the broken shape of Existentialist suffering: Maud screams, waking from her nightmare.   Kinnell sleepwalks to her, takes her up, holds her in the moonlight.   The child clings to him, hard "as if clinging could save us. " He says that she thinks he "will never die. " He seems to "exude" to her "the permanence of smoke or stars"--all the while his "broken arms" are healing themselves around her.   In section 3, the clever "caca, caca" section, Kinnell moves through the cuteness of indulgent parenthood to some slick writing, comparing his own eventual trip into oblivion as going with his daughter down

          the path of vanished alpha-
                         bets,
     the roadlessness

              to the other side of the dark-
                     ness. . . .

I imagine Dylan Thomas' ghost standing somewhere in the
shade examining the contents of his nose. Momentosity is
the word I invent for this writing ... and it is an affliction
that has also hit W. S. Merwin, who similarly strains after
monumentalities he apparently no longer feels, but which his
readers have come to expect. Momentosity. I invite the
reader to compare also the various passages in Nightmares
where Kinnell rides on the fame (back) of his Bear--the mag-
nificent figure lifted from the earlier Body Rags.

       Kinnell, to me, seems mired midway. I sincerely
hope that his new work will indicate fresh turnings free of
self-pity, stale romantic writing, and a stifling Existentialism.
There is a principle of art that the more you struggle for
momentousness the less likely you are to bring it off. There's
an ease to the rising of every biscuit (poem); there's a leav-
ening somewhere in most nightmares.

ROBERT CREELEY'S FOR LOVE REVISITED

Robert Creeley's For Love (1962) contains poems writ-
ten between 1950 and 1960. In its influence on younger writ-
ers it ranks with Ginsberg's Howl and Olson's Maximus
Poems. I still recall the excitement I felt on first reading
the book. I was working on a final version of my own Songs
for a Son (W. W. Norton, 1967), and had not yet read the
Black Mountain Poets. Since my poems commemorated a
deceased son, I wanted to give the illusion that a child could
understand the poems; in other words, my diction was to be
fairly pure and comprehensible. I had no idea that poets
were writing a style of the kind I required for my own needs.
For Love was there when I needed it. Since I haven't read
Creeley's book for several years, I approach this reassess-
ment with some of the apprehension one feels when an old
friend turns up. Will he be a bore? Will he be absurd?
Will everything be said in half an hour? The critical con-
sensus on Creeley's later poetry has it that he is a pallid
carbon of his early efforts. I am pleased to find the impact
of For Love undiminished. In this reassessment I shall de-
scribe some of the features that still strike me as seminal;
I shall not pretend to say everything that needs saying. My
discussion is organized around these topics: Grace, Empti-
ness, Play, Is/It, Kids, and Thomas Hardy.

Grace

In "Le Fou, " dedicated to Charles Olson, Creeley de-
scribes Olson's breath-group poems as vehicles of grace.
Of course, Creeley reveals as much about his own work as
about Olson's; and his evocation of the motions of the breath-
group, projective verse style is a better means into that
style than any prose essay I have read on the subject. Grace,
Creeley says, in keeping with the slow rhythms of the breath,
"comes slowly"; a length of breath determines the beat of the
lines. Grace implies a form so effortless in its effects we
are unaware of the poet's struggle with resistant materials.

Obviously, the notion that the artist maintains a tension be-
tween the grace he creates and the resistances of subject
matter and language is central to most aesthetic systems,
particularly of classical ones.   And here is a bone: in an
odd way both Creeley and Olson are classical writers.

   In "Le Fou" Creeley's hesitancies suggest a voice
getting the beat exactly right.   A careful, thorough examina-
tion of masculine in relation to feminine feet, and of mono-
syllabic to polysyllabic words, would produce an accurate
descriptive log of the poem's flow.   Creeley's line-spacings
too, allow the individual breath-groups sinuosity.   Interest-
ingly, this is the purest formally Olsonesque poem in the
book; Creeley (at least here) prefers the more traditional
stanza form to the explosive arranging of breathgroups in
varying positions on the page.   Always, whether he is writ-
ing in an unabashed projective manner or in a more tradi-
tional one, Creeley senses that kineticism must be trans-
mitted (the energy, to use Olson's word) from the charged
first syllable all the way, line by line, through the living
body of the poem.   "Le Fou" resembles a charged, sinuous
dance.   As it moves within its form, we move in time out
from it, to new earscapes, eyescapes, tonguescapes.   We
leave the poem ("goodbye") as we "go by" the poem--a grace-
fully waving plant, a moving dancer.   Yeatsian? Yes.   The
question: is the poem the dance, or is the poem the dancer?
Some of each condition seems appropriate.   The idea teases.

Emptiness

   For Love doesn't whine or snivel as Creeley confronts
a "universal emptiness. "   Poems ride between poet and the
void.   Wallace Stevens would have approved.   Yet we must
set the ground.   It's as if each poet/artist has his piece of
desert to display his works against.   The desert blooms
with canvases, posters, books--all affixed to stakes driven
into difficult, resistant soil.   To create art, says Creeley,
"is the courage necessary. "   Only then is the poet free from
debilitating, consuming sterilities of place and time.   De-
fiance, or, rather, indifference, is the appropriate stance,
symbolized for Creeley in the act of the mailman who steals
and burns letters.   Creeley doesn't care; let the mailman
destruct; there's no way he can harm you.   Meaninglessness,
hence, assumes meaning.

   "The End, " a funny improvisation on loneliness, turns

a famous passage from Walt Whitman to its advantage. Cree-
ley's speaker buys a new hat, in order better to touch the
world by being entertaining and distinctive. But he bombs,
is ignored, and is left with "a feeling like being choked. "
He can't absorb the rejection. His new gray hat sickens him,
and he has, he reports, "no purpose no longer distinguish-
able. " Paradoxically, Creeley, an intensely self-obsessed
poet--one of his severe limitations, finally, seldom imposes
that ego on the world. He deciphers the world on its terms
as much as he can. Perhaps this is why his triumphs are
so often incomplete: his own ego blinds him to what the
world really demands of him. In "The Innocence" he fum-
bles to re-see, to re-teach himself. The brutalities of a
competitive society derive from church, family, and state.
Symbolically the poet must learn all over that fire burns and
water drowns.

        "The Innocence" opens with obvious, child-like defini-
tions: the sea is a "line / of unbroken mountains" as the
waves freeze into visual patterns.   The sky "is the sky. "
The ground "is the ground. " Our life-line is here, on that
ground--a fact requiring persistent reaffirmations. On the
earth-line we experience whatever there is of the mystical.
Mist shrouds real shapes in strangeness. Considering the
amorphous shapes, we sense "another quiet, " the mystic en-
ergies of the universe. Slowly, the speaker grows aware of
leaves, rock, and other parts of the visible landscape he
hasn't hitherto noted. His vision, although his own, remains
imperfect. This is in a sense the poet's triumph: for only
through haze does an existential sterility yield beauty.

                            Play

        Fun/play is a most attractive feature of For Love.
Sophisticated allusions to medieval love lyrics appear.   In
"Chanson" a warm intelligence informs the refrains--one re-
frain is archaically playful, the other stark and contemporary.
Lady and madame, wife and mistress, are polarities.   The
gentleness (perhaps I should say gentilesse) of looking back-
wards is conveyed by this line: "one hoists up a window shut
many years. " Why? To allow a lark (remnant of an older
poetic convention) to appear. The image of the bird is subtle,
gentle, tender.

        The most playful of these poems, and perhaps the
most famous, treats the disruption of a marriage in which

the woman is a crude, contemptuous, emasculating beast and
the man a sensitive, feminine, courtly creature. Shades of
Jungian animus and anima. Here are some of the trappings:
"things went on right merrily, " "little cheer, " violets in the
spring, heavenly mercy shining down on the lovers, the lady
aloof and remote from the blandishments of her lover, the
lady vengeful. Chansonesque rhymes joyously wielded turn
nicely gross:

> Oh come home soon, I write to her.
> Go screw yourself, is her answer.
> Now what is that, for Christian word?
> I hope she feeds on dried goose turd.

The poem is not, however, a putdown of the medieval genre
from which it derives. It celebrates the form as a device
for exposing a modern conflict. The concluding section, a
panegyric, is a marvellous tour de force evocation of the
earlier genre, Chaucerian, chansonesque. Creeley delights
in fractured tenses--another facet of his humor. We skip
as he laughs, daring us to catch him as he romps through
his verse field. "Don't sign anything, " is one of the best of
these poems. It begins with these lines:

> Riding the horse as was my wont,
> There was a bunch of cows in a field.

Bad grammar, yes. Anti-romantic, yes. Perhaps the anti-
romanticism is the primary fun: the first line could be the
beginning of a medieval poem, albeit badly executed. But
Creeley kicks the traces. And his range matters: to bring
off his contrast is no small triumph. The playful, obstreper-
ous child. The mirror always looks backwards and forwards
simultaneously. Grotesqueries of language, illiteracies of
feeling and speech, displace the enamelled past. Creeley
forces us to see how far we have come, or how far we have
fallen, from traditional order. His horse decides to chase
the cows, and the speaker in the saddle must follow as "un-
easy accompanist. " In other poems also Creeley produces a
sudden blister of grossness: "a greasy hand, lover's nuts";
"the trees, goddamn them"--W. Wordsworth turns in his
grave; "I have to take a piss"; "tits raised high / in the
sky, " etc.

Is/It

These are two of Creeley's favorite words. Is is

staunchly and simply being, clipped and vigorously assertive.
It is the object pointed to before it is named, the abstraction
(riddle) stated before the finger-poet-god-Adam points to the
object naming it. It is, together, are signposts in the des-
ert, the created thing delimiting existential space.

"The Riddle" is a skillful plosive feast. Grace in
the hesitancies, philosophy in the tone. It and its echoes
are almost always accentuated, providing small stress-peaks
for playing less-clipped rolling sounds. The rhythm/sound
patterns are subtle, to be heard with the outer ear, with the
inner ear, feasting: wealth--a pickup of rushing and mean-
ing threading quickly over from one line to the next, an ex-
citement rare in poetry. The "question, " as I read it, is
the eternal enigma of the male-female connection: Creeley's
speaker, maddeningly hesitant, gives the impression he'd be
really boring in bed. The woman is commanding, "impera-
tive, " while the man is "lost in stern/thought. "

Kids

Reading Creeley is to re-experience our minds as
children, when nonsense and fantasy were as real as stubbing
toes. A story then was never a lie. Cracks in the pave-
ment were magic crevices--if you stepped on them you might
disappear forever. In Creeley's "The Cracks, " a children's
game becomes a rendition of a nasty adult relationship.
"Jack's Blues" depends upon our fantasies working to a log-
ical truth. Exaggeration:

> I'm going to roll up
> a monkey and smoke it, put
> an elephant in the pot. I'm going out
> and never come back.

So, Jack disappears from his troubles by playing child, mad-
deningly passive. When you want to berate him he won't be
there.

Other poems, particularly some of the love poems,
employ fantasy to contrast the speaker's dissatisfaction with
the real world of his flesh and blood female. "The Whip"
is one of the best. Speaker in bed with his woman who is
"very white / and quiet" sleeping. Fantasy-woman appears
on the roof. At this point, real woman utters an entirely
unromantic, unfantastic "ugh" and puts her hand on the speak-

er's back.   The touch restores him.   The fantasy-woman
dissolves.   He feels guilt that his mind has betrayed the
flesh-and-blood woman.   And it is she he turns to, for love.

Thomas Hardy

Part 3 of For Love reveals affinities of tone, diction,
and manner with Thomas Hardy's poetry.   Creeley has ab-
sorbed the older poet well.   My feeling is that if the truth
were known Hardy would prove one of the most influential of
all turn-of-the-century poets on later poets.   But critics gen-
erally remain myopic.   In Creeley's "Song" the agents, like
Hardy's, are elemental forces, sparely realized.   Rivers,
land, sea, wind, trees ... these are the agents against which
the weather of the poet's feelings prevail.   The simple qua-
train stanzas provide an illusion of concreteness, and are
forms loved by Hardy; the elemental force of wind finding
trees to move is curiously specific.   Whether the setting is
Dorset or New Mexico doesn't matter.   The sudden personal,
philosophical turn is also reminiscent of Hardy, as are the
hesitancies behind the questions and the direct simple
rhymes:

> And me, why me
> on any day might be
> favored with kind prosperity
> or sunk in wretched misery.

The simplicity of the form: dimeter, trimeter, followed by
two tetrameters; the simple rhymes--two plain monosyllables
set against two polysyllabic rhymes; the use of old-fashioned
phrases--"kind prosperity, " "wretched misery. "   And what
could be simpler than the response to the question "why me?"
An apothegm: "be natural, while alive. "   And once dead we
"go on another/course, I hope. "   Creeley's tentativeness re-
flects a similar stance frequent with Hardy.

"Kore" similarly deals with simple, elemental acts.
The first stanza risks the sort of inversion Hardy liked to
include as part of his poetic carpentry; it was as if he wished
to maintain some mark of the crude, of the adze, on his
work.   Here is Creeley:

> As I was walking
>   I came upon
> chance, walking
>   the same road upon.

Even the most casual reader of Hardy is aware of chance as
a prime mover. In "Kore" chance produces a vision in a
light green wood of a lady led by goat men, moving to a
flute. "The Rain, " as in Hardy's poems about rain, is the
occasion for self-reflection and an uneasiness about that self,
implicitly religious, implicitly romantic. Love, like rain,
enables the poet to escape fatuousness, fatigue, indifference.
The problem is to soften the ego's edge--finding one's self
at last 'wet / with a decent happiness. " For both Hardy
and Creeley time is essentially one. The present is for
questioning one's purpose and destiny. Past and future, as
parts of the present, yield some comfort in the fact that
they are cut from the same die. The questionings never end.
Hardy's "Ah no, the years, oh, " the refrain of "During Wind
and Rain, " his finest lyric, finds echo in the concluding
stanza of Creeley's "The Plan":

> the way, the way
> it was yesterday, will
> be also today
> and tomorrow.

Hardy called himself a meliorist, which means that things
are bad but that in a mysterious way they are getting better.
Creeley puts the idea thus in "The Immoral Proposition, " on
behalf of the "unsure egoist" who knows that "God knows /
nothing is competent nothing is / all there is. " One's salva-
tion and strength, it seems, reside in one's ego. Says
Creeley, the healthy egoist must be sure; the 'unsure egoist
is not good for himself. " For Love is an impressive reveal-
ing of one hesitant poet's effort to vivify and starch-up his
ego. Perhaps because Creeley's ego fails as often as it ad-
vances these poems remain human and poignant, despite the
passing of over twenty years.

THE POEM AS SPIRIT-MEAT

or

Michael McClure's Corpus of Poems Are Delecti*

AIM: McClure's poetry has been better understood by the lions at the San Francisco Zoo at feeding time than by American poetry-lovers.

BLAST: No contemporary poet has
1. written with more energy than Michael McClure.

2. celebrated a sheer physical existence as a means of spiritual enlightenment so persistently and so tellingly.

3. better synthesized the conflicting female-male elements of our natures--Jean Harlow and Billy the Kid being archetypal. McClure is a major love poet.

4. moved as deeply into a vehement madness: he destroys in order to recreate a vibrant sanity.

5. allowed sheer sound to exist as Mantra: McClure writes a pure Mantric Poetry without any trappings OM-wise, etc., from the far east or from Jeremiah and other ranting Old Testament prophets.

6. been so unabashedly romantic in these days of cynicism and depression: McClure is a son of Blake, Swedenborg, Shelley, Whitman, Cummings.

7. Etc., etc., etc.

THEREFORE: McClure's writing is like action painting:

*Reprinted by permission from NEW, No. 24 (1974) pp. 84-91; Copyright © 1974 by John Gill.

spontaneous.   The reader is to re-experience the excitement
McClure felt writing the poems.   The energy screaming (at
times) streaming (at others) is as important as any direct
poetic statement the reader might receive, of a traditional
sort.   McClure fractures the expected and the preconditioned
poetic response.   Communication, obviously, is a tone, an
excitement, a fear, a sexual connection, a discharge.   The
act of the Poem is Mantric: chanting, caressing, shouting,
shitting, or breathing.   The poem is cleansing and spiritual.
Communication is also the conveying of non-verbal ideas
spread like warm honey on the slabsurfaces of the mind,
giving it from my mind over to yours, from McClure's mind
over to ours.

As mammalian communicator, McClure ennobles Man, since
he (man) reachieves or recognizes the Mantric Force of lan-
guage.   The Lamb's baa responds lovingly to the graaah of
the lion and meshes with it.   Jean Harlow responds with
lascivious purrs to Billy the Kid's growlings and chest-beat-
ings.   Declaiming the delicious sound graaah freshens our
spirit-nodes; we vibrate with recharged life.

McClure's beast (mammal) language is love: we are to form
these strange sounds with abandon and pleasure, with love-
explosives, love-verbal-fun-ejaculations:

> THE PINE CONE IS PERFECT.   IT STANDS BY
> THE FOOT OF THE MAIDEN.
> No, it is upon the table.   The furniture is
> grahoor.   The light is grahoor.
> This is in bliss eternity.   Oh calm gahrr groooh
> nahrr
> la ahhr NOOOHH!   Marr sum vahhr grahrraiee
> hrahhr
> nok-thorp naharr.   No rise up!   No stand out!
> BUT STEADY!
> STEADY!   STEADY
> as she goes
> I am thy-my flagged flesh ship.
> GRUHH.   NOOOOH!   HAHHR!   BLOOW!
> Bluhh
> !

> (Ghost Tantras No. 30)

Like "The Pine Cone Is Perfect," the 99th of the Ghost
Tantras must be read according to its individual sounds,

without our worrying about whether we have them right or
not.   We abandon our common puritanic notions about poems.
Poems are not necessarily always meant to be recollected in
tranquility, rendered into prose equivalents, read in vicar-
esque tones, or worshipped: they are to be lived as part of
one's blood stream, fingers and/or genitals.   We experience
founts of energy welling within ourselves and we luxuriate in
pure sounds of animal excitement freed of objects.   Our re-
sponse is spontaneous, sensuous (sensual).   Our abandon is
childlike, trusting, innocent, Blakean.   We resonate spirit,
body, mind as joy.   Life may be bleared and seared but it
is not hopelessly contaminated.

McClure's poems are healthful and restorative, and if we are
into them the actor in us emerges.   And this actor is the
agent extension of our meatspirit selves: without him we
would be zombies.   A primal scream releases us into life.
McClure would free this actor-agent, thereby enhancing po-
etry as a sung-shouted-declaimed-primal experience.   Here
is a portion of Ghost Tantras No. 99, the final one of the
long series:

> IN TRANQUILITY THY GRAHRR AYOHH
> ROOHOOERING
> GRAHAYAOR GAHARRR GRAHHR GAHHR
> THWOSH NARR GAHROOOOOOOOH GAHRR
> GRAH GAHRRR! GRAYHEEOARR GRAHRGM
> THAHRR NEEOWSH DYE YEOR GAHRR
> grah grooom gahhr nowrt thowtoom obleeomosh.

The poem is strangely formalist in its structure and design
of sounds.

In his essay "Reason" (in Meat Science Essays) McClure
describes his spontaneous man: he lies in sunlight on the
forest floor with his eyes closed.   He exercises, stretching
as yogis do.   His mind is a large blackness.   He gives him-
self completely to the sheer pleasure of his muscle-life.
"He groans, writhes, twists, denies himself nothing that the
sinew and tendons and lung and heart request. "   His con-
sciousness is a "blank field. "   He ceases to measure time.
His life is the splendid animal play of muscles establishing
a subcurrent rhythm, creating a pattern in space.   (Numer-
ous of McClure's most avant-garde poems have neo-classic
rhythm patterns, and echo Milton, Marvell, Dryden, etc.).
He repeats the pattern endlessly, allowing his body muscles
to create variations on a basic pattern.   A delicious animal

heat moves through his skull; he sees delicious colors in-
side his skull.   He growls satisfaction and raises his arms
to the sun's heat.   He makes animal-pleasure noises at the
sun, playing, "fulfilling the muscles' demands, " and, there-
by, experiencing his human consciousness anew: "He feels
himself as a mammal!   He does not think of himself as man
but as his weight and size and shape in muscles and organs
of sense and consciousness. "   He has touched on "a ball of
silence" within himself.   He knows he is Man, but he is also
like a tiger and a lion.   His instinct turns primal.   Through
a myth consciousness he senses what his primitive forbears
felt.   He experiences deep reason, a Reason unrelated to the
"intellect ... except that it furnishes the notes by means of
which the melody of reason is played in life. "   Reason is
"the liberty of human flesh moving in the universe. "

To McClure, poetry "comes straight in through the senses
and combines imagination with distortion. "   And there must
be "joy and pleasure. "   McClure's equation is: the greater
the joy and pleasure one experiences, the greater the energy
one feels in one's life.   He is an enemy of moderation.   The
human on the floor stretching his muscles and snarling mam-
mal sounds in sunlight acknowledges the fact that there have
always been "secret hopes and desires. "   The notion of "lev-
els of existence" McClure rejects as a "kind of modern
psychological folklore. "   The stretching mammal-man via his
physical act portrays his belief "that matter is spirit and the
meat is the container. "   We are so conditioned to think of
meat as something cut up to be sold in supermarkets or fed
to lions, cats, and dogs that we have almost entirely lost the
positive connotations of the word--these McClure restores.
His aware, alive man requires no logic to comprehend his
destiny: "stretching his leg and twisting the muscles of his
arm in pleasure creates reason.   The pearl gleaming on
flesh in the light is an act of reason!"

I find this statement absolutely central to receiving McClure's
plays and his poems.   Until we are willing to enjoy the spon-
taneity of the human-mammal on the forest floor, and dispense
with commonplace notions of what poems and plays are sup-
posed to do, we shall miss a truly unique poetic experience.
Poetry is Action.   Poetry is Explosion.

Of course, there are earlier models for McClure's ecstasy.
Shelley and Walt Whitman, to name two: Shelley's romantic
exclamations and his willingness to risk overstatement for
the sake of a fervid personal truth.   Whitman's unabashed

energy: his "urge, urge, urge" is reflected in McClure's "The Surge" (Star). McClure's own note below suggests his fascination with the poetic act as engendering a physical protein organism. The poem, he implies, must fall short of an absolute beauty--it remains a step towards a "fully achieved" or perfect life:

> This is the failure of an attempt to write a beautiful poem. I would like to have it looked at as the mindless coiling of a protein that has not fully achieved life --but one that is, or might be, a step towards living-being.

"The Surge" begins:

> THE SURGE! THE SURGE! THE SURGE!
> IT IS THE SURGE OF LIFE
> I SEEK
> TO VIEW...

In "Under The Black Trees," his daring to declare his pain and his joy without reservation or apology is Shelleyan and Whitmanesque:

> My chest is weeping--and I do not cry longer.
> There is only the kneading of my chest
> and I know it is moaning. The lobes
> of my lungs draw upon one another.

And "White Bread Gleams upon Heavy Tables" lovingly and humorously imitates Whitman's fondness for the Frenchified word to convey an emotion an English word wouldn't quite convey: the puns on "ass" and "massage" are quite marvelous:

> The smoothness of thy toes,
> thy chin...
> THY AMBASSAGE ! !

McClure's perpetual use of OH OH OH OH reflects a Romantic self-declaration. Here is one example taken at random from Dark Brown: "OH BRAIN OH LOVE OH GOD SHIT PAIN OH HEAT FIRE OF CONFUSIONS." Such explosions (with their attendant humor) are a "BUILDING," McClure writes, "TO A HUGE GLORIA ROMANTIC CRY, NEW BAROQUE SHAPE / halls of graciousness and beauty unseen before."

McClure's cries move towards that baroque shape.   Their
frequency, and their sequential juxtapositions with crude
words prevent a Romantic sentimentality.   Yes.   But how
are we to respond to such stark, unrestrained emotion.   Is
he a put-on?   Should we run and hide?   Go to another cor-
ner of the cocktail-party room?   Go home?   Talk about Mc-
Clure behind his back as a super-romantic slob and lousy
poet?

McClure insists that we FREAK OUT alive with feeling.

> MANTRIC WORDS AND SOUNDS
> UNBLOCK THE CHOKED AND
> CLOGGED BODY CHANNELS TO THE
> SPIRIT!

If these poems were merely one long personal wail they
wouldn't be worth reading.   But see the love and humor!
And relish the grandeur majestioso swirling mammalian joy
sounds!

The headline technique McClure borrows, obviously, from
pop culture: movies, comics, tabloid newspapers, posters.
Life is a perpetual circus.   The poet as barker.

The loving McClure reader laughs as he experiences the
giantism as well as the mouseness of these works.   Lion and
Mouse play together in Eden.   As do Devil and Angel.   Jean
Harlow and Billy the Kid.   The here and now is potentially
an Eden, in the sense that in some of the world's nooks and
crannies we can re-experience our lost Paradise, and that
lost echelon of senses Blake insisted we shucked at the time
of the Fall.

At the Fall, Adam put away his cock and persuaded Eve to
cover her cunt with a fig leaf.   From that moment man de-
nied his muscle-knowledge and his muscle-grandeur, and
rarely thereafter experienced mammalian joy, stretching,
bathed in sun, knowing that superb orgasms can simply hap-
pen ... jert, jert, jert.   You needn't pump, bump, jump,
grind, and sweat to get them.   You don't even require any body
but your own.   Your ecstasy is effortless and spontaneous.
You don't feel or see the pool of honey on your belly until
you return to the human (from the mammal) state.   Push the
honey around with your fingers.   Smell it.   Taste it.   A
Gift from god.   Poems are sperm and maiden come meant to
be eaten!

I have the feeling that the poem McClure wants to bring off
(and he may very well do it) is one that will stimulate this
super-orgasm, where you can't contain your joy, and your
vesicles spontaneously runneth over!

I don't think anyone writing today is a better love poet than
McClure. Foils and poignards? "Valentine's Day Sonnet"
is representative of his feelings about women and their roles
with men. As a hymn to Woman it is ostensibly conventional,
suggests Blake in its language (and not merely because Mc-
Clure says lambliness), and suggests in its playfulness E. E.
Cummings at his best. The sonnet is tender, intense, and
Venusian. I quote the beginning of it:

> GLORIOUS DIVINE CREATURE, I'VE JUST
>   SEEN YOUR NAKEDNESS,
>   Your womanly-muscled flesh, and lambliness
>   again
>   in a new light
> I SMELL THE SULFUR AND SPRUCE
> in your hair. And the dream-scent of your sleek
>   waist.
> but it is the relaxed light upon your brow and
>   cheeks
>   that tells me
> YOU MUST BE PROTECTED
> from Rippers and Devourers.

And here is a more erotic moment from his ambitious "Fuck
Ode" (the ode concludes Dark Brown):

> ALL IS QUIET BUT MY SONG TO ME, YOUR
>   SONG
>   to you. This is our touching. This
>   is the vast hall that we inhabit. Coiling,
>   standing. Cock into rose-black meat. Tongue
>   into rose meat. Come upon your breasts, Come
>   upon your tongue, come in your borrow
>   Cavern love snail breath strange arm line

I see McClure as the Jim Dine of poetry. "Oh Fucking
Lover Roar with Joy--I, Lion Man!" incorporates the con-
temporary pop mode with the traditional. In one passage
there is an echo of the popular song "I'd walk a million
miles for one of your smiles," etc. The image of the "two
meat clouds" is humorous, surreal, and loving, and some-
what Magritte-esque. The third line is a parody of Shelley's

line in "West Wind." Amusing is McClure's playfulness with
Oversoul as Undersoul:

> I GROAN, I AM, UPON THE CONE SHAPED
>   BREASTS
>   & tossing thighs!
> --AND SEND MY THOUGHTS INTO A
>   BLACKER UNIVERSE
>   OF SUGAR!
>
> Thy face is a strained sheer Heart twisted
>   to fine beauty by thy coming.
> It is a million miles from toes to thighs!
>   (Our bodies beat like the ultimate movie
> slowed to blurs of two meat clouds becoming
>   one--and the Undersoul is joined
>   by kissing mouths.)
>
>   OH!
>   OH!

McClure's use of pop motifs, I should say, is both playful
and serious, and affects me with a joy similar to that I ex-
perience at a Claes Oldenberg show: the artist's love for
life triumphs over the absurdities he finds in it. A gener-
ous, childlike spirit asserts the worth of the human self in
disaster and pain. Both Oldenberg and McClure transmute
their direct confrontations with the threatening, the dessi-
cated, the horrible, the funky, and the ugly into joyousness.
What a triumph!

"Grahar Mantra," a celebration poem, reveals McClure's
technique of individual Concrete-Word Power.   Letters of
the alphabet in combination are Mantras.   Grahhr is a joyous
emotional release concretized by the adjectives surrounding,
or attached to it.   Grahhr has to do with celestial matters,
since it rides space as a rainbow. It is vapor. It is sex-
ual: a "White Mount," and it is kissed. One receives here
the illusion of concreteness. In actuality, the image re-
mains vague. It's as if Blood Wisdom concretizes the ab-
straction: paramount is the joy or pleasure felt in simply
mammalizing the word as muscle play of vocal chords de-
tached from bread-and-butter meanings. And that, for Mc-
Clure, makes the word concrete. Here is the concluding
stanza:

> Blue Black Winged Space Rainbow GRAHHR

> Black Winged GRAHHR Toes Kiss
> Pink Leather GRAHHR Blue Rainbow
> Vapor GRAHHR Vapor GRAHHR
> Hahr Rainbow Space Black Yahr
>   GRAH!   GRAH!
> White Mount Toes Kiss
> Toes Kiss Star.

McClure's general avoidance of self-pity is refreshing, which
is not to say that he does not experience despair, anguish,
etc. His Dark Brown almost exclusively deals with personal
torment. Beneath his awareness of the tremendous mounds
of shit and debris piled everywhere on this planet (and in
most human psyches) resides a touching celebration of him-
self as a kind of Vesalian man, at home in a fucked universe.
McClure's revolt is via his self-assertiveness:

> THAT I AM A FLOWER DOES NOT MEAN
> THAT I AM RESPONSIBLE
> FOR THE AGONY OF THE ROOTS!--
> > ("Poisoned Wheat")

> Sickness and guilt must be cast off!
>   Guilt is a luxury.
> Being sickened is meaningless.
> > ("Poisoned Wheat")

> Each man is a mess and a fuck-up
>   with hideous ideals
> serving his perverted individual
>   HOLY GHOST
>   with a twisted smile!
> BUT HOW BEAUTIFUL! HOW BEAUTIFUL!
>   --And what grace!
> > ("For Anger")

"Mad Sonnet 3" (there are 13 in the series) reveals McClure
at his finest: delicate, gentle, fantasizing. His language
moves freely among levels (tits to dew-drop). An immensely
skillful use of rhymes (McClure handles these effects as su-
perb camp and as straightforwardly complex rhyming effects;
sometimes he is self-consciously archaic, at other times he
is experimentally fresh: hollyhock, thought, stalk, not).
There is an incredible image: these tiny mammals of the
sonnet "are there hearing the sugar run in the stalk of the
lily." Finally, meat is beauty, the very inner source of our
energetic, vital spirit-beings:

TINY MAMMALS WALK ON WHITE BE-
TWEEN THE YELLOW
BOULDER GRAINS OF THE LILY'S
POLLEN. . . .

I am obsessed with the thought
THAT I AM SANE
and men are not

IF BEAUTY IS NOT MEAT THEN WHAT IS
ALIVE
is not imagination!
AND IF MEAT IS NOT BEAUTY
then save condemnation
and drop your bombs

&
spray
the rays!

PEEK OUT!   PEEK OUT!

There are many clues to McClure's aims as poet buried in
his numerous prose pieces, most of them gathered in his
Meat Science Essays.   These were published 10 years ago,
and remain one of the crucial documents of the poetic scene
in the early 'sixties.   Here is his conclusion to "Revolt":

There is no Cynicism that may stand in judgment.
Revolt pushes to life--it is the degree farthest from
death.   Stones do not revolt.   There are no an-
swers.   Acts and violence with cause are sweet
destruction.   And the sadness that there must be
any death.   There is no plan to follow.   All is lib-
erty.   There are physical voices and the Voice of
Meatspirit speaking.   There are physical voices of
the dead and the inert speaking.   The dead is the
non-vital past that lives within us and about us.
There is liberty of choice, and there is, or is not,
a greater Liberty beyond this.   But there is con-
stantly revolt and regimen of freshness.

Yes, BROTHER: praise to all things that bring closeness
to the UNIVERSE!   Praise Michael.   Praise Us.
GAAHHHHHHHHHHR! ! !

MOLECULAR RAINBOWS:

Harold Norse*

To say of Norse's remarkable poems that they are
primarily of the gay imagination is to limit them.   True,
few of Norse's poems are free of either homosexual celebra-
tion or angst; but their range is immense both geographical-
ly and spiritually.   Norse's fifteen years of expatriate wan-
dering throughout Europe and northern Africa, simply in
terms of psychic and sense exposure, have provided him with
the materials for his work of a variety and depth rare among
poets.   It does matter that he has wandered through some of
the most beautiful physical and sexual landscapes in the world.
His feelings of being an outcast from his own New York/
American culture were and remain obviously profound.   The
appearance of Norse's Selected Poems: Hotel Nirvana, under
the City Lights imprint, is cause for rejoicing; for the first
time this gifted poet's work is easily available to the wide
audience it should have.   Karma Circuit is republished by
Panjandrum, after a limited edition published hitherto only
in England.   His translations and adaptations of The Roman
Sonnets of Giuseppe Gioacchino Belli will appear shortly in
a new edition.   Recently, a several-page interview with Norse
appeared in Gay Sunshine #18, and for its thoroughness and
frankness has already become something of a classic.

I

"Classic frieze in a garage, " the opening poem of
Karma Circuit, shows Norse's fascination with faces from
the Classical past alive in the present.   The contrast is
simple: an ancient frieze imposed upon a modern garage
with its young intent mechanics and its broken cars.   As he

*Reprinted by permission from Fag Rag/Gay Sunshine, No.
22 (Summer 1974) pp. 20-21; Copyright © 1974 by Winston
Leyland & Salvatore Farinella.

gazes at "the brown wiry youths" busy with the cars, Norse
flashes on Hermes, sees him actually "in the rainbow / of
the dark oil on the floor. " He sees "the wild" Sibyl also,
her words bubbling, drowned "beneath the motor's roar. "

Surface meanings are quite accessible here, even to
non-poetry readers ... and this is one of Norse's triumphs
as a poet: he locates readers easily (on the surface) and
then proceeds to his interior magic. In "Classic frieze, " for
example, Norse's preoccupations are old: we have always
hungered for ancient Greece, that time of fantasized loves be-
tween men and boys, men and men. Also, to contrast the
present as junkyard-mechanized time with an idealized past is
not news. By directing the poem in towards his own fanta-
sies (Hermes and Sibyl) Norse translates stock material into
poignant revelation.

Obviously, the past in Hotel Nirvana symbolizes beau-
ty, silence, order, love, introspection; the present stands as
the antithesis of these civilized values.   "The Business of
Poetry, " one of Norse's shorter poems, presents the issue.
A youth and a girl making love share a silent joy and despair.
The present is full of "savage and brutal men" who rend life.

The title poem, "Hotel Nirvana, " moves from "The
Business of Poetry" to an appropriate rage. Violence, mad-
ness, butchery, poison induce our rage:

>   i could not rise to the god or demon
>   of a dying planet
>   corpses try to contact each other
>   with helpless gestures
>   lovers go mad in cannibal beds
>   gnaw each other's flesh
>
>   dead mouths dribble worms
>   of sound
>   hips explode
>   hot membranes into throats
>   that grope the crotch for god
>   lipstick passions breathe into blue carbonic fumes
>   streaked with tobacco haze
>   as macedonian helmets of the police
>   glitter with hate
>   the international cripples huddle together
>   dying
>   of universal butchery

seeking the light
the way out

     Yes, Nirvana in a hotel! Something tacky going on
here ... sweaty sheets ... international set gathered in from
America, Europe, eating one another out in sad sperm-girl-
Kum-hotel rooms. Yes, guru-This or guru-That sell illusions
of magic carpets, monk-fucks, nun bellies on the ground,
maintaining monalisa smiles of "disinterested mystery."
Norse sees the sad bullshit of it all, the decadence as in a
Fellini movie. Guru-followers appear. Swami in lotus-
posture under philodendron leaves, gentle mind, devoted to
vedas, science & bible, near the funicular on Mt. Lycabet-
tos, Swami flown in from Paris to unravel crisis between
husband & wife (metaphysical jetset). Swami, Norse asks,
"what can you tell us / from hotel nirvana?"

     Response: his message doesn't get through: "that
thing / between the legs / and between the ears / got in the
way." Marvelous! Swami looks at his followers and says:
"turn off the ventriloquist's voice / flush out the snakeoil in
the blood / your bible / your gita / your gems / your guns /
your flags / your death." But "at night they went to the nite
clubs gobbling and soaking / up the suds / while that thing /
between the legs / became / more urgent."

     "Hotel Nirvana" is a deep pain memory celebration
lostness poem. The threat amidst the decay is "the void."
Norse is an anguished Whitman reversed. His sexuality is
a molecular rainbow; his mouth swims with sperm. And
these are joy motifs, destroyed by lies. What is brother-
hood? gayhood? humanhood? whitmanhood? He seems to re-
ject his own emotions as so much "bullshit." Does he, Norse,
stand tall among the liars in the desert, the crying child,
the man betrayed? Yes and no. Nor should this ambiguity
disturb us; life is seldom clearly negative as against positive,
or clearly joy against pain. Norse is willing always to nail
himself up, if the pain and the act promise even a half-il-
lumination. His undergoing is ruthless and profound.

     Norse is aware that the times are viciously hostile to
poets and "faggots." An amazing poem, "We Bumped Off
Your Friend the Poet," is spoken by the Spaniard Ruiz Alon-
so, ex-typographer, who fired two bullets into Lorca's ass
and expects Franco to give him a medal. Not only was Lor-
ca a poet but "he was a queer with Leftist leanings ... a
queer Communist poet":

We left him in a ditch
I fired 2 bullets into his ass
for being queer

II

Norse shares something of Whitman's sense of an en-
compassing vision.   "Zombie Fix" is Spanish in its locale.
There is a sense of amazing life and energy throughout this
ambitious poem.   I feel secure here, as I do in all of these
poems, in the presence of a first-rate poetic talent, technical-
ly sure and adept, metaphysically mature.   Little escapes his
eye.   Death is a presence: "all over Spain i shook the clam-
my hand of executed souls / kissed sweet mouths of corpses
spoke with the vanquished / spirit of revolution walked with
unspoken fear. "   The "zombie fix" is not the "lust in the
johns of Malaga, " "dark rustlings in doorways off the ram-
blas, " or "fandangos of fuck in hotels that stank of fish. "
The zombie fix is the glass and steel life of Manhattan, with
its "vapid saurian heights of shiny nightmare script written
for all / with breakdown nerves of power mad executives /
running the world on alcohol & sex. "   And this remains
Norse's position on American life throughout his books.

Norse's talent is highly visual.   Portions seem de-
scriptions of snapshots or paintings.   And Norse himself is
highly aware of his visual sense.   "The Boy, the Birds, the
Concierge and Verlaine" is a poignant expression of reality
as turn-on dissolved.   A series of street pictures is the
occasion.   Poet wanders from the Parisian Latin quarter of
St. Germain with its firm asses, beer-drinking, "a mimic
movie of lips and tits / and swollen jeans padded in the right
places, " where "copcars cruise like leprosy" ... poet wan-
ders to "a quiet little square / Place de Furstembourg" with
its four planetrees and its streetlamp.   He passes Delacroix's
studio, now closed for repairs, and finds

on a bench flat on his belly
a lotus boy with radiant tan
and very dirty feet

dozing beside a folder of drawings.   "Everyone stares / at
him. "

The antidote to the world's viciousness and insanity is,
as one might expect, love.   But, particularly in the gay world,

loves are ephemeral and relationships dissolve in pain and
hurt.   No news here either, of course.   Painfully private is
"You Must Have Been a Sensational Baby. "   As we age, lust
fails to diminish, and the fulfilling of lust (in the gay world)
becomes increasingly impossible.   The poem is in two parts.
The first part quickly sketches the poet's sense of his own
aging:

> I love your eyebrows, said one.
> the distribution of your bodyhair
> is sensational.   what teeth, said two.
> your mouth is cocaine, said three.
> your lips, said four, look like sexual organs.
> they are, I said.
> as I got older features thickened.
> the body grew flabby.   then
> thin in the wrong places.   they
> all shut up or spoke about life.

In part 2, the speaker's frustration is edged with humor.
A ruthless honesty of feeling is chillingly realized in the
final lust-symbol.   A pair of muscular calves drives him
crazy.   He asks the youth if he is a dancer.   "Oh, no, " he
responds, 'I was born with them. "   The youth goes on read-
ing his newspaper.   Norse is not relieved.   "The whole
place trembles with lust. "

    The very pain of such an attraction Norse remarked
on in the Gay Sunshine interview, where he explained that
beauty in the young bestows on that person "a kind of godlike
superhuman quality to be worshipped and admired rather than
to be comfortable with.   It's a gift like genius.   The pos-
sessor can get away with almost anything.   But the beauty
must also get old and die.   I've never been comfortable in
the presence of great beauty.   If I have sex with a great
beauty, it is always followed by a kind of sadness, and I'm
sure that this is because it could not continue forever" (p. 7).
Obviously, there must be alternatives to aging in the presence
of such attractions, particularly in America where youth is
ipso facto Divine!   Norse seems to be working towards pos-
sible accommodations in his latest poetry: the fact of his
poetry is more than an adequate compensation for the fading
and mellowing of sinew and muscle.   To connect with the
spirit is not bullshit!   It doth matter how one defineth Beauty
vs. Beast!   The ephemeral fuck is available, in the bars,
baths, for hire.   The lasting fuck is a totality, built over
months of loving and caring.   The young, I'm beginning to

find, are attracted and fascinated by older folk, particularly
if the latter have created beautiful poems, pictures, music
out of personal risk, courage and fearlessness. Harold, you
are there!

A handful of poems in the central section of Selected
Poems celebrate a fulfilling love. These are the Mohammed
poems, commemorating a friendship with a seventeen-year-
old Moroccan youth. Norse and Mohammed journey through
the mountains to Taroudant. They buy alabaster kif bowls
and watch dancing boys in cafes.

Sexual joy becomes a way of "leaving the mind"--"To
Mohammed in the Hotel of the Palms." But such departures
are ephemeral, as are peregrinations over the faces of
Europe and Africa. Restlessness and the driven self seem
sexual ... and if there is a thematic progress in Norse's
body of work it is towards the wisdom that one can't keep
running as a working out (victim) of our sex drives. The
flash of a train is sexual. A sleek metallic plane ... a
swift speedboat ... a streaking horse. Norse says (in "Now
France"), 'I've chosen orgasm / feeling / smell / soul."
He implies a progression here from body-lust to soul-ex-
perience. We might quarrel with the sequence of these
stages; we can't quarrel with their authenticity. Poetry, for
Norse, is sanity. Poetry is movement towards beauty and
belief. Sexuality in its affinities with spirituality endows an
absurd world with meaning. Norse reports this experience:
in the midst of writing a poem "& feeling absurd, " he goes
to the window and sees a "lonely weirdo / in priestly garb /
ratty & black" scribbling on a wall. Norse runs downstairs
to find what is surely a rationale for his own life:

> WE ARE SEARCHING
> FOR RATIONAL REASONS
> FOR BELIEVING
> IN THE ABSURD

We feel strengthened because Harold Norse is here, and be-
cause he has seen so fully and so well, sparing neither him-
self nor us. His energies are both Boschian and calming,
wild and controlled.

ANGELS WITH GENITALS:

Clayton Eshleman's Coils*

    Coils is a demanding book. Clayton Eshleman has a probing, original mind, and once he has you into his poems (and if we can appropriately see a book of poems as female, receptor) he doesn't let go until you finally drop off exhilarated and spent, exhausted and nourished. And nourished is apt for Coils. Eshleman is a creator of personal myth par excellence. His energy is contagious and undiminishing. His absorption of Whitman, Blake, Vallejo, and Reich is feeling, encompassing, resolved, and astute. And as he spins out psychic explorations and ravishments his voice is his own. Few poets seem to grow so impressively within the pages of a single book. Coils is a living through of the sexual, cerebral, metaphysical, mythic love coils of a single, complex, creative life. Coiling is a spiralling. One thinks of Yeats' gyres spinning throughout history. Coiling and twisting generate force, force generates motion; the result is a danse vital, a potent liberation of selves.

II

    I think first of Mrs. William Blake as an extension of Mr. William Blake's penis. For Mr. Blake loved Mrs. Blake. And no part of himself, I'd assume, did Mr. Blake love more than he loved his penis. Even tiny it aroused his favor, since he loved playing Adam and Eve naked in the Garden. He and Mrs. Blake were their own angels. Swedenborg would have been pleased. For whatever thing we love we long to hold--books, fruit, landscapes, heart-groin stimulators, persons. . . .

*Reprinted by permission from Margins, No. 9-11 (Fall 1975) pp. 49-51; 193; Copyright © 1975 by Margins.

In this sense all loving is mysteriously tactile. The
finger and the palm convey their special breath to the body
or the object they are about to touch. As the finger moves
a thin centimeter from a surface, tingling occurs and within
that infitesimal space a landscape of angels turn on to one
another in joy. Can we ever truly understand the distribu-
tions of our sexual energies? We jet the stuff of burgeoning
and of dying republics, as Whitman would have put it. Each
of us creates his/her sexual republic, setting out towns,
country seats, forests, establishing beloved persons beside
lakes, placing persons hostile to us (we require them for the
growth of our energies) in less hospitable sites. In a sense,
we are adepts, as William Blake was, at creating gardens,
private mythologies. The rivers, streams, rills of our sexu-
ality keep that landscape verdant. The healthier our sexual-
ity the more abundant and beautiful our created country. The
totality of Blake's Bible (all of his writings and drawings)
directs itself as life rather than death. Blake garbed the
naked body with the gossamer fur of sex. In his sense, to
trust the imagination was to trust the body. Both his rage
and his joy were extensions of his body knowing and loving
itself. His discharged energies were his oeuvre-orgasms.
Nothing is sour in Blake. All his loving and hating are ex-
tensions of his vital penis. And with this ready rod to hand
he saw the universe as vagina. In this vastness he found
joy, his sexuality assuming both male and female aspects.
As he pumped the universe, he was mystically enveloped by
labia, stroked all over by these lips, as much recipient as
giver, as much giver as recipient.

III

I stress Blake because Eshleman has been criticized
for being too attentive to his penis. So, let's examine the
matter: mid-twentieth-century American/European meta-
physics feasts on sexuality as its manna. A going into the
roots of the human. Vesalius threw in the veins and arteries,
provided genitalia, defined the substructure and some of the
cutaneous realities; but then he allowed the Pope to shroud
man's splendid nudity in mists of incense, blood spilled from
Christ's wounds, cloaked/choked bodies in wimples, ugly
rough-worsteds, chains. And the ensuing wars have been
vicious peregrinations after misplaced penises. One of the
major disasters of Christianity is that angels were created
sexless and without navels. We feel much less uptight about
strange eyes witnessing our chests and buttocks than our
penises, vaginas, and navels. Predictable? Of course.

IV

We pay dearly for these dismal castrations; and Eshle-
man's anguish (personal and universal) over the sexual is a
human testament to the risks a creative mind takes restor-
ing genitals hitherto culturally butchered. One of Eshleman's
masters Whitman insisted that the poet be a conscience for
his time. Gifted with psychical insight beyond the ordinary,
the poet writes large, to use one of Walt's favored words;
his own private experience symbolizes the harrowing strivings
of his age. In Camden, New Jersey (Beulah-land?) the stub-
ble on Warren Fritzinger's face is the stubble on Adam's,
the plaid laprobe covering the stricken poet in his wheelchair
is the universal ether-robe cooling and protecting him from
the sun's rays. To sing of the stubble on a handsome chin
is to sing the body electric--cutaneously; to sing of the plaid
robe is to chant hymns to the beneficient / destructive / rav-
ishing sun.

V

In this Whitmanic sense of large-writing, Eshleman's
scope makes most poetry today look anemic. Perhaps the
very deadness and sterility poets complain of happens be-
cause our best-known poets are simply rehearsing old stances.
A new book by any of the poets I mention below (and the list
could be longer) sounds like books they've already published.
Merwin offers up his penis on the altar of pallid universal
abstractions. Kinnell stumbles trying to hold his guts in
with his hands, digging the sexual/existential pain as some-
how indigenous to man--the pain relieved somewhat by senti-
mental feelings engendered by loving children. Bukowski
hungers for the good lay he's never had, and doesn't realize
he's misplaced his cock (it's up there on top of the old Nash
Kelvinator with the empty Bud cans). James Tate and Bill
Knott stick pieces of glitter all over their bodies and think
it's physical. John Ashbery continues to feel that we are
all angels obsessed with the verbal scintillations of light and
impressionist color shimmering in the tops of gigantic trees,
or off the roofs of skyscrapers. James Wright grows beaver-
somnolent in that hammock.

Poets who haven't resolved their sexuality cripple
themselves as artists; or, poets who've become too comfort-
able with their sexuality stifle themselves. Resolving our

sexuality is essential, and the resolving is a perpetual al-
most spiritual discipline/exercise. We move nowhere as
artists unless we free ourselves from the emasculations of
past centuries, reassemble our genitals, and then move as
integrated selves, honoring, as Eshleman puts it, the energy
on the body as well as the energy within it. Coils is, in
these senses, a catalyst work.

VI

      Why does it matter so much where poets were and
are? Is much gained by naming the actual streets where they
walked, the countries they visited, the housekeeping details
of their lives in all of their non-visionary splendor? Are
poets who incorporate such details being self-indulgent? or,
in Michael McClure's terms, is the creating of a personal
universe via a personal universe deck of cards (one card per
detail from the poet's life) the strata out of which eventual
transcendence emerge?

      In Eshleman's earlier book, Indiana, I felt such detail
indulgent, meant for friends, better kept in journals. I felt
excluded. In Coils, on the other hand, these good house-
keeping details work. That they do has led me to some
postulates about this kind of poetry. First, if the poems in
a single book lend energies one to the other, backwards and
forwards, downwards as well as upwards, no details are ir-
relevant; and interdependent energies create larger energies.
Here Mrs. Blake mounteth William again, and the lions start
stroking the lambs with their loving velvet tongues. Second,
the plain and the humdrum must constitute a base for more
encompassing concerns; i.e., if a poet remains commonplace
the poems will mire there. Coils gleams with Blakean over-
tones of the mystical, rife with Vallejo's pains translated in-
to Eshleman's, burgeoning with Whitmanic force. The syn-
thesis of these energies occurs, I feel, because Eshleman
folds them all in skillfully with the albumin and yolk of him-
self.

VII

      I have some trouble comprehending the mystical drift
of Coils, a drift towards an original insight--that the act of
love is a potent giving of and a receiving of vast energies
spun out of the self. I simplify, obviously, and underplay

Eshleman's almost mystic regard for rich energies exchanged
and transmogrified.   And what I say about love is so far a
truism.   The considerable stress of Coils is directed towards
(or resolved into) a far more original consummation: what I
call the cutaneous self, or what Eshleman sees as the ener-
gy on the body, is both male and female; similarly, the en-
ergy within the body shares this duality.   Yes, duality is
inimical to awareness, and a fusion of these opposites must
occur.   But in a special way: opposition (as Blake and Whit-
man knew well) results in energy which moves like fertile smoke
and fuses the imagination into the creative act.   To write a
good poem becomes an exciting metaphorical sexual congress
with the universe, resolving negative and hostile forces.

VIII

        To score with a female is to score with the female in
both one's psyche and in one's physical self.   One senses
that Eshleman feels because his body cells are both biolog-
ically male and female, and that only recently has he allowed
them a balanced interplay.   Finally, their chemistries inter-
weave and charge his whole being with energies of the sort
he has never known hitherto.   If entering the vagina is an
entering of the self, it is also an orgasmic receiving of en-
ergies from that foreign self.   Coils is unified in good part
by Eshleman's growing with and through the women para-
mount in his life--and on a different level with his male
friends, among them Paul Blackburn, Robert Kelly, and Cid
Corman.   The various sections of Coils build around a grow-
ing wisdom of the body achieved through congress with these
people, and, hence, around a growing wisdom of the soul as
well--a wisdom felt in joy/pain rather than intellectualized.

IX

        Another omnipresent theme is a resolving of the moth-
er in us--a mythic earth mother, destroyer and lifegiver, a
personal presence always.   Gladys Eshleman, loving and po-
tent midwesterner, moves grandly throughout Coils, attend-
ing lovingly to the shreds and tatters of her life and her
son's life, stripping off pieces with her teeth, restoring the
pieces later, her own needs overwhelming as she faces death
by cancer.   The mother is an aspect of the female within us.
And, biologically, cells in our bodies are hers; and since she
is both male and female some of those cells we inherit from

her are male as well, bearing in their fragile walls (wills)
the cripplings and repressions bestowed by the mother's
psyche; ditto, for the father.   One wonders how we manage
to function as well as we do.   I see Eshleman's seminal
poem "Mokpo" as an absorbing and a transforming recogni-
tion of the male genes inherited from his progenitors, re-
garded through the mask of the figure Mokpo who seduces
Eshleman.   Another crucial fragment is the annealing of the
healthy psyche.   The conflict to identify and honor these
stressful thrusts, both physical and psychic, in Coils as-
sumes vital metaphysical overtones.   The surge here is ex-
actly of the sort more contemporary poets should be making;
the result in Coils is a poetry of scope.   The book deserves
numerous readers, particularly among young poets who are
dissatisfied with the celebrities who keep writing the same
poem over and over again.   A plea for attention for Eshle-
man from these poets would largely be a waste of time.
Coils, and the rest of Eshleman's work will reach its audi-
ence.   And the complaints made in the desert by poets who
insist that contemporary poetry is dead will burrow in at the
roots of some yucca in the Mojave and die.

THERE IS AN ATWATER KENT IN THE LIVING ROOM:

Jack Spicer*

Billy the Kid is to Jack Spicer what Adonis, Childe Harold, Alastor, and Werther were to the nineteenth century romantics. Prettify him, forget the fact that B. the Kid was an idiot, a moron, sadist, and incredibly naive; pretend that as a symbol for the POET he stands against the bad guys of the outside world who think that poets are faggots or worse, and who are out to git 'em; assume that Billy's body is so pure that he never needs to bathe it--no jockey shorts beneath his tight, worn jeans. And, yes, he's out there confronting vast panoramas of nature: the Western U.S. landscape is Spicer's equivalent for Byron's Alps or Shelley's Euganean Hills. Billy even represents Poet as Christ: Billy has stigmata, bulletholes, three in the groin and one in the head, "dancing right below the left eyebrow." Billy as Romantic Poet-Figure has a touch of the comicbook person about him; but Spicer's writing is too good, and his shifts of voice between speaker and Billy too subtle to cardboard-bastardize Billy. Spicer writes a terrific kaleidoscopic poem, or, rather, to use a word he liked to characterize his own work, a collage. In Billy the Kid, Part II, Spicer characterizes the poem:

> A sprinkling of gold leaf looking like hell flowers
> A flat piece of wrapping paper, already wrinkled, but
>   wrinkled again by hand, smoothed into
>   shape by an electric iron
> A painting
> Which told me about the death of Billy the Kid.
> Collage   a binding together
> Of the real
> Which flat colors

*Reprinted by permission from Manroot, No. 10 (1974-75) pp. 181-91; Copyright © 1975 by Paul Mariah for the authors.

> Tell us what heroes
>   really come by.

Once, though, he has set up the collage motif, with a char-
acteristic fondness, Zen-like Spicer contrasts the opposite of
what he's just said, and produces an irresolvable paradox:

> No, it is not a collage.   Hell flowers
> Fall from the hands of heroes
>   fall from all of our hands
>   flat
> As if we were not ever able quite to include them.
> His gun
>   does not shoot real bullets
>   his death
> Being done is unimportant.
> Being done
> In those flat colors
> Not a collage
> A binding together, a
> Memory.

Yes, Billy is Spicer's invention.   Yes, the bullets he shoots
aren't real, etc.   But since a collage is made up of real
swatches of paper, cloth, plaster, if a poem is its inventions
and, hence, imagined, you can't have a collage.   Yet, at the
same time, one has a collage.   Clear?

What of Billy as enamoratus?   Spicer underplays the
homosexual motif.   His speaker is rather mindless in his
love for butch Billy.   Love feelings are expressed with the
directness of a romantic valentine:

> Billy the Kid
> I love you
> Billy the Kid
> I back anything you say
> And there was the desert
> And the mouth of the river
> Billy the Kid
> (In spite of your death notices)
> There is honey in the groin
> Billy.

In homosexual parlance, of course, "honey in the groin" is
sperm.

Spicer was sufficiently touched by Robert Duncan and
Charles Olson to appreciate various romantic myth-motifs as
helpful to his own work.   Among them are the eternal river,
the holy grail, and the poet as a shaman-figure and sensitive
plant.   Let's examine how Spicer employed the river image:
Billy the Kid reaches the river where he is to be shot.   Dry
grass and cotton candy appear at the river's edge--death mo-
tifs, possibly, of the real world (grass) and of a fantasy
world (cotton candy), the latter, essential fluff imagination
material derived from natural fact, for the look of cotton-
wood trees from a distance resembles cotton candy.   Ahem.

As he approaches the river, Billy, aware of his doom,
meets his Romantic double, his doppelgänger and secret shar-
er Alias.   Bill tells Alias that "somebody" wants him "to
drink the river / Somebody wants to thirst us. " Alias says
it's not the river that desires their deaths:

> No river
> Wants to trap men.   There ain't no malice in it.   Try
> To understand.

Billy and Alias take off their shirts, a sort of courtly/
knightly exchange with homosexual overtones.   Billy says:

> I was never real.   Alias was never real.
> Or that big cotton tree or the ground.
> Or the little river.

Flashing on sophisticated neo-Platonic Shelleyan notions of
the Real and the non-Real, Billy opts for a way of driving
deep into the perplexed cortices of despised Philistines the
inference that art/poetry has the true Reality and that all
else is woeful illusion and fantasy.   And, again, Spicer wants
it both ways: illusion and fantasy (dancing) are fun:

> Our lady
> Stands as a kind of dancing partner for the memory.
> Will you dance, Our Lady,
> Dead and unexpected?
> Billy wants you to dance
> Billy
> Will shoot the heels off your shoes if you don't dance
> Billy
> Being dead also   wants
> Fun.

(Billy the Kid, VIII)

I find Spicer's tripping with these notions of Shelleyan
Platonism valuable towards an understanding of his work--
especially since at least two giants war in his imagination:
one giant (both are lucky and green) represents Reality as
Absolute shot off and beyond and towards and eventually into
some Hyperionesque over-world of Intimation and Intuition.
Giant two is earthly, concrete, Williamsesque (and Olson-
esque). This giant speaks through Spicer in one of the bril-
liant letters to García Lorca (After Lorca, pp. 34-5):

> I would like to make poems out of real ob-
> jects. The lemon to be a lemon that the reader
> could cut or squeeze or taste--a real lemon like a
> newspaper in a collage is a real newspaper. I
> would like the moon in my poems to be a real
> moon, one which could be suddenly covered with a
> cloud that has nothing to do with the poem--a moon
> utterly independent of images. The imagination pic-
> tures the real. I would like to point to the real,
> disclose it, to make a poem that has no sound in it
> but the pointing of a finger.

Here is his poem (#4 of "For Poetry Chicago, " Book of
Magazine Verse) about the problems he confronts with lemon
as image:

> The rind (also called the skin)
>   the lemon is difficult to understand
> It goes around itself in an oval
>   quite unlike the orange which,
>   as anyone can tell, is a fruit
>   easily to be eaten.
> It can be crushed in canneries into
>   all sorts of extracts which are
>   still not lemons. Oranges
>   have no such fate. They're pretty
>   much the same as they were. Culls
>   become frozen orange juice. The best
>   oranges are eaten.
> It's the shape of the lemon, I
>   guess that causes trouble.
>   It's ovalness, it's rind. This
>   is where my love, somehow, stops.

Fascinating! Particularly the notion of the poem "that has
no sound in it but the pointing of a finger. " Spicer's ideal
poem is no further away from us than our nearest camera

loaded with film. Wind film forward to hand with finger
pointing towards up-coming #1 photograph. The finger-hand
predicts the dozen or twenty photographs to follow, even be-
fore they are recorded. This ultimate poem (the hand-finger
on the film) allows, nay, demands the most complete Ro-
mantic act from the reader: reader creates his own poem/
poem sequence. To use one of Spicer's words characterizing
his poems, the reader creates a serial: there are as many
frames/parts as one would care to invent to lead on after
the hand/finger appears on the film. And these poems would
contain marvellous objects sensitively rendered: lemons,
moons, etc., having quite the illusion of the vegetable and
mineral existences they enjoy in nature.

> To experiment, let's try moving our mind around the
object lemon. Make of the lemon a kind of third eye of the
citrus world, anent Spicer's fondness for layers of transcen-
dental romantical meanings. First, though, circulate your
mind over, around, under, and through (vertically and hori-
zontally) the lemon. Taste, touch, lick, bite, pinch, hit,
smell, squash, suck lemon. Make rhymes for lemon: one,
done, swimmin', wimmin, agamemnon, etc. Have lemon
drop from branch of lemon tree onto soft grass. Carry
lemon into house. Lemonade, hand lotion, fuck lotion, etc.

> What I'm saying is that I don't quite understand--to
my satisfaction at least--how Spicer's lemon can become the
pure detached object in the poem/qua poem he means it to
be. I am more perplexed by this romantic vagueness when
I try to see Billy the Kid as O B J E C T, or Merlin, or
García Lorca, or Henry Rago, or Huntz, or God as Coleridg-
ean-type ommjects. I conclude that Spicer was struck with
Lorca's special talent for allowing objects to determine fresh
routes within a poem, an earth-talent route for earth-objects.
Perhaps a Ph.D. linguist loses along the way towards de-
termining his own poems; they resist and flop over as blatant
morpheme-addicts. No wonder, therefore, that Spicer's best
poems are the translations of and improvisations on Lorca.

> Spicer himself best characterized his failure to achieve
that superb clarity of image that passeth all understanding in
part 10 of his "15 False Propositions about God" (Published
only, so far as I know, in the English The Wivenhoe Park
Review, No. 1, Winter 1964, pp. 84-91):

> > I do not remember the poem well but I know that
> > beauty

> Will always become fuzzy
> And love fuzzy
> And the fact of death itself fuzzy
> Like a big tree.

The "blurred forest" frustrates and angers him. He wants
to decimate, to chop it apart, with his bare hands. And in
the concluding portion of the letter to Lorca mentioned above,
he tellingly explored the connection between the natural ob-
ject in its full-blown maturity and in its awful decay:

> But things decay, reason argues. Real
> things become garbage. The piece of lemon you
> shellac to the canvas begins to develop a mold,
> the newspaper tells of incredibly ancient events in
> forgotten slang, the boy becomes a grandfather.
> Yes, but the garbage of the real still reaches out
> into the current world making its objects, in turn,
> visible--lemon calls to lemon, newspaper to news-
> paper, boy to boy. As things decay they bring
> their equivalents into being.

He finds his resolution in a principle of correspondences,
much like the <u>correspondances</u> that turned Baudelaire on:

> Things do not connect; they correspond. That is what
> makes it possible for a poet to translate real objects,
> to bring them across language as easily as he can bring
> them across time. That tree you saw in Spain is a
> tree I could never have seen in California, that lemon
> has a different smell and a different taste, BUT the
> answer is this--every place and every time has a real
> object to correspond with your real object--that lemon
> may become this lemon, or it may even become this
> piece of seaweed, or this particular color of gray in
> this ocean. One does not need to imagine that lemon;
> one needs to discover it.
> Even these letters. They correspond with some-
> thing (I don't know what) that you have written (perhaps
> as unapparently as that lemon corresponds to this piece
> of seaweed) and, in turn, some future poet will write
> something which corresponds to them. That is how we
> dead men write to each other.

> Love,

> Jack

II

In his conflict between illusion and reality, Spicer
found an out: a burrow with two exits and two entrances.
Actually there are two openings, and one may either exit or
enter by either of them.   Both are located at the base of a
tree Spicer liked to call "God. "

By exiting from one hole, the poet takes complete re-
sponsibility for the success and/or failure of his poems ...
as verbal constructs (phoneme/morpheme-delights) conveying
images, thoughts, mythic material Jungian, etc.   From the
next exit he emerges as--and this is Spicer's metaphor--"a
counterpunching radio" ("Sporting Life, " Language, p. 2).
The poet writes Spicer

> is a radio, the poet is a liar.   The poet is a
> counterpunching radio.
> And those messages (God would not damn them) do
> not even know they are champions.

In a portion of "Vancouver Lecture #1" Spicer ampli-
fied the metaphor.   Essentially, again, the idea resembles
ideas proclaimed by Shelley and Wordsworth, albeit Spicer's
are couched in modern lingo.   Spicer dissociates the radio
program from the radio set: "I don't think the messages are
for the poet ... any more than a radio program is for the
radio set.   And I think that the radio set doesn't really wor-
ry about whether anyone is listening to it or not and neither
does the poet.   And I don't know what the poem does. "   The
radio program, obviously, has a sponsor who does his
thing(s) to get his program heard.   The quality of the pro-
gram, the Neilsen ratings, don't affect the radios themselves.
So, if poet is radio set (yes, emerging like bunny or squir-
rel from a hole under tree "God"), what poet transmits orig-
inates somewhere outside him, in some New York City or
Chicago Studio of the Soul directed, paid for, and arranged
by numerous ghostly (since radio set or person listening to
radio don't see the sponsors) sponsors.

Later in the lecture Spicer deals with these ghosts.
First, metaphors aren't meant for humans; they are meant
for "ghosts. "   Metaphors concretize the individual wires (as
in radios) reaching all silver, from "the end of the beautiful
as if elsewhere. "   This remark has the lucidity of a sentence
tossed off by Gertrude Stein as she observes Toklas whipping
up another batch of those cookies.   Spicer's wires seem to

be whatever of <u>eternal</u> (my word) exists in whatever objects
strike the poet <u>as worth</u> placing in a poem.   Says Spicer:
"The wires in the rose are beautiful. "   Which I like, and I
think understand.   Platonism.   There is an absolute <u>beautiful.</u>
Wires run from <u>beautiful</u> to objects in <u>the</u> concrete <u>universe.</u>
Silver wire <u>filaments set</u> up quiverings and noises in radio-
poet who gives them audibility.   His readers tune-in.

     Yes, but who are these sponsors?   Ghosts: "Poems
were written for ghosts.   The ghosts the poems were written
for are the ghosts of the poems.   We have it second-hand.
They cannot hear the noise they have been making":

> Finally the messages penetrate
> There is a corpse of an image--they
> >   penetrate
> The corpse of a radio.   Cocteau used a
> >   car radio on account of NO SPEED
> >   LIMIT.   In any case the messages
> >   penetrate the radio and render it
> >   (and the radio) ultimately useless.
> Prayer
> Is exactly that
> The kneeling radio down to the tomb
> >   of some saint
> Uselessness sung and danced (the
> >   radio dead but alive it can
> >   connect things
> Into sound.   Their prayer
> Its only connection.
> >   ("Thing Language, " <u>Language</u>, p. 6.)

     Is this all clear?   Spicer seems to say that whatever
tremblings of Beauty-Sound-Grave/Past/Death quiver in our
poems constitute the individual "ghosts" of each of our indi-
vidual poems.   Yet, there are ghosts, or a super-ghost, outside
the poem too.   Spicer uneasily names this super-ghost "God, "
and devotes his "15 False Propositions about God" to the
problem.   The question supporting it all is: to what extent
is the poet responsible for his writing, good and bad?   Is
he simply the receptacle, the radio?

     A motif of the "God" sequence (or <u>serial</u>) is from
Ezra Pound:

> Beauty is so rare a thing,
> So few drink at my fountain.

The lines become a refrain in the early sections.   God, King
of the Forest (Oh! shades of Regenerative Myths, Vegetable
and Fisher Kings, etc.) is a cripple with one leg longer than
the other.   His forest seems made up of poets and their
lovers: young trees are young lovers, old trees are old
lovers, etc.   The poet intent upon his art struggles to find
"a new Song/Real/Music." He has trouble: "A pain in the
eyebrows. A visiting card." Spicer's private lament that
a lover is gone is the occasion for a complaint to God.   At
the moment when the serial turns metaphysical, or meat-a-
physical, Spicer asks:

> Why
> Does
> Your absence seem so real or your presences
> So uninviting?

The question's not subtle, Sandy. "Arf.   Arf." Send the
beautiful young hustler packing, Jack, and find yourself a
young, honest-to-god poet to love.   But when Spicer does in
the next section, where he engages Old Daddy Warbucks in the
Sky in argument, is subtle.   God begins by judging Spicer's
poems: "Real bad poems." Spicer responds: "Dear Sir:
I should like to...." But God interrupts, informing him that
hate and love, since they are clarifications enough of them-
selves, don't belong in poetry and merely embarrass reader
and poet and "lack Dignity." Spicer:

> Dear Sir: I should like to make sure that everything
>   that I said about you in my poetry was true, that
>   you really existed....
> That you were not an occasion
> In a real bad scene
> That what the poems said had meaning
> Apart from what the poems said.

This sounds like a romantic copout, since the easiest way to
dissuade your opponent from cornering you is simply to say
that after all you didn't intend to argue: my poems have
meanings quite apart from what their words say, and, you,
incredible dummy (D, if the Dummy is the Deity) you should
understand them.

        Perhaps I am obtuse; but I suspect poets who excuse
their sleazy thought and sleazy image-making this way; or
who masquerade a lack of profundity by saying that their pro-
fundity exists but can't be verbalized.   This is a mere step

away from the slap-the-forehead-gad-I'm-sensitive-school of
poetry and criticism: the impact of a work of art is so eso-
teric and so removed, and yet so real, that any attempt to
describe it sullies it, like raping a virgin or a boy. Obvi-
ously, to lack a substrata or structure of intellect towards
some larger awareness, aesthetic or religious, is a delusion.
To a degree, Spicer deludes himself that he's more profound
than he is. Stance does not equal Substance.

And Spicer with his Ph.D. in Linguistics and his wide
reading understands the dilemma without really resolving it,
except in vague romantic terms. God, he says, is the near-
est tree. OK, wander outside--I happen to be at Yaddo in
Saratoga Springs, New York, right now. I walk up to the
nearest impressive tree, a large white pine. Obviously it
has its concrete properties, and if the tree is my God, God
is for me a living organism--my God is vegetable qua vege-
table, etc.

So far, so good. What do I do with my tree, though?
Climb it? Pray to it? Rub against it until I come? Chop
it down? There are other possibilities. I think, dear Jack,
that I'll let the tree stand, for the nonce.

In concluding the fifteen poem series on God, Spicer
takes ambiguity as his resolution. In a rather sloppily writ-
ten line he reports his own psychic state at the time: "No
thought coheres or sensation." Perhaps he wrote the poem--
or, since he believed in dictated poetry, perhaps he received
the poem at one sitting, and, since it is lengthy, was ex-
hausted at the end. His inability to realize God beyond "tree-
ness" he blames on the "abysmal toyshop" of the world, full,
as it is, of the gawds and geegaws, distractions and enter-
tainments that fill up our days and victimize us. Spicer as
victim addresses "Dear Sir" again, confessing that he once
believed in a "three-headed God ... sometimes both when
talking with you and living with you." Nothing is resolved.
Rather there is a sense of things vaguely and evanescently
put right, and with a flicker of self-pity. Spicer doesn't
fall exactly upon the thorns of life and bleed; he rather steps
among them scratching an ankle or a calf now and then.

III

There is something old-fashioned and non-progressive
in another of his ideas. In the Vancouver Lecture, he ex-

plored the idea of the dictated poem.   A poem, he reports,
nudges him on the back and starts coming through, scaring
him, particularly when it delivers the opposite of what he
had meant to say.   Now, "even a practicing bad poet," Spicer
declares, knows that "something from outside" produces these
results, sneaking effects and details into our poems we never
intended.

I won't analyze the ramifications of Spicer's theory in
much detail (see the treatment of it in Caterpillar 12), but
will simply suggest that his idea, and he admits this, is as
old as the proverbial hills.   Does he advance the idea with
fresh insight?   No.   But his statement of it is valuable since
it transpired under conditions of direct stress with a live
audience--no ghosts this time.   He is unabashedly romantic,
and makes connections with Olson, Creeley, and Projective
Verse.   Interesting also is that Spicer attaches to his idea
of a push from something outside a notion like the Words-
worthian notion of the wisdom of the primitive and/or child.
Such folk are better poets than educated, well-read persons.
Says Spicer: when you're "hooked up" with the universal
power sources and set out to write a poem, it's best if you
are uneducated and a little dumb: "because an uneducated
person often can write a better poem than an educated per-
son, simply because there are only so many building blocks,
so many ways of arranging them ... in the long run, for
really just good poetry and sometimes really great poetry--
an infinitely small vocabulary is what you want...." Of
course, there is always the possibility Jack may be putting
us on.   But I don't think so.

The judgment we must make, finally, of course, is
of Spicer's poetry: what sort of house did Jack build?

My own feeling is that he knew too much about lan-
guage--and, in this sense, his primitivist theory works: for
he never quite convincingly stood as the primitive poet of his
fantasies.   The Vancouver Lecture shows his awareness of
and his distrust for his learning.   Here is one of his best
linguist poems, #3 of the series "Graphemics" from Lan-
guage.   The strings freshly recall: the image we saw earli-
er of these universal silver threads; the idea of a false or
plastic reality; the function of the object as a red light warn-
ing the poet that he must see and feel limits; the connections
between crossing a street against a traffic light, tying a shoe
with a granny knot, and the need to snarl--all of these meta-
phors for the poetic act:

Let us tie the strings on this bit of reality.
Graphemes.   Once wax now plastic, showing
        the ends.   Like a red light.
One feels or sees limits.
They are warning graphemes but also meaning
        graphemes because without the marked
        ends of the shoelace or the traffic signal
        one would not know how to tie a
        shoe or cross a street--which is like
        making a sentence.
Crossing a street against the light or tying
        a shoe with a granny knot is all right
        Freedom, in fact, providing one sees
        or feels the warning graphemes.   Let
        them snarl at you then and you snarl
        back at them.   You'll be dead sooner
But so will they.   They
Disappear when you die.

The poem is hardly primitive or simple and represents
Spicer at his most original and best.

When Spicer tries to be simple, as he does in his
poem to Ginsberg (#10, "For Down Beat, " Book of Magazine
Verse), he allows the simple-minded statement to suffice for
simplicity.   What does one do with this opening line: "At
least we both know how shitty the world is. "?   Answer:
"Blush. "   And the concluding sentiment is an inept reflection
of Whitman's cranky twists of language: "Fight the combine
of your heart and my heart or anybody's heart.   People are
starving. "   On the other hand, this insight from the same
serial poem is right on: "The poet has an arid parch of his
reality and the others. / Things desert him. "   For some rea-
son, Spicer proceeds to a bit of bathos, the occasion his ob-
session with a lover: "I thought of you / as a butterfly to-
night with clipped wings. "   Not only is the sentiment silly,
but "with clipped wings" hangs out there sloppily remote from
its subject you.

The start of one of his God-poems (#4, "For the St.
Louis Sporting News, Book of Magazine Verse) is a refresh-
ing contrast:

God is a big white baseball that has nothing to do
        but go in a curve or a straight line.   I studied
        geometry in highschool and know that this is true.
Given these facts the pitcher, the batter, and the
        catcher all look pretty silly.

This is uncomplicated, simple, profound, humorous.   And
there are many moments of this quality in Spicer's work.
One listens and one finds that aesthetic Silence he loved, a
silence, in fact, he wrote a book, A Book of Music, to cele-
brate:

> Ridiculous
> How the space between three violins
> Can threaten all of our poetry.
>
> ("Cantata")

> And we
> Can learn our names from our mouths
> Name our names
> In the middle of the same music
>   ("Duet for a Chair and a Table")

Heard sounds are sweet, but those unheard are sweeter, etc....

IV

        Throughout Spicer's poetry recurs the situation of the
poet in a threatening, collapsing world.   The poet tries to
maintain his sanity through his art, knowing, at the same
time, that there is little or no audience for it.   (It is inter-
esting that Spicer apparently never put his few published
books in copyright).   This theme Spicer treats as movingly
as any poet of his time, and by my focusing on aspects of
his Romanticism, I leave out much in his poetry that moves
and delights.   He is a master-writer, and it is no small
wonder that so many young poets, particularly on the West
Coast, revere him and read him, often.   One might call him
the West Coast Frank O'Hara despite the scarcity of his
books.   His For Lorca, in my own case, arrived propitious-
ly and kept me high for a week and led to my writing some
thirty poems.   I shall always be grateful to him.

        Spicer's sense of a collapsing world was real: shredded
wheat and paper maché (sic), and fuzzy trees and fuzzy peo-
ple, and war, and revolution.   His fine, ostensibly Arthurian
poem, "The Book of Merlin" (In Leary and Kelly, A Contro-
versy of Poets) is his most completely revolutionary poem.
He uses passages from a German romantic marching song popu-
lar with the Army of the Second Internationale during the 1930's:
"Heimat, du bist wieder mein, " references to Sacco and Vanzet-
ti, and to Hitler's Koncentrationslage ... these surround the cen-

tral motif of the Holy Grail. In brief, the choice we have in the modern world is between the Grail (Love) and the Bomb. Spicer is pessimistic about which of the pair it will be.

Confronted by collapse and immanent disaster, the poet, nevertheless, prompted by "someone" out there, proceeds to build his house. The best statement of this occurs in the 5th section of "15 False Propositions. " The passage is uncomplicated, at least on the surface. There are two houses: the house you live in (or the world), and the house you construct with your poems, a modest palace of art, perhaps. The first house falls down. You find yourself shivering in the timbers alone with "the vacant lumber of your poetry. " The rarity of Beauty--a final Romantic concept implicit in my earlier comments is a sad consolation; yet, it is a consolation:

> When the house falls you wonder
> If there will ever be poetry
> And you shiver in the timbers wondering
> If there will ever be poetry
> When the house falls you shiver
> In the vacant lumber of your poetry.
> Beauty is so rare a thing, Pound sang.
> So few drink at my fountain.

Far more durable and joined than this passage suggests is the house that Jack built--or at least as much of it as we've seen in print. And here is the place to add my complaint to those already made for the continuing failure to publish a definitive, accessible Spicer. (I drew a parallel with Frank O'Hara a few paragraphs ago: if Spicer had only been as lucky in his editors!).

Romanticism determines the decor and the central unifying timbers of Spicer's house; and these concepts of creativity, god, and passion are varied by occasional pieces of furniture and bits of decor from the twentieth century world. His house, therefore, gives the illusion of contemporaneity. And his rooms are spacious, and the best are filled with air and energy, beautiful and well-made. Spicer was a fine carpenter. I shall conclude with a nicely relevant bit of his carpentry:

> This is the melancholy Dane
> That built all the houses that lived in the lane
> Across from the house that Jack built.

> This is the maiden all forlorn, a
>   crumpled cow with a crumpled horn
> Who lived in the house that Jack built.
> This is the crab-god shiny and bright
>   who sunned by day and wrote by night
>   and lived in the house that Jack built.
> This is the end of it, very dear friend, this
>   is the end of us.

NOTE: Since I wrote this essay, The Collected Books of Jack Spicer has appeared, edited and with a commentary by Robin Blaser, published by Black Sparrow Press.

THE HITHERTO NEGLECTED WORKS

OF AMNESIA GLASSCOCK:

John Steinbeck*

At age thirty-two John Steinbeck reputedly published eight poems in the now defunct Monterey Beacon, under the pseudonym Amnesia Glasscock. The poems divide equally between the January 5th and the 26th numbers of the paper. These works border on doggerel; in fact, at times they are doggerel. There is little sophistication of technique or theme. They read much like productions of a gifted but nasty high-schooler getting his kicks from admiring men, in the consciousness of a woman, while pretending to despise homosexuals. It has been fair game, of course, to detect homosexual leanings in almost every modern male writer of note: Hemingway resolving his gay feelings via suicide, Mailer accommodating his flamboyant love-hate for women, ditto for James Dickey, T. S. Eliot journeying with those magi in drag, Jack London onanistically supreme in his heaven of sailors, toughs, stevedores, Fitzgerald burnishing his love/fear of men in alcohol.... Such speculations, whether parlor game or no, have validity. Artists are sensitive--as the cliché goes. Sensitivity implies a quickening of the anima, or female self. The female self responds to male sexuality. The writer of merit can't avoid reflecting his fascination with other males. The anima will be heard.

In the mid nineteen-thirties, an ambitious writer in America would hardly risk publishing overtly homosexual poems, and especially in a small-town journal, no matter how sophisticated that town (Monterey was not and never has been Carmel). The device of masquerading as a woman provides protection, obviously. The poet as chameleon. The

*Reprinted by permission from the foreword to Collected Poems of Amnesia Glasscock, San Francisco, Manroot Press, 1976; Copyright © 1976 by Manroot Books.

poet as ventriloquist.   The nineteenth-century poets, except
for Whitman who was up-front, managed the problem via
masquerade.   John Addington Symonds, whom Swinburne in
a less than generous moment derogated as "John Soddington
Symonds ... that amorist of blue-breeched gondoliers, " wrote
several volumes of sonnets and other poems to various men
and boys, concealing their true gender behind various female-
gender pronouns.   The problem fascinates.

     Steinbeck's poems use satire to protect what appears
to be his own macho-threatened image.   By showing that he
despises the esthete (and hence the "pansy") he insists on his
own hairy-chested male self.   The artist-genius caught in
Romantic weltschmerz is a figure of ridicule:

          The artist has a perfect right, I say,
          To wear a sword-stock--or a green
               toupee,
          To pace the floor arrayed in velvet
               cape,
          Indulge in sodomy or rape
          While yokels from the midlands gape.
                                        ("The Genius")

The artist has a right to suffer; his art though is "obviously
hot-house grown" and worthless.

     "Ivanhoe" is another attack on the esthetic androgy-
nous artist.   "Fair Rosalind" as prototype of the esthete sits
in her tower distraught.   Her father thinks some male has
wronged her.   Not true.   She weeps for "all the little lambs
/ And virgins yet unborn. "   She weeps for "broken daisies, "
forlorn minstrels, mankind's dead hopes, the transitoriness
of life.   Here is the father's response--no esthete-sympathizer
he:

          Her father scarce restrained a sob,
          His fine old face turned pale.
          He turned fair Rosalind about,
          And kicked her in the tail.

Glasscock is vicious in " Song of the Disgusted Modern. "
She laments that the old days are gone when men, like moun-
taineers, had hairy ears and were "strong as oaken trees. "
Modern men, alas, wear "marcel waves" and boast "dimpled
knees. "   We are too cerebral; heroic feats have given way to
Nietzche, Jung, Kant, and Freud.   "Lilting love songs" sang
to passing sailors now supplant whooped battle-cries:

> Our men grow more emasculate
>   Through every passing hour.
> For men were men in those dead days,
>   And a pansy was a flower.

"The Visitor" is a Thomas Hardyesque ballad, in which dear
Amnesia ironically laments the passing of romantic love from
her life.   A lad of great beauty sitting gaily on his "milk-
white steed" turns up at her door.   He stays for twenty years,
and now "sits with a yearning face / Acatching dust and a
'filling space. "   The romantic illusion in time dissolves and
sinks as so much collapsing bread-dough.

"Mammy, " with an atrociously written final stanza, is
an utterly unsympathetic, clichéd attempt by Glasscock to ex-
plain how faggots get that way.   Sonny is eleven before mam-
my cuts his curls.   She's always wanted daughters, so taught
him to cook and sew, kept him from "rude boys, " saw that
he had plenty of books and toys.   In that doggerel-ridden last
stanza she laments:

> And he has always come to me
>   As to a sanctuary.
> And now I wonder if I've raised--
>   Another little dearie.

In two poems Amnesia drops her pants.   Amnesia is
thoroughly turned on.   "Thoughts on Seeing A Stevedore" is
Lady Chatterlyesque in its fascination with a huge hairy bloke
from "another sphere. "   Here is the whole poem:

> Great bronze ape-man
> Man from another sphere,
> Who knows but that you, too,
> Could be taught to lilt a song?

"Four Shades of Navy-Blue" is an ostensibly humorous romp
in ballad measure extolling the turn-on power of sailors' pos-
teriors.   Assuming that Steinbeck had satiric intentions in
mind--the artist as Amnesia Glasscock is carried away by
her "aesthetic" feelings for sailor breeches.   She has read
her John Addington Symonds (his Essays in a Key of Blue in-
cludes an essay on the bluish tones of a gondolier's clothes),
Oscar Wilde, and Arthur Symons (Symons preciously adapted
James McNeill Whistler's titles for his poems); viz., "studies
in white, " "nocturnes, " "symphonies, " in various colors,
usually pale, and meticulously described.   Also, Gilbert and

Sullivan's parody of the Wildean-Paterean esthete Bunthorne, in Patience, comes to mind. Yet, when I combine Stein-beck's (if indeed these are his works) viciousness towards gays (his esthetes are automatically homosexual), so I can't help but conclude that his own feelings for men were power-ful, perhaps even frightening, and that he hid behind the simper and the snigger, proffering a quick teasing glimpse of his true feelings in the "Stevedore" and in "Four Shades of Navy-Blue. " The latter is the best realized of the eight poems:

Four Shades of Navy-Blue

I

I sing the beauty of breeches on sailors,
The pants of the navy, songs of the sea.
Those round little seats in their snug woolen casings
Have rhythm and color and pure symmetry.

II

I cannot chant the glories of the dawn,
To me it brings no perfect ecstacy.
Instead I find I'm very strangely drawn
To sing of the breeches
Of the king's navee.

III

The progress of each rhythmic, swinging seat
I follow, dazed, with half-enchanted eyes,
I wonder, if recruiting for the fleet
Consists in grading fannys for their size?

IV

Being a girl who was never addicted
To picking up sailors in dance-hall or street,
I feel that my speech can be quite unrestricted.
There's beauty to me in the pants on the fleet.

V

I say it without any personal feeling,
I truly adore every navy-clad seat,
My aesthetic thrill I'm no longer concealing,
There's beauty to me in the pants on the fleet.

VI

That insolent swagger is utterly charming,
I'm lost in a rapture that's full and complete.

        I say it with frankness that <u>should</u> be disarming,
        There's beauty to me in the <u>pants</u> on the fleet.

A common ploy among closet queens is, of course, to outdo
macho males at being macho. Ridicule and snigger at gays
is a means of rubbing off your own mental phallus. How
else explain Steinbeck's perpetrations of these poems? At
thirty-two one would expect him to have arrived, more or
less, as a writer. Perhaps he sensed that the art colony at
Carmel (The <u>Beacon</u> included news of Carmel) needed a few
lumps. Though near in actual miles, Cannery Row was
metaphorically far over the seas from Carmel--or was it the
other way around. Carmel, in Steinbeck's mind, may have
been Paris. I don't know if anyone ever managed to count
the hairs on Steinbeck's chest, or those on his crotch, ears,
and in his beard; my guess is that they were far less numer-
ous, and far less wiry than he supposed.

Note: I am aware that Mrs. Steinbeck, upset by the reap-
pearance of these poems, now claims that she wrote them.
Obviously, her saying so doesn't constitute absolute proof.
My feeling is that the issue is vexed, and it is in that spirit
that I offer my analysis of these poems. I appreciate that
their authorship is conjectural.

I, ME, MYSELF, ET CETERA:

Dan Gerber's Departures*

I

Blurb quote on back of book following hip picture and hip autobiographical statement by Gerber: "... finely honed poetry, pure and unadorned. "--Jim Harrison.

Dedication page: "for Jim Harrison. "

II

A gathering of possessives from Departures: my early promise ... my profile ... my way ... my mother ... my life ... my name ... my respectable novel ... my biography ... my gladstone bag ... my hands ... my chin ... my family crest ... my labor ... my grief ... my taxes ... my boat ... my snow shoes ... my palm ... my face ... my skin ... my wife ... my music ... my desire ... my god ... my body ... my head ... my eye ... my heart ... my window ... my shadow ... my desk ... my ear ... my delight ... my boredom ... my fire ... my paintings ... my overstuffed soul ... my table ... my peas ... my knife ... my grin ... my possessions ... my reflection ... my insane lust ... my need to be left alone ... my all American boy.

III

A gathering of verbs (first person subject) from Departures: I've wanted ... I've wasted ... I've dreamed ...

*Reprinted by permission from Margins, No. 13 (Aug. -Sept. 1974) p. 68; Copyright © 1974 by Margins.

I'd like ... I've spent ... I watch ... I never learn ... I've
read ... I know ... I read ... I'm rocked ... I remem-
bered ... I imagine ... I begin ... I travel ... I grow sad
... I've acquired ... I dream ... I am loving a woman ...
I hold two fingers ... I enter the book. I think ... I have
no use for ... I've had a lot of unhappiness ... I decided
... I'll buy ... I suffer ... I don't know yet ... I buried
... I've forgotten ... I covered ... I'm back ... I suspect
... I suspect even ... I dreamed ... I'm tired of poems ...
I want ... I'm not ashamed ... I'm bored ... I put on my
trousers ... I came to important things ... I say goodbye ...

THE POEM AS DILDO:

Leonard Cohen's The Energy of Slaves*

Where hath the magic gone that informed Spice Box of Earth, some of Cohen's songs, and Beautiful Losers? Taking The Energy of Slaves for itself, these formulas for writing poems emerge, apparently representing LC's present state as poet:

      1.   Inculcate poems with a sleazy romantic jargon: thee, thou, etc.

      2.   Make your ugly-duckling fifteen-year-old readers (female) feel that you've assumed the burden of their ugliness and pain, and that you love them: see "Portrait of a Girl": here the teenie-sweetie thinks she is too fat-assed and hairy, and she sweats too much.

      3.   Luxuriate in your own self-pity and crippled states of mind. Imagine you are a dwarf addressing your nymphette: "You could love me as an embalmed child / if my legs were not so thick and short. "

      4.   Sink deeper and deeper into moaning. A teenage girl I used to know played LC's albums interminably during a difficult period when she was contemplating suicide. You need never be specific about why "we are the wretched ones. "

      5.   Drop in bits of hip bad grammar: "Keep me waiting in Room 801 / like you did that night when we were young. "

      6.   Be a bit gross, become increasingly grosser, become turn-on so that poems become dildos for teenage nymphettes fantasizing about you whilst doing themselves:

*Reprinted by permission from Margins, No. 13 (Aug. -Sept. 1974) pp. 66-67; Copyright © 1974 by Margins.

Since you had "a perfect ass" you'll have to forgive my
not falling for "your face or your conversation"

or

the way you hold your cunt
is old-fashioned

or

I'm going to burn down your house
and fuck you in the ass
                    (the big bad wolf to the little pig?)

7.   Avoid punctuation so that your "craft of verse"
gives a superficial illusion of sophistication.   Also use the
clumsy connective "that" a lot, so that becomes a clue that
you can use a prose that almost sings:

nor is it a foreign claw
that sears this from my first and only heart

8.   For the sake of wide sales in places like Wool-
worths, Sears, B. Daltons, and Simpsons, keep the anatomy
of your love pretty much on a valentine level:

"The only wisdom I want to have" is to know whether
or not I am the only one you love.

9.   Always, persist in vagueness: "I have nothing in
mind for you, " "I am the ghost of Joan of Arc, " "the one
cunt sunk like an imperial bathtub / in my slippery conversa-
tion. "   Good poems, according to LC, are apples with blood
on them: "There is always blood on your apple / and only
sometimes on mine. "

10.   By down-grading your talent imply that it is in
reality gigantic: you create "in that shabby little laboratory /
called my talent. "

11.   Attack poets and writers of a larger talent than
your own, viz., in the verses "On Hearing That Irving
Layton Was Kissed By Allen Ginsberg At A Toronto
Poetry Reading. "   Cohen reports that shortly after Pat-
rick Kavanagh received "the blessings" of Allen Ginsberg,
he, Kavanagh, died.   Or, in a neatie described in the back-
cover blurb as "an unforgettable, acidly poignant 'letter' to

one Norman Mailer, " Cohen declares that if Norman Mailer ever fucks with him or comes up and punches him in the gut he'll "k--l" Mailer and his "entire family. "

12. An, occasionally, but rarely, drop in a fine poem reminiscent of your earlier best: this one begins with an awful cliché (Love is a fire) and turns quite fine: Love's fire 'disfigures everyone / It is the world's excuse / for being ugly. "

13. Yes, but then return to the I-don't-give-a-fuck tone: as the lovers lie together in Acapulco, "young monks" proceed through the snows of Mt. Baldy single-file, "shivering and farting in the moonlight. "

Instead of fulfilling T. S. Eliot's projection for the world's end as a whimper rather than a bang, Cohen's poetry shimmers off with a shiver and a fart.

VERSES WITH POINTED EARS

Leonard Nimoy's Will I Think of You*

What kinds of poems would you write if you were
Leonard Nimoy and had little pointed ears? Would the mas-
tications of your soul via verse be drenched in soul-other
planetary cosmic schlock? Or would you have somehow by
ultra-sensitive radar tapped into the celestial rhythms of the
universe in a superhuman way? Well, dear reader, you won't
have to go far to find the answer; for Leonard Nimoy of
Star Trek fame presents himself to the world in a couple of
volumes of poems that won't quit. I bought one of them the
other day. It is called Will I Think of You? An absolutely
darling collection of soul belches and eructations, accom-
panied by photographs arranged and snapped by Nimoy.

Before moving into Will I Think of You, let me specu-
late about the fantasy some celebrities in other media enjoy
--that they are poets. Has the hitherto lowly role of poet
exalted itself? Nimoy is one of several non-poet folk who
have presented their various orifice-verse-pickings to the
world. John Boy of "The Waltons" is another; his slender
volume Poems actually isn't too bad. I gather that most of
them he wrote before he was famous. Then, I understand
that Robert Mitchum published a book of poems too. These
I haven't seen; but since he is the greatest actor in Holly-
wood, they might just be good. I'd like to hear from anyone
out there who could lend me a copy of Mitchum's book. And
novelists, too, try their hand at writing poetry. John Stein-
beck reputedly did it, under the pseudonym Amnesia Glass-
cock--a baker's half-dozen poems extolling the virtues of the
"beauty of breeches on sailors," etc. And Ernest Heming-
way. And James Joyce. And good old Ray Bradbury billows
along on his numerous laurels and presents "poetry" to the

---

*Reprinted by permission from Foco, Vol. 1 (Oct. 12, 1976)
p. 5; Copyright © 1976 by Foco.

world. He hires big orchestras to orchestrate them, folks.
I heard him read one of his concoctions at a Comicbook Fair
in San Diego last November; it was absolutely embarrassing,
actually bad derivative Swinburne, bad nineteenth-century.
And the ideas were slick, superficial, on the level an aver-
age undergraduate of no particular promise would write. And
yet, Ray Bradbury will go far with this terrible stuff: I
can't remember what orchestra leader ... I think it was
Previn ... he "commanded" to produce music to accompany
his interminable poem. And then the host of rock and pop
singers: Donovan liked calling himself "Your Bard. " Jim
Morrison wrote and published a book of middling verses.
And teachers and professors hoping to be in with their stu-
dents include Dylan's songs in their poetry courses. One
horrible aspect of all this is that these poetasting dabblers
assume that they need not be in touch with the serious po-
etry of their time: poetry is like masturbating--the fact that
you whip off your own batch makes it good and worth some-
body's attention. It's like Sunday painting, and every serious
poet knows now what serious painters must feel about the
hordes of hobbyists who could care less about discipline,
craft, training and yet who regard themselves as "serious"
painters.

Why do these celebrities want to be poets? Does
this mean that poets have supplanted architects, doctors,
politicians, singers as the ultimate in turn-on professions?
In a dismal world crashing to the ground (as we are so fre-
quently reminded), does the pursuit of poetry, implying as it
does the sensitive, the ethereal, the inspired, the released
and free, does the pursuit of poetry now rank as the highest
of human pursuits? As a practicing poet myself I like the
idea. Soon the ladies' magazines will heroize poets as ro-
mantic interests, forgetting that Dylan Thomas was a slob with
women, that Robert Lowell was a supreme toad-stabber of
female parts, that James Dickey is said to devour women
the way other men devour tootsie rolls, that Robert Frost
was probably very colorless in bed. Poets are not all Cho-
pins, my dear. Nor are they all Byrons. Byron, you re-
call, spurning his wife's marriage proposals, finally accepted
her, then tormented her on their wedding night, screaming
that he was in hell, keeping a candle burning by their bed-
side all night, and declaring that he didn't mind sleeping with
women as long as they weren't too plain.

It seems, in short, that poets are in. And this in-
cludes the grubby ones.

So Leonard Nimoy joins the ranks of the exalted. Via
the good publishing hands of Dell, one of the largest of mass
media publishers. According to the cover-blurb, Nimoy ad-
dresses his beloved, "hoping that somehow she will hear.
These are the eyes of a man seeking his beloved in every
place where life and beauty dwell. This is the magic of love
itself, transforming our world into a place of miracles. "

Why the lover doesn't turn up seems to me obvious:
these poems are too shameless, embarrassing, and tediously
awful. The worst of them quiver on that old fiddle of ro-
mantic sentiments. The absent lover seems to have taste
when it comes to poetry. Perhaps it helps to imagine a kind
of verse (don't dignify it with the name poetry) cuts below
Benton or Rod McKuen. Cold-cuts below! The utter pom-
posity of Nimoy's conceptions comes through in the el slicko
titles he gives to his parts: "Daybreak and Darkness, " "Sea-
sons, " "Joys and Sorrows, " "In Places, " "At Times. "

Here is an example of a jug-gurgling verse, where the
beloved is a jug of fire-juice and the poet is another: fire-
jugjuice female fills up firejugjuice male:

> Will I think of you?
> Only when it's cold
>
> and I'm shivering
>
> Against the wind
>
> And suddenly from inside
> The core of me
> From my deepest depth:
> Comes
> A small warming flame
> Which wants to grow
> And I fight it
> Until I realize I need it
> Want it
> To flow through me
> To fill me
> because
> It is you.

If you glance at Nimoy's language you'll see that Ni-
moy has never once thought about the cliché as despicable:
"You shiver in the wind, " "deep inside the core of me, " "a
small warming flame, " "deepest depths. "

There is also an utterly coy image of rain on a window

as God's tears drenching the universe of Nimoy's misery,
because the hero's soul is aching and his heart is crying ...
a sort of forgetmenot poem: 'If this you see, remember
me. " Yes, these poems resemble those maudlin lines
raunchy country schoolboys scribbled on pencil tablets and
wadded up and flung across the aisle at Becky Thatcher.
What these poems crave is some of the juice those same boys
carved into the walls of the country school outhouse!

Nor does Nimoy, despite his trekking amidst all those
specific stars know how to be precise and use a telling im-
age. Here's the Good Samaritan theme once again:

<blockquote>
If we can help One Who finds the way
                    Too hard or too long
Then it is worth All of being
        And I will try to help
    Because someone helped me
Someone who cared more
    About the brothers on the road
                    Than about
the Gifts at the end
        And that someone was you
        So I will think of you
</blockquote>

Who is the you? What brothers on the road? What
Gift at the end? What way is lost? At least the parables
in the Bible had an original cadence and a vital language.
Nimoy's poems are cheap dimestore paste-pearl rings.   Love
for Nimoy is a matter of much sexless mutual weeping.   You
have to be something of a cretin to turn on to them.   Or, if
it is still true that love via fantasy is blind, then I suppose
you can fantasize that handsome dude with the funny ears,
the Star Trek happiest, speaking all these nothings into your
ears.   But that's a trip I'm not into.   And as a serious poet,
I resent the glutting of what little poetry market-audience ex-
ists with such verse as Will I Think of You.   I've been for-
tunate myself in finding publishers, so my response to Ni-
moy's verse isn't sour grapes.   Rather I hope that I speak
for a host of poets I know who can't find publishers for their
work, and who are turned down by the biggies--Dell, Random
House, Simon and Schuster--who say there's no money in
poetry and then publish work like Nimoy's.   My crit-
ic's role is less than well-served if I slide along and see
such publishing without a protest.   For what efficacy my
scream may have, I make it loud and clear.   So, dear read-
er, consider yourself witness to a gigantic and horrible
scream of rage.

A RUSTY ROSE:

Eric Greinke*

> I, Robert D. Swets, did not write a word
> of the quotation from the Grand Rapids
> Press on the dustjacket of Iron Rose which
> has, for reasons unknown, been attributed
> to me by L. Eric Greinke. --R. Swets, 30
> August 74

Is $4.50 for a book of some 28 slight poems a rip-off? Is the fact that the author of Iron Rose is also a moving force behind Pilot Press Books an instance of unsubtle vanity enterprise? Does the fact that Greinke is the poetry editor of Amaranthus which he uses for one of the jacket blurbs to push his book also smack of vanity?

The answer to Question 1 is, obviously, that if the 28 poems are rifted with Keatsian gold, the book is not a rip-off. I am afraid that these poems are self-indulgent, slight, and clichéd. They are also carelessly printed: howlers like pathes for paths and "course black curtains" get through. One poem, "The Moon is Red," contains these clichés: the river runs to the sea, a woman breathes hard, deep things take place deep inside the woman; snow falls to earth; the night is cold; the road is long. Also, I feel unsure of Greinke's technical skill. Why, for example, does he hide the obvious wear-hair rhyme and pretend he doesn't have a couplet?

> I gave my love black roses
> to wear in her bloodblack hair.

Grammar Problems: in "The Snowy Fields" (yes, dedicated

---

*Reprinted by permission from Margins, No. 13 (Aug. -Sept. 1974) p. 63; Copyright © 1974 by Margins.

to Robert Bly who is not responsible for poems dedicated to
him) this line occurs: "If I was to walk across that field
.... " I suppose that avoiding the conditional sounds hip, but
I, for one, find it distasteful.   Also, Greinke writes: "It's
like when / you mark a coin. " This hip-fashion language
isn't literate and serves no purpose other than to sound "in. "
There is also a lot of self-congratulation in the book: Greinke
plants a lot of seed (cliché for sperm, right?); Greinke is in-
dulgent in his thinking, and assumes that mental confusion of
an image is art: in the title poem, for example, the speak-
er's pistol shoots bullets, stones, and the ubiquitous seeds
into "the postal wind, " whatever that is.   "The postal wind"
carries these rocks, stones, bullets, seeds to the woman's
"black rose" and enters the rose of teeth and hard leaves.
Inside, the "seed" welds new roses "into your thighs. " Ugh.

Finally, most of the poems are dedicated to friends,
including two to Donald Hall.   I find these dedications ego-
trips.   It's as if poets who do this are saying: this poem is
timeless and deathless, and, because it is so good, and since
your name is attached to it, you too shall be timeless and
deathless.   I'm not against writing poems for friends, or
against giving them; if most of a collection though is made
up of poems to various anonymous people, I feel excluded.
One solution is to put a special list at the back of the book
somewhere saying "the following poems are for the friends
and poets indicated. " Or something like that.

I'm sorry to be so negative.   I am suspicious of pub-
lishers who publish their own work, and always assume that
no other press would publish it.   This may be my problem.
If Greinke's poems were better I would have less complaint.
Also, I am unimpressed by the wild jacket endorsements by
critics from the Traverse City Eagle, the Sault Evening News,
the Grand Rapids Press, and Greinke's own magazine Ama-
ranthus.

WHIPPIN' IT OFF OVER THE MIND AND ART

OF ARTIE BREMER

Stephen Vincent*

Time so encapsulates these days that Artie Bremer has already slipped from being a household name to a semi-anonymity. Was it Martin Luther King, or was it George Wallace? No, that one was Sirhan. If you were to take a poll on your local street, you'd probably find that five out of ten people, or fewer, remember Artie. How long does it take for an assassin to become a folk hero? My hypothesis is that a killer becomes the subject matter of art as soon as he proceeds (or regresses) towards his anonymity, where, if the assassin hasn't been fixed in the amber of art, he slips off pretty much forever. For example, where are the ballads and elegies for the doctor who shot Huey Long? The Austrian Archduke? Who celebrated Gandhi's killer?

Something in a poet's psyche refuses to let certain ones of these vermin-folk disappear into the limbo of weirdos, misfits, and assassins. The reason may be that poets need to rub against turn-on Satans as a means of resolving their own fears--including the need to fulfill the murderer's role. Isn't the act of the poem an act of murder, or, at least, of violation--if it commemorates a presence or a memory fascinating to the poet?

There are so many ways of death, as the Good Book says: some are picturesque, some are aesthetic. Others are crude, gross, and violent. Surely, our hope is understandable--if we ever appear in someone's poem let the poet be sufficiently competent so as not to intensify our suffering at his/her hands via inept craftsmanship. If we are to be

*Reprinted by permission from Margins, No. 19 (April 1974) pp. 44-45; Copyright © 1974 by Margins.

tacked up (or pinned wriggling to the walls of the poem) let
it be, we pray, firmly and well. I'm sure that Artie Brem-
er, Charlie Manson, etc., would also share this prayer.

   Consider the attractiveness villains had for Shake-
speare, Satan for Milton, Faust for Goethe, and Renaissance
murderers for Robert Browning. The list is indefinite. Per-
haps some keen death-wish emits poufs of regret from poets
fascinated by criminals, regret that they--the poets--were not,
alas, among the victims. It's actually very sexual. Since
murder is a form of rape, since fantasizing that the murder-
er is coming to get you is an aid to masturbation and love
palpitations, the crush and shimmer of death are stimuli for
one's orgasm (and for one's art) whether via a hand or via a
responsive orifice. The love-strokings by the poet of the
murderer, in poems, are obviously a simulation of flesh-
pleasure-pain. A sort of Bremer's Law follows: the greater
one's sexual frustration, the easier it is to frighten oneself
by imagining the intrusion of robbers and rapists coming to
get you: viz., widowers and virgins on TV reporting imag-
ined and real close-calls to the police. The poem becomes
a safety-valve, allowing the poet to release his special frus-
trations on stage before portions of the world's poetry reader-
ship. Bremer's Law moves into the holiest of places.

   Recently I heard an argument for death as the ulti-
mate sex act. For natural as well as for unnatural deaths.
The arguer had apparently stumbled onto an idea she hadn't
thought carefully about; for, when pressed to clarify, she
couldn't. Not that the idea is particularly novel; but it does
seem worth exploring as it affects poetry, and as it relates
to Stephen Vincent's poem. The risk I take, of course, is
that like the woman who argues that death is sexual and there-
by reveals her own necrophiliac proclivities, I too may be so
accused. A good critic lowers the bucket to whatever depths
he feels he must. It is true that in these more or less per-
missive days we shall eventually see necrophiliacs marching
for their rights, for understanding, and for access to their
own cemeteries and mausoleums, bodies being willed there
for a price by indifferent or needy families. Now, admitted-
ly, this gross, vaguely Jonathan Swiftian idea, on the surface
has little to do with poetry or with Vincent's chapbook. But,
if we are open-minded about how death affects us, we will
admit that death is in good measure a groin-vulva experience.

   Notice the next time you share the news with some-
one, of a common acquaintance's suicide, how the breath

heightens, the eyeballs dilate and the voice trembles. Your
hair may even stand on end. The sharing (commiseration)
reaches a pitch until nervous laughter occurs. And then we
fall back into the evenness of the day's normal hours. Shock,
I am saying, is sexual--as is fear. By extension, hairs
standing on end are paradigms for the rising clitoris and the
rigid penis. Further, the stiffness of a corpse is the rigid-
ity of sex organs frozen hard awaiting mold and decay. To
look at a dead person rigid is like regarding that person sud-
denly exposed in a private sexual act, resolving itself. The
rigidity of the body, even as it turns blue, is a paradigm for
the assassin-rapist's weapon ... the pistol or knife or axe.
Our psyches are lured to the attack-weapon much as we are
lured to commiserate (for ourselves, actually) beside the stiff
remains of the departed one. Our own pleasure-pain antici-
pates our own final orgasm-death-expenditure of sexlife mus-
cle energy. And we have all noticed how the odor of funer-
al parlors, produced primarily by massed gladioli, resemble
the odor of kum.

It would appear, also, that each witnessing of a death
or a murder enables us more courageously to confront our
own death, whether by fire, water, axe, pistol, or disease.
Sex as violence. Death as violence. Death as sex. And
another syllogism: all sex contains some pleasure blent with
pain. Death is sex. Therefore, death contains both pleas-
ure and pain. Now, substitute the esthetic experience for
death and sex to see how art and creativity interweave with
death and sex.

Poems about murderers and outlaws are almost al-
ways either overtly or implicitly, sexual. Michael McClure's
splendid series on Billy the Kid and Jean Harlow develop a
manic sexual tension out of contrasting erotic daimons. My
own "What John Dillinger Meant to Me" is a rendering of
adolescent fantasies about an outrageously sexual outlaw/
killer who shot up my hometown. And let's hear it out there
for "Frankie and Johnnie, " "Jack the Ripper" and "Lizzie
Borden. " But why labor the obvious.

What fascinates me about Vincent's "The Ballad of
Artie Bremer" is its style. It's the only "ballad" or com-
memorative poem I know adapting cadences and spacings to
a masturbatory jert-jert rhythm. And it doesn't stop until
the final "You Blew Up / You Blew UP.... " But I antici-
pate. Observe Vincent's opening:

```
        Bremer    Bremer   Bremer
        Bremer    Bakery
        Bremer    Bazooka
        Bremer    Battle The Father Plan

        Bremer    Invite Your Father Home
        Bremer    Bomb
        Bremer    Boom
        Bremer    Behave Yourself
        Bremer    Bathe Yourself

        Is There A Tongue
        I Would Not Touch

        Bremer   Beauty
        Beau Bald   Bremer   I Scald You
                             I Scald You

        Bremer   Blood
        Bremer   Blood
        Bremer's Blood
             Brim
             Brim
             Brim
```

Throughout, the rhythms are essentially hand-regular, so reg-
ular, in fact, that you can switch hands without missing a
beat.   The slight variations in words (Bakery as distinct
from Bazooka, for example) represent varying fingerpad pres-
sures and/or dildo angles.   And note the intense caressing
physicality of what's already transpired: the commands to
Bremer, nicely sadistic--behave yourself, bathe yourself, I
scald you, etc., culminate in the Tongue/Touch moment, and
lead to the marvelous whip-whip of Blood ... Brim.   These
stroke-accelerations prepare us for the father and state
lashings that follow, and the release via this highly physical,
Bremer-Caress passage:

```
        Take A Bremer To
        Sleep With A Bremer
        Talk To A Bremer
        There Was A Young Bremer
        Who Came
```

Later, the poem turns marvelously raunchy, our onanistic
joys heightened by the odor of Bremer's socks and the pos-
sibility that our fantasy-Bremer has eluded us:

Bremer
Where Is Your Body
Bremer
   Dirty Socks
    On Cheap Broom Floor
Where Is Your

I Have A Duty To Touch
And To Hold
And To

Where Is Your Body
Bremer
Where Is Your

Blood Blood Blood
Three Men In A

Bremer In The Laurel
Not For Your Head
Poet
Not For Your Head
Blood
Brother
Blood

    Here Vincent makes the equation exact: Poet is broth-
er to Bremer.

THE RUSSIAN ROD MCKUEN:

Yevgeny Yevtushenko

From Desire to Desire is a collection of over a hun-
dred love poems, written by Russia's stellar gift to world
poetry Yevgeny Yevtushenko. In paper, this new collection
sells for two dollars fifty, which isn't that much of a rip-off.
There's a nice introspective portrait on the back cover of
the poet sweatered and casual. And the prestigious trans-
lators include James Dickey, Lawrence Ferlinghetti, Stanley
Kunitz, Peter Levi, John Updike, and Richard Wilbur--each
in his way injecting a few hormones from his own poetic
system into this pallid writing. All of these translators, I
should add, apparently do not read Russian, or, at least do
not read it well enough to translate from it. They have been
"helped"--that's the word--by non-poets who know the lan-
guage. Isn't there a matter of ethics here, or of profes-
sionalism? Should translators know the language of the work
they translate? Perhaps because of these translators' ignor-
ance of the language, Yevtushenko's poems sound worse than
they should. But I don't think so.

We all remember how popular Yevtushenko's readings
were in this country a few years ago. Hyped by Time-Life,
Inc., masses attended his readings in gymnasiums, music-
halls, theaters. He was a Russian Rod McKuen: undergoing,
sentimental, self-revealing, egotistic, facile. Serious poets
and the universities and colleges picked up on him, anxious
to rub against a contemporary Russian consciousness, even
a mediocre one. My guess is that secretly everybody wished
that Mr. Bliss would find America so great and wonderful he
would abandon Russia and live here. His fees, I'm told,
were enormous. Twenty-five American poets could have been
paid handsomely for readings. I felt then that Yevtushenko
delivered little; and this current volume convinces me that he
still delivers embarrassingly little, considering his enormous
reputation.

He's an entirely non-controversial poet. The innocent adolescent will find nothing here to blush over. The adult prurience-hunter will see nothing to complain of to the censoring authorities. I suppose it takes a certain talent to write love-poems this low on the erotic thermometer. More important, there's nothing that would in any way lend itself to liberalizing the Russian climate for writers and thinkers. Poets I know have been distressed by Yevtushenko's failure (one assumes that his immense world-wide reputation would give him some immunity from political harrassment in his homeland) to speak out, however tepidly, against Russian persecutions of writers, thinkers, and Jews.

His constant theme is himself. Yevtushenko strikes me as one of the most narcissistic poets writing today. Here, for example, are the first-person references in a simple poem "Deep Snow":

> I ask
> I do
> I peer
> I know
> I am skiing
> I can spy
> I feel troubled
> I have to go
> I'll not get lost
> I feel like smoking
> I'm weary of running from myself
> I'll ride home instead
> my skiis
> I'll arrive
> She yearned for me
> I'll answer
> I'll begin to think
> I don't understand
> I shake my head
> I answer
> I reply
> I am skiing over the white snow

His approach to women as love objects is mindless and clichéd. His women behave in the worst nineteenth-century role-playings. Masha "understands everything / though she doesn't understand a thing." Masha is a serious "wide-eyed being / and the room of my mouth goes dry when her slender boyish legs ... bear her helplessly to me.... I

kiss all that Masha's arms are--from elbow to the rose-
petals of her nails.   The woman in "The Incendiary" is a
sort of Willi who is both here and not here.   Note the cli-
chés:

> You're here with me, and yet not here.
> In fact you have abandoned me.   You glide
> through the smoldering wreckage of the past,
> holding aloft a bluish light in your hand.

Here, in "A Moment Half-Winter Half-Fall, " Yevtushenko
matches Leonard Cohen's teeny-bopper, dildoesque poems:

> Like a defenseless, little animal,
> Your shoe nuzzled its mouth against my shoe,
> but, embarrassed and a little dead,
> it, too, kept itself from a reply.

Another woman, Irene, sits "shining with goodness, all shy
and childlike. " She is the prostitute with the heart of gold.
She has people to sleep with, but no one to wake up with.
Her brown eyes, once clear, are now "sad. "

   Many of Yevtushenko's poems are sullied by mindless
abstractions, one of his hallmarks.   "Early Illusions" con-
tains these goodies; an undergraduate of modest talent writ-
ing these in a workshop would be asked to switch majors to
biology:

> Early illusions are beautiful
> Early illusions are wounding
> But what does it matter!   We are above vanity,
> we embrace the highest knowledge,
> saved by our happy blindness. . . .

The best of these poems is "On the Death of a Dog. " Here
Yevtushenko's sentimentality and egoism are restrained by the
vigorous theme of the dog's death.   Yevtushenko even seemed
to care.   But such poems are few.

   I hope I have not been too unkind in my responses to
this widely-heralded poet.   Yevtushenko condemns himself,
actually, in words which I feel his prestigious translators will
ignore--perhaps because they were probably paid good dollars
by the publisher to ignore them.   Yevtushenko writes: "To
be sentimental is not a weakness but a crime. " And here is
his final lament.   Perhaps even he realizes that clichés don't
really do the work they're intended to:

> What good thing then has all my fiery declaiming
>   stirred,
> if, scattering myself from the stage, making the
>   clichés roll,
> I wanted to give happiness to the whole world
> and found I could not give it to one living soul?

I'm afraid I'm one of those living souls his clichés have
failed to penetrate.   Moreover, I lament and resent the costs
lavished on publishing such mediocre work.   There are a
hundred American poets around who deserve an audience ...
and as many good foreign ones ... who won't find one via
Yevtushenko's publisher.   But isn't that, folks, what money
and publishing are all about?

EAGLES AND SUNS:

Octavio Paz

The fascination of American poets with Spanish-speaking poets puzzles me. With some poets--particularly Lorca, Neruda, and Parra--this adulation amounts to an obsession. Big American poets have translated them: Robert Bly, W. S. Merwin, Clayton Eshleman, Edwin Honig. Incredibly fancy editions (usually bilingual) seem to appear monthly. You're nowhere in American poetry, or, so it seems, unless you've written your Neruda, Parra, Lorca or Paz poems. Reasons for this obsession? One is that the proximity of Latin countries to our own borders helps American poets feel a kinship. Two: Spanish is an easier language to master than French, German, or Russian--so it is easier for American poets (few of them are gifted at foreign languages) to appear to read, or read at, Spanish. Three: American poets feel deficient because they lack the breadth and cultural sweep European poets possess--you assume that European poets, including the English ones, are bi- or tri-lingual. Four: Spanish poets have been political martyrs: Neruda's recent victimization by Allende's slaughterers; Lorca's assassination by Franco's thugs; etc. Major twentieth-century poet-martyrs. Where many poets feel they are outcasts in their own culture, an affection for poet-martyrs comes naturally.

The occasion for these reflections is the appearance of Mexican poet Octavio Paz's Eagle or Sun. These poems were written and published during 1949-1950, some twenty-seven years ago--which may explain why their surrealism seems so warmed over, and why they seem so boring-- tedium is one of Paz's favorite words and favorite states of mind. Paz himself supposedly explained that Eagle or Sun is an "exploration" of Mexico. At the same time, it is an "exploration of the relations between language and the poet, reality and language, the poet and history. " I find Paz's Eagle or Sun almost consistently dull, except for a pair of prose poems. Frankly, I don't know what all the shouting is

101

about, or why this book deserves publication.   Is it the
bucks?

Elusiveness and vagueness characterize the book.   The
image of the mythical "messengers of Someone, capital S"
who does not appear but who dominates an entire sequence is
an example.   The Someone seems at best a figment of the
poet's shadow-mind.   In one of his more rambling pieces,
Paz oscillates around the problem in this maddening way:

> A little reflection has made me see that you are
> not a memory, not even something forgotten: I
> do not feel you as the one that I was, but rather
> as the one that I will be, as the one that is being
> ....   In sum, I don't know you, I've never seen
> you, and yet I have never felt alone, without you.

There is an uneasy sense that both Paz and his daimon are
victims caught in a sterile debilitation--tedium.   "True Life"
he sees nihilistically.   The phrase is his, and his rendering
of it is for me facile: the sophomoric mind weaves in and
around itself, a mind in love with philosophy, but mistaking
that discipline for the mere piling on of antitheses, ending
with verbal play as the positive force.   No conclusions are
possible, only a verbal embroidery.

I suppose, as the jacket declares, that these poems
do have political dimensions.   But, they are in the voice of
a talented man who has given up, even on politics.   He re-
calls his loves, conversations, friendships.   All are over.
He is melancholy, hopeless.   He quits "the nevertheless, the
even, the in spite of everything."   He knows "the trap of
morality and the drowsiness of certain words."   He has "lost
faith in all those constructions of stone, ideas, ciphers.   I
quit.   I await the event."

Rather drastic 1940's Existentialism?   One can't help
recalling that "Myth of Sisyphus."   Paz is a hothouse Exis-
tentialist.   At the base of that accursed mountain he lies
whimpering, flashing multi-colored flowers and demons.   He
fails, unlike Camus' hero, to rise with dignity once more to
push that blasted stone back up the mountain.   "There's no
use," Paz writes, "going out or staying at home.   No use
erecting walls against the impalpable.   A mouth will extin-
guish all the fires, a doubt will root up all the decisions.
It will be everywhere without being anywhere."   He is left
with his memories.   Yes, they never quit him.   They feed

his tedium.   He is the big-little man who once had illusions
of being entirely big: but, alas, he's been chopped down.
"It's true, " he writes, "I haven't triumphed in life, that I
never leave my retreat unless disguised and impelled by hard
necessity.   But when I am alone, and envy and spite show
their horrible faces, the memory of those hours pacifies and
calms me. "

Towards the end of the series there are some good
surrealist pieces.   One, "Exit, " avoids the excesses of sur-
realist writing--the easy facile associative images of minds
freaked out or freaking out.   But these good moments don't
redeem the book--for me, at least.

Paz emerges as a self-obsessed man.   Every page
reflects his fascination, almost fecal, with bits and scroung-
ings of his bowels-psyche.   It occurs to me that a poet re-
stricting his boundaries so severely is perverse.   One of
these narcissitic poems, "My Life with the Wave, " does,
however, despite a coy beginning, seem to work.   We sus-
pend disbelief and imagine that the poet brings a wave home
from the sea to live with him in his apartment.   He takes
the wave home on a train, dumping it into the water-cooler
for the space of the journey, thereby salting the drinking
water.   He's arrested, accused of poisoning the water.   The
investigation lasts a year.   He's sentenced, and months later
released.   He arrives home, hears laughter and singing com-
ing from his apartment.   The effect on him is "like the
smack of a wave of surprise when surprise smacks us in the
chest. " The wave has lived all this while in his apartment,
waiting for him.   He loves her light, fragrance, color.
"Love was a game, a perpetual creation.   Everything was
beach, sand, a bed with sheets that were always fresh.
Plunging into her waters, I would be drenched to the socks
and then find myself high above, at a dizzying height, mys-
teriously suspended, to fall like a stone.... "

But, alas, he never reaches the center of her being.
He never touches "the nakedness of pain and of death.   Per-
haps it does not exist in waves ... she had no center, just
an emptiness like a whirlwind that sucked me in and smoth-
ered me. " From this point forwards things worsen: the
wave is bored with him.   He tries to amuse her by installing
a colony of fish in the house.   She adores a couple of piran-
has.   He's jealous.   He kills the fish.   The wave beats and
pounds him until he nearly drowns.   Finally, winter comes
and she turns to ice.   He is unmoved and puts the ice in a

canvas bag and sells it to a waiter in a restaurant who chops
the wave into little pieces and puts them in buckets for chill-
ing wine.   Obviously, salt in your ice-water doesn't matter
here.

Another successful piece is a delightfully grim se-
quence, worthy of a Jodorowsky film, about a little girl who
loses her head and, who, after much blood and torture, finds
it.   An occasional authentic sado-masochism isn't enough,
alas, to redeem an otherwise passive, self-obsessive book of
poems.   I remain unconvinced that Eagle or Sun is very con-
sequential.

A RIGHT FINE PORK ROAST, FOLKS:

J. D. Reed*

Part One of these Odes concludes by helping us get
to sleep: pretend we can stay seven years old forever.
Part Two makes the rounds and concludes that we're lucky
we can't see the backs of our necks since there's a "big
wheel" turning there, "proud, mechanical, the circus lost in
rubble." Part Three concludes with an Ode by the Poet as
Pimp, declaring that he's going to the country and build
"snow angels by the roadhouse." Part Four winds down
with the image of a road coming towards us out of the mist,
a "powerful, black river." Part Five pays homage to Ne-
ruda's Woodcutter, the poet finding himself "fish-eyed / in
the bubble of spit" on the Woodcutter's mouth. Conclusion
to this part, and to the entire book: "My God. This is a
separate world."

This rough attempt to find hooking points for Fatback
Odes doesn't do justice to the book. Every page crackles
with the unexpected. Reed has wasted neither feelings nor
language. The poems usually operate on a level that says as
much about Reed's feelings of himself as a poet, and about
the function of poetry, as it does about the whores, friends,
and memories. Somehow Reed brings off touches that in
lesser poets would simply be clever:

> Dora Sue's perineum
> is nailed to my Levis.
>> ("Ode on Ron's Holiday Lounge")

> And night fell like a bull dike
> on a girl scout.
> You labored over a couplet

*Reprinted by permission from Margins, No. 18 (March
1975) pp. 69-70, 72; Copyright © 1975 by Margins.

which had to contain
two images of rebirth.
　　　　　　　("If you See Yourself from the Corner of the
　　　　　　　　　Study While At Work At Your Desk Ode")

Both of these moments work: in the first Dora Sue has
treated the speaker badly, and he's getting even. In the sec-
ond, Reed confronts the awful problem of writing when the
imagination flags and the writer has the urge to dredge up
some stock romantic images.

"Under Mons Veneris" is a tour de force, containing,
as it does, a neatly arranged series of epithets for the va-
gina. Reed is capable of a nice ironic dimension in the final
line:

Flap　flange
gash　hole
rill　oyster
bearded clam,
and one-eyed tiger

pin wallet　slash
the brillo pads
mouth-in-the-bloomers
sausage grinder

crack gap
slit　cave
old red dugout
camembert trench

snack　mussel
wet tunnel　cock throttle
tube and snatch
honeypot and rhubarb pie

tank　twat
dipper and fluff
dork necklace　dick-choke

vaseline valve and vagina of course
it's not just your body I adore.

A sensual sensual image of linked tongues evokes Reed's feel-
ings about his parents, their duelling with tongues, and "that
tongue / on my tongue a while longer, thinking."

The grotesque material of a bar, in "The Busy Bee," says something about our deaths. The central figure is of an old alcoholic, Betty, who gives men blow jobs, and finally dies, her liver destroyed. Skinny is one of her men:

> Skinny   sweet   you said
> that they're all lovely people
> and we're dying
> right alongside like tankers.

Here is an example of Reed's fondness for juxtaposing a beautiful romantic line (the first one) with a campy effect:

> Trout mouths dimple this long pool
> as if the Manistee had acne.
>   ("Your Complimentary River Ode")

As a reader I feel secure with Reed.   I think this happens because of Reed's control.

The final section of Fatback Odes, the "Ode" on Neruda's Woodcutter, works least well of the sections. Reed's imitation of Neruda's cataloguing doesn't work, and the impression is disjointed and careless.   Also, a peculiar surreal quality doesn't work: "I would come riding into Chile / on a styrofoam mare, her name / tangled in my hair." I'm not impressed.   This stanza is almost a parody of Neruda:

> Here's the death of a young moron
> in a county hospital,
> choking on his own drool
> until the drugged attendant comes
> to finish the job

If Reed's book is a good pork roast--which the back-cover blurb suggests it is--he has roasted it well.   Says Reed: "The crackling skin of a good pork roast is the only thing keeping the blade from the meat.   The heavy air cuts us open." Fatback Odes may not cut you open, but it will give you a few good scratches and bites--and that's a lot more than you get from most poems you read these days.

STRAW DREAMS:

Roxie Powell*

I don't know Roxie Powell (he? she? young? old?),
but I am relieved that the marvelous chapbook Dreams of
Straw has not disappeared from the face of the earth. It
almost did, apparently. Published by Dave Haselwood and
Charles Plymell originally in 1963 in a "project edition" of
few copies. First edition rare. To reprint, or rather to
do this fresh edition, the editors borrowed Allen Ginsberg's
personal copy: "the only one we found." Anyone anxious for
an original experience in poetry will love Dreams of Straw.
Non-workshop, non-Iowa, non-NYcity-clever, non-anything.
They read as if they had come up out of some fantasy root-
cellar where R. Powell had kept child-creatures a la crazy
dingdong school: Mr. and Mrs. Cow, Candy Bear, a dog
who likes to sit on spiders, etc. A sort of Grandma Moses
poems with balls--unselfconsciously crude, poignant, funny.
Here is "Spider":

> Across the street
> And under the tree,
>
> My dog sits upon a spider I caught.
>
> Tomorrow, I must take my spider to bathe
>
> And wash him clean.
>
> My dog doesn't know my spider is dirty.

A couple of the poems are ironic jibes at Mr. and
Mrs. Camperunit mentality people, dead from crown of head
down, yet capable of coming alive, if appropriately jolted:

*Reprinted by permission from Northeast Rising Sun, Vol. 1
(Jan. 1976) pp. 12, 14; Copyright © 1976 by Cherry Valley
Editions.

Sing, I'm Shit-face, a young Kansas
                                    boy, and
I've come to sing with grunt-farts of joy;
To sing of my country and beat off my
                                    tom-tom,
To sing you a sweet song
That's your dear Uncle's swan song.

Now that's political, dead-folk political.   Here is how
a real treat of a poem "Eye-Breaker" begins:

The undies are a little stained on the
                                    line,
Eye-breakers for the Mr. and Mrs. Cow
Whose children don't mind,

A windy day, all the same, is
To an undie what stain should be ...

There's a special wisdom too, dropped in with the
nonchalance of a yo-yo bouncing against a windowpane:

Well, if your collar's not starched
How can your neck stand straight.
It can, and that's how I'll hold it,
Unless some zipper undoes it again.

Another example, from "Run Little Child" (the child's
mother is waiting to beat him/her):

But do not forget who you are.
There is among you a fence to be
                                    painted,
A toilet to be flushed, a head to be
                                    shaved
And a mind still alive.
Go now and parade your virtue, I am
                                    tired,
Tomorrow they will lay me to rest in a
                                    casket
Made of bottles.

At his/her best, Powell has a crazy, child-like inno-
cence; it's as if he/she doesn't know how astute and incisive
he/she is.   What, for example, does one do with a poem like
this?

I Had a Whore

I had a whore wrapped up so tight
In my arms that
Christmas came late.

Santa Claus stood out my window
Pissing on the pane,
And damned if my only christmas card
Unglued with his pissy steam.

    The syntax of the last two lines belongs to a primitive writer, one who's learned his art from old family post cards and from newspaper verse reminiscent of that great writer Julia Moore, the Sweet Singer of Michigan. The childlike roll and timbre take over best though in "There is a Time":

There is a time for fish to woo
For clouds blue
Time is funny that way.

Sometimes windows true are really you,
Their hands are soft their panes are
                      blue

And if you try
Someday you'll cry
And all the rains will fade the time
                  away.

    I dig this poetry, obviously; I derive more pleasure from its scant pages than from hundreds of pages turned out by Atheneum Press, Black Sparrow, etc.... Someone should produce an anthology of American primitive verse, including pieces from this book, and generous chunks of Alfred Starr Hamilton. There must be dozens of poets like these around, generally neglected by sophisticated critics and poets. If one insists that one of the major functions of poetry is to deliver joy, then Roxie Powell earns numerous brownie points towards that super poetry badge in the sky. I want to see more of his (or her) work published. I hope he or she is still alive and writing up the proverbial storm. Will the real Roxie Powell please stand up!

GLUTEAL VS. MAMMARY POEMS:

A NICE MATTER OF AESTHETICS:

W. A. Roecker's You Know Me*

In a revealing poem buried towards the back of his
book, Roecker expresses his distaste for the work of "an-
other rhyming poet, an old man revered in the east, " whose
poems incense Roecker: "the issue's carcass ossified for
centuries. "   Who the old poet is, of course, is not revealed;
and it is fun, if pointless, to speculate on his identity.   The
old boy's poems are like girls "walking by in couplets / and
quatrains, all breasts / and no ass. "

The obvious implication is that the best poems have
both breasts and asses.   The implication, further, is that
such poems are Roecker's.   Are they?

Despite their economy, Roecker's poems are seldom
more than tantalizers: occasionally drink-sodden, usually
lonely (one of R.'s favorite words).   Further, almost all of
these poems deal in one way or another with the question of
the poet-speaker's male identity: hunting, fishing, drinking,
screwing.   They are non-intellectual, except insofar as
flashes of insight occur: "The worst must be over / when
pain loses its freshness. "   "Let's agree there's no one road
/ or uncontaminated eye to see it. "   Shibboleths of sorts,
but hardly wildly exciting as insights.

I guess it's the self-conscious Hemingwayesque male-
ness I dislike, finding Roecker's statements of it easy and
superficial.   Here are some examples: "... I was male as
always last night / and enjoying it for that ... drunk, / my
friends became brothers, we / leaned on each other and

*Reprinted by permission from Margins, No. 12 (June-July
1974) pp. 54-55; Copyright © 1974 by Margins.

laughed / when we could see / we were no longer apart. "
Or "And lie to your friends / about hard manly affections, /
throw punches, guard your crotch.... "

Roecker's pose is dual: "you know me ... I'm a
playful slob: remember how I used to pull chairs from un-
der my friends in high school? Remember the parties? Re-
member those good hangovers when we danced with one an-
other's wives, passed out, etcetera?" The speaker can't
maintain his toughness, and like a man steeped in drink feels
self-pity. Roecker ain't exactly maudlin about it, but rather
takes little excursions in that direction, the precipitators
being grief or drink: "To Tim Hardin" is a good example;
here is the final stanza:

> I don't know where you are now
> but what's coming out is proof
> we're in the same place often enough
> to learn if we can put death aside,
> help each other
> with what we want
> from song or poem, the power
> a man can find in himself or a rock,
> putting the world back into one.

In "The Silver Dolphin" the self-potent assurance is marred
by the easy word pain. The word is somehow meant to carry
much more than it can ever begin to: tacking the dolphin
image to it doesn't work:

> I keep my feet, my direction,
> hear the water hiss, taste the salt
> of my own choosing and follow pain,
> the silver dolphin.

An otherwise good long poem "Elegy for John Phillip Mer-
win" is marred by sentimentality. A portrait of an incred-
ible man emerges; and Roecker's detail is expressive of his
own grief. But these lines are a letdown: "We are all in-
sane. / The way we hurt each other, destroy the world. "
The fine image of the brown moth "looking like a small wide
teepee" can't begin to save those lines. And, a few moments
earlier in the same poem the allusions to Christ and John
(appropriate because John is the name of the subject of the
elegy) in combination with the uninhibited weeping fail.

On the back cover of You Know Me Roecker calls

113

himself a "romantic moralist." I'll buy that. The risks he
takes are substantial, and I think greater than those the old
rhyming poet takes: it is possible to say, following Roecker's
own metaphor, that Roecker's poems are far more gluteal
than mammary; the old rhyming guy's poems are far more
mammary than gluteal. My point is that breasts, finally,
are far more fascinating and interesting than asses; you can
simply do more with them--can't you? or can you?

SURREALIST EQUATIONS:

Nanos Valaoritis*

　　In reviewing Nanos Valaoritis' Diplomatic Relations,
a reviewer must account for the poet's surrealism in both
his poems and his collages.　Much-regarded and much ad-
mired in the San Francisco Bay area as a leading Surrealist,
Valaoritis asks for treatment other than the kind of hero-
worship I sense when San Francisco poets talk about him.
I write, therefore, out of my own immediate perception of
these poems, and without any personal sense of his personal
ambience or knowledge of his courage in matters political.
One gets a sense from his books of a playful yet serious and
splendid person.　This said, I proceed to the poems.

　　Diplomatic Relations is in general a better book than
his Hired Hieroglyphs (Kayak Books, 1971).　Diplomatic Re-
lations is better formed and less surrealistically sloppy and
coy.　Unless Surrealism is superbly done it bores; and I
must say that a heavy proportion of Valaoritis' poems bore
me, because they are over-weighted with images that are
either obviously surreal or with lines that come easily and
were allowed to stand unselfcritically.　An equation is pos-
sible: the success of a Surrealist poem moves in proportion
to the richness of the creative intelligence producing the poem.
No news, of course.　Actually, I've seen few Surrealist poems
worth a second reading, or even a first.　Perhaps that is
why, if modern art and literary critics hadn't inflated the
movement, it would have remained a fairly brief episode in
European art.　Obviously, my prejudices show.

　　Here are the opening lines of "Funeral Rites":

　　The invisible serpent of revolt

*Reprinted by permission from Margins, No. 10 (Feb. -March
1974) pp.　46-47; Copyright © 1974 by Margins.

> Eats up the rabbit of my voice
> Contaminates my speech with gangrene
> Stops me from crossing the road with a dead arm
> Lays a thick dictatorship of clouds on sunny after-
>   noons
> Makes poisonous fumes come out of my mouth
> Drifting battle-ship in a surreal sea
> Desperately I look for my beloved possessions
> In the ruins of dilapidated sensations
> Where poets like tragic rats
> Drown in the deafening silence of their poems.

How confusing! A serpent of revolt (invisible) devours the
rabbit of the speaker's voice, thereby contaminating his
speech with gangrene. As a result he (speaker) can't cross
the road with a dead arm. Meaning what? A dictatorship of
clouds creating noxious fumes doesn't help much.

There is madness and there is fine madness. The
latter is required for good Surrealist poems; the former is
chaos, pretension, sleaziness. The poem must, amid the
fertile irrational chaos, flow with images and emotions that
cohere in some formal way. Valaoritis' poem is woefully
and carelessly spun. Like most of his work, this poem has
a laudable political direction, a statement to make, and this
is, in a sense, a saving grace. One of the best of these po-
litical poems is "Factual Poem III," although this too has
the slackness of a first-draft poem crowded with images and
deadwood. Why, for example, is this entire line necessary:
"Eternal ostriches with your heads in the sand"? In context,
merely to say "eternal ostriches" says it all; the sand is
implied. The political situation of the world (and, for Valao-
ritis, particularly in Greece) is shit, and engenders madness
as the only sanity-saving stance. But I come again to the
fact of the individual poem's artistry: Valaoritis too often
sacrifices expedience for the sake of emotion. He should
have worked the poems over more.

There are good poems. "The Poet & the Other Man:
A Creation Myth: For Harold Norse" works extremely well.
It complements Norse's fire and energy beautifully, and sug-
gests his struggle to be heard against the indifference of es-
tablishment critics and publishers. Finally, the poem is de-
pressing: the poet's poems become Laws of Nature:

> The Poet was sitting in his bed
> Propped up with pillows of birds' feathers

> And he dictated poem after poem
> To his secretary
> His poems were immediately turned into
> LAWS OF NATURE
> and
> They were obeyed by minerals
> Stones birds reptiles elephants monkeys
> Atoms crystals fish and plants
> All creatures of the poet's mind
> All except one, who turned a deaf ear

A dissident figure refuses to accept the poet's Laws and,
from his igloo in the North Pole, creates his own. These
overwhelm the world. The Fascist mind overwhelms and
overcomes:

> And the Fish dived deep in the Ocean to hide
> And the Elephant joins the Plants
> In the Forests for protection
> and the Crystals become rare
> And the Atoms become so small
> That no one could see them any longer
> and the Monkeys forgot how to speak
> and started chattering in an unknown tongue
> and the Reptiles began to crawl
> so that HE wouldn't notice them

> He who shouted so loud
> That everyone became deaf
> His voice booming over loudspeakers
> Drowning everything and especially what the poet
>   had said
> In a Universal Roar

The title poem "Diplomatic Relations" works well as a zany
surrealistic trip, and beautifully indicts political negotiations
for their incredible Marx Brothers stupidities and inanities.
Humor infuses the seriousness. The poem has an ease about
it lacking in most of the other poems.

The collages are numerous. I don't find them very
interesting. A pop tone emerges built from figures found in
old books and comic strips. They catch the eye at first;
but I soon find myself moving swiftly over them. I guess
what I'm saying is that books of poems with pictures are
schizophrenic, almost always. Is Valaoritis sneaking in the
collages, or is he sneaking in the poems? Valaoritis has en-
ergy, passion, and humor. Few of these poems do him justice.

FROMAGE, AMIABLY:

Gertrude Stein*

As Gertrude Stein says: "Two fishes are enough for
three people," so two of Gertrude Stein's books are enough
for multitudes. Nuns riding in an omnibus and hyacinths act-
ing vertically rather than finally does tell us something about
writing, and also perhaps about war. Since this newly re-
published How to Write seems to have something to do with
how words rain (paragraphs are emotional, sentences are not)
on people wanting to write, or informing them of themes like:
"when china lilies smell like chinamen," or being angry for
two or three days, depending upon your mother's grocery
baskets and the freshness of kumquats in grease outofdoors
truthfully. Or: "Sentences are made with to be slowly."
Eaten? screwed? caressed? written? mangled? Or, this
seems the answer (an answer): "That is what sentences are
for in a way made slower." The teeth here are of the fin-
est, logically, as are the gums--so dance the spruces
thoughtful towards hares.

This book of some nearly 400 pages requires a Sam-
sonesque dedication, and was meant to be read while eating
macaroons and glazed snails--barrels of them. If you read
it entirely at a sitting without going forwards or into sen-
tences ('likes make likes") until your mind is extortionately
widened as a sentenced-mind-amiably ... there is little hope.
Yes, maudlin: "It is very pretty to love a pretty person and
to think of her when she is feeling very pretty." No, not to
be ignored. And Yes/No to allow her mountains to sit on
your face thinking they are sixes and sevens. I do not know,
Gertrude, whether chocolate or fromage, amiably,

robert

*Reprinted by permission from Margins, No. 10 (Feb. -
March 1974) p. 65; Copyright © 1974 by Margins.

TO BLEED OR NOT TO BLEED:

William Meredith's Hazard, the Painter

Meredith's latest book is most consistently enjoyable.
Refreshingly, Meredith creates an intriguing persona--an in-
trospective, ironic, bemused, somewhat under-achieving paint-
er who for two years has worked on a painting of a parachut-
ist.   There's no sense that this will be his masterpiece.
Through the painter Hazard, Meredith may be exposing the
dilatory recalcitrance many of us experience in forcing our-
selves to settle down to work.   Hazard is the arch-procras-
tinator--and yet he manages to accomplish a body of work.
And there are obvious connections between Hazard and Mere-
dith: both men were Navy pilots in World War II, both are
artists, both have a place in the country, both are observant
of nature and the ironies of man's brief tenure on the uni-
versal plane, etc.   As Meredith says in an opening note:
these connections are "much fewer than the author would
like. "   Hazard's delightful wit is memorable--and this is
something much needed if he is to serve as one "in charge
of morale in a morbid time. "   Hazard is a colorful fumbler.

In "Hazard's Optimism" Hazard does air-work on his
painting of the parachutist.   It appears that he's actually got-
ten himself into a jumpsuit (after lying to his wife), ascends,
and tumbles safely towards earth.   He rejoices in his fall:

> He calls out to the sky, his voice
> the voice of an animal that makes no words
> but a happy incorrigible noise, not
> of this time.

Hazard knows that because he has to make the fall in order
to get the painting right, he's not the world's most gifted
painter.   He considers the great masters of the past--Bruegel,
the Elder, rendered landscapes as if they were all seen from
above the earth.   Bruegel didn't require jumps to get his per-

spective right.   But, "dull Hazard must be taken up again
and dropped. "

Hazard moves into a neat reminiscence of his child-
hood: his mother is hoovering the livingroom rug.   Hazard
is indoors with a cold, sprawling on the hoovered part of the
rug with his dog, playing Jessica Dragonette on an old wind-
up victrola.   Dear Jessica!   Now almost forgotten, yet at
one time a glory-singer translating the manner of grand opera
into art-songs for the American family radio.   Note how skill-
fully Meredith manages the cadences in his lines--there is
energy and a fine doubling back of sounds:

> Shocked at the death of Jessica Dragonette,
> he slipped her black corpse back into one of the
>   books
> and thought of the heavy cost an artist paid.
> Then he thought how queer it was to own
> all those pressed singers and a gramophone
> and not be able to afford a live maid.

At a musical supporting McGovern for president, held
in his house, bored, Hazard grows horny.   As his mind
drifts over his lust and on to his painting (which hasn't been
going well) and to his own aging, note the force of the death-
camp image:

> Hazard desires his wife, the way people
> on the trains to the death-camps were seized
> by irrational lust.   She is the youngest woman
> in the room, he would like to be in bed
> with her now, he would like to be president.

Meredith wields the verse-line with skill: his sense
of when to close a line is always apt, and his interior hatch-
ings of half-rhymes and assonances are highly satisfying.
His tone is basically colloquial, in the sense that Robert
Frost's tone was; and there is also something of Frost's win-
some irony here.

On another occasion, Hazard takes a walk through his
wooded acres.   He meditates upon the boulders, dropped in
place by their glacial "ice-barges. "   Then there were no
trees, no topsoil, no "cerebral hemisphere / that could hold
coordinates. "   Now, Hazard observes whimsically, he a
"freeholder" owns this place and the stones--with, of course,
the bank's mortgage.   Smaller stones he imagines deposited

by "flesh-barges" rather than "ice-barges"--stones "wrestled
to earth / by rabbit or deer," or shoved into place by "hun-
grier men" with sticks.   His meditation ends with a poignant
sense of himself against these stones.   The air he breathes,
as it swiftly passes through his lungs and mouth, is more
his to keep than these amazing, timeless stones, stones he
owns merely on paper.

      In "Rhode Island," Hazard takes one of his numerous
leaves from painting.   I have the impression almost that
painting is his avocation.   Here his enjoyment of a semi-
slumbering ease opens with a choice piece of wit:

> Here at the seashore they use the clouds over &
>   over
> again, like the rented animals in Aida.

He submits to the ocean's eroticism, balancing his two worlds
of dream and reality:

> No matter how often you make love
> in August you're always aware of genitalia,
> your own and the half-naked others'.
> Even with the gracefulest bathers
> you're aware of their kinship with porpoises,
> mammals disporting themselves in a blue element,
> smelling slightly of fish.

      He is also capable of intense non-satiric feeling.   In
"Nausea," a sparrow chasing a butterfly in a Milanese court-
yard reminds him of his experiences as an aviator in World
War II.   Bird and butterfly turn and weave "like pilots in a
dog-fight" around an enormous statue of a "buck-naked" Na-
poleon.   During practice dog-fights in the Navy, "scared
shitless," Hazard used to vomit:

> He had a fearful vision,
> a memory it was, really:
> in a cockpit full of chili
> with cold terror in his gut
> he flies round and round and round
> a blue oblong in Texas,
> trying to escape his friend.

      I find reading Hazard, the Painter an antidote to the
books full of snivelling first-persons I've been reading lately.
The bleeding heart syndrome, despite Shelley's falling on the

thorns of life, seems peculiarly American.   Perhaps the
syndrome goes back to Thomas Wolfe and the homeward look-
ing angel, and to displaying your guts out there under the
stars, as if they were crammed with gentle-smelling, choice
ambergris.   I don't know.   Too few American poets move
towards other personae.   Meredith proves that fine poetry
happens this way; and that in the process of distancing the
self, enough of the self remains for the reader to enjoy the
connections.   I feel I know more, or have sensed more of
Meredith, in these poems, than I would have in poems un-
abashedly of himself; in the latter, the temptation is to lie
in order to make the heart bleed more.   I'll remember
Hazard the painter, choice non-bleeder that he is, a long
time.

WATERS POUND UPON THE DOOR:

Arthur Gregor's The Past Now

In this, his seventh book of poems, Arthur Gregor
writes of himself in his middle years, as he continues to
sort out the hungers assailing him.   First, he writes of his
displacement from his Austrian origins--his family fled the
Nazis. Second, he writes of sexual irresolutions.   And,
third, he writes of aging, and the primacy of the philosoph-
ical self.   While Gregor is known chiefly as a trade-press
poet, the majority of these poems appeared in small maga-
zines--in The Southern Review, Mill Mountain Review, Crazy
Horse, Hellcoal Annual, Poetry Now, Pembroke Magazine,
South Carolina Review, and Michigan Quarterly.   He sustains
poets of all persuasions.

In "The Hand upon His Head," European culture main-
tains its touch on him--and there is pain.   Gregor stumbles,
hurting, through his years in American exile, the fastidious
culture of castles, villas, superb food, wine, classical music,
and intellectuality all possessing him still, but threatened by
a gray America:

> Heavy waters pound upon the door.
> All at once they feel they understand.
> The residue of centuries hangs on their eyes.
> They applaud to say
> what they could never say in words,
> and then they leave.

The residue of these early years strengthens him, allows
him to fight his displacement, and enables him to "flow":

> And it is important
> this be done.   A flag over a camp, vast lands,
> announces a country's dominance.
> The personal self brought up, freed,
> waving over one's being like a flag,

> declares this conquest: to allow
> the terrains, the crevices to be filled;
> to open one's being
> so the waters may flow.

He craves to be a superb lover. As he wanders postured in
landscapes, he continues to prowl for sexual connections, and,
in a larger sense, for the encompassing love-absorption that
will tell him that he has, indeed, returned to his warm
home. Intimations from the past fog through, distressing
him. He turns in pain, his intellectualizing self pondering
his experiences and cravings as so many hot rubies growing
colder and colder. This past, Gregor eventually discerns,
is not located in "a worldly place." There is no returning,
except via art and reveries. And Gregor writes a highly
reverie-laden poetry:

Man Weeping

> I have erred in this:
> in attempting to find my place
> in terms the world defines.
> Once again I beat my fists
> as though on doors of steel.
> Which do not turn to mist
> unless he who entreats
> remembers where diffusion lies,
> that the locale he seeks
> is none but where he stands.
>
> I asked again for happiness
> where all is momentary,
> for calm and airy views
> where all is thick and muddy,
> blocked the gates ahead.
> I had forgotten that
> return is not a worldly place.
>
> What weeps in man, faced by
> what he cannot control,
> is that in him that's more
> than man, how else could he
> feel solaced by his sorrow?
> The blue calm of airy views
> originates in him, in antique
> memories. No place is there
> to go but where I am. Seeing

a man weeping, and sensing
his suffering and relief
brought me back to this.

        Since he cannot literally return to his past, Gregor
assumes the posture of a European poet-intellectual, locating
his pain and resolving whatever he can of it in terms of his
soul, of contraries partially meshed, and of the doppelgänger:
a handsome face seen at a highway intersection, on the beach,
or in a crowded street is a facet of the poet's aching, quest-
ing self. The sexual hunger he feels for these ephemeral
faces and bodies is what we might call the Cavafy Ache: an
intense hunger for classical beauty rendered in male form,
the ancient Greek ideal materialized. I do not read this
hunger as overtly sexual, or Uranian; rather, it allows its
perceiver to read the material world quite exclusively in
terms of an ideal world--a beautiful mortal youth is an ap-
proximate for an ancient Praxitelean youth. But finally Gre-
gor's hunger for cultured Europe does fade into a sexual
ache. The same fig leaves. "The Guide" serves the dis-
cussion well. In its closing stanzas, the speaker assumes
an almost feminine passivity partly sexual, partly abstract
... the tension resolved as anima pitted against "earthling."
Some readers may feel uneasy over the unabashed roman-
ticism of the last lines--I, however, enjoy it:

            ... for I know that I cannot alone
            accomplish the next step,
            cannot guess where the next crossing is
            the landing where
            what is needed for
            the deepening I crave
            is right and ready for me.
            Can only plead

            that it may be,
            can break
            the hold of security,
            keep one foot raised in readiness
            but must wait, wait
            until the guide
            I've come to trust
            places it
            on what I will accept
            as the right track.

Who must surely shudder with

delight
which in this life
only the anticipated lover knows
as--cradling me as air does--
he--the bodiless--
takes me further, on to

where I yearn to get.
What mission of unearthly love!
To help an ignorant earthling on
to the radiance that he--the bodiless--
is now possessed of!

In "Two Shapes" lust is sexual failure: the lovers
fail to spin off into empyreans of ecstasy. The tangle on the
bed is "detrimental." The lovers feel "cast out." A reverie
transpires ostensibly while the lovers are in their lust-tangle,
during one of the sexual pauses, when their energies are mo-
mentarily exhausted, and the bridge to the new stage of their
loving is unpredictable. The phallus may fall limp, or it
may reinvigorate itself afresh. In a marvelous line, the
speaker realizes that his cerebrations impede a full loving,
and he disposes of the "shapes" hovering in the air above
the lovers:

the shapes are as flecks of ash
adrift in an unnecessary waste.

The last poem of the book, "A Return," is best when
Gregor drops the colloquial tone (it's addressed to friends at
Yaddo) and proceeds to confront bewilderment and yearning.
He is always a skilled craftsman. Few poets are as honest
in their explorations of the mind's force as a potential be-
trayer. In "A Defiance" he casts away the mind as the force
depriving him of spontaneity--the mind creates that vast area
of pain between the ideal and the real, the intense wish and
the only partial fulfillment. Ironically, the mind will con-
tinue to torment him until he dies:

The mind shall be cast upon
the ground where I walk.
Let it be like fruit
that falls when it must.
Let it spill itself
as it does if it must.
The mind shall have no preference.
I shall carry it under my arm

like a helmet or a hat.
I shall put it on when it rains,
against destructive heat or stones.
I shall lay it beside me in the grass.
I shall forget it
when the sun has closed my eyes.

Perfection, Gregor says, is always frail. As I read
his poems, I find this as his most persistent theme: the
creative psyche struggling to translate fragility into harder
substance, to metamorphose the flickering shadow of one's
double into blood and sinew.   Love then discovers itself not
in Platonic realms, but in engagements of the flesh and heart
with other, taut, breathing selves. Gregor's forte is the pre-
sentation of these flickerings of consciousness, these pain-
teasers, perpetually nagging because so little of ourselves
finds fulfillment--our ideals promise so much better.   Gre-
gor's idealism fails to shield him as it might; and here is
where I find him unforgettable--when his considerable lyric
gift flows over and around his psychical intensities.

IMPASSIONED COWS:

Katy Akin*

Katy Akin remains something of a mystery. I knew
her some years back when I was living in Riverside, Cali-
fornia, and she, then in high school, came to poetry read-
ings, lived a heavy counter-culture life-style, and wrote
poems stunning in their promise, intensity, and craft. I
heard that after a consuming love affair or two she left this
country and exported her various talents (including her phys-
ical beauty) to Europe, where she wanders, always on the
margins of poverty, living by her wits in whatever ways she
can. Some stories say that she sells her body when she runs
out of bread; others that she is a nude dancer in go-go bars
in Amsterdam and other salacious European dives. She has
dropped out, all the way, it seems.

About 4 years ago I happened to see an issue of Hang-
ing Loose, and was amazed to find poems by Katy Akin.
Yes, it was the same Katy Akin of Riverside. I wrote to
Hanging Loose to find out about her: she was in Europe,
they had not heard of her before her poems appeared in the
mail. No address. She struck them as one of the most
original poets they had ever published. Apparently, for what-
ever reasons, she sent her work only to Hanging Loose.
And it is exciting now to have her first book Impassioned
Cows By Moonlight published by them.

Akin skillfully juxtaposes pain and joy, with commun-
ity. And the latter word is important--she is one of the bed-
spread wearing, long-haired nomads of her generation. Their
rebelliousness produces joy; and a sense of belonging to one
another, of trust, develops, foreign to the non-counterculture
world. The pain emerges simply from being displaced, from

*Reprinted by permission from Margins, No. 28-30 (Jan. -
March 1976) pp. 76-78; Copyright © 1976 by Margins.

starvation, from moving through the vagabond layers of life
where the non-vagabonds have dumped most of their merde.
Her poem "The Crows" says it beautifully.   Note the orig-
inal way she handles her various images: dust-filled egg,
crow with his beak in tar, the feeling a crow has as a train
(life) blows past, the crow's eye as a "fish-roe eye." I
feel this poem.   Here is "The Crows" in its entirety:

The Crows

> We are the crows.
> We stroll between railroad tracks
> trading brown coins.
> We rise to the wires
> when a train blows by
> it storms and sucks at our feet
> which are like stolen twigs
> rasping their scales together, crowding.
>
> In the morning
> warehouses pile just inside our vision.
> The grey lights switch all day
> and we shake from our feathers
> broken dust and walnut shells.
> We peck between steel thighs.
>
> Once one of us
> jabbed his beak in tar.
> Gravel stuck to it;
> he slowly starved.
> His fish-roe eye
> was desperate, he clung
> to a glittering telephone pole.
>
> When he fell through the dusk
> we were the crows
> watching the train-light slice him
> like a dust-filled egg.
>
> Shifting on the wires at night
> our heads are filled
> with our dreams, which thunder through the streets
> swollen huge and runaway,
> soot slapping the trees.
> Winter is upon us.
>
> the trees are crabs

in the turning sky.
each day another ring
slips from my lengthening fingers.
I welcome the months
that rattle in the dry wisteria like wings.

Akin's empathy with others is deep and felt with considerable
originality, and the majority of these poems (as well as the
3 prose-pieces) are experiences of affection; she has a spe-
cial way of moving somehow into the skin of the people (men
and women) she loves.   One of the most poignant poems is
about her mother.   She feels "august" as her mother is Au-
gust--fall--fading, etc.   School "led" Akin "like a big dis-
tracted dog ... I was close to the huge suction of thunder-
heads."   She longed to be her mother: "I knew wet leaves /
in my mother's red hair, and her mother's name / was im-
mediate. / August. / I feel my stomach. / my dreams are
explicit with / too many faces."

A panegyric to a friend begins:

entering you
our wings slide together
you are unplanned
as rips in leather, smoke in eyes.
you smell your own recent love
and gift me with your mouth.

("To Beth")

To one of her men, Jim, "My Sixteenth," she writes:

I had missed him insanely,
crouched on the braided rug
in the heat
writing poems to his balls.

god knows I detested them,
the warm slime
they gagged me with,
I swallowed
pretending to like....

Her "Night Poem No. 93" is to me a major poem-state-
ment of mother-hunger, of betrayal, of pain.

Normally, in reviewing I resist quoting poems in their
entirety.   Akin, though, is so little known, and her book dif-

ficult to get, it seems appropriate to quote rather fully from
her. If the mark of a good poem is its power to produce
chills in a reader, this poem is, for me, a splendid one:

Night Poem No. 93

I can't find my mother, my mama, oh
skirt on hairy calves in Woolworth's, oh
christmas,
    oh dead oh dead, she has green shoots
and black bruises, oh mama
    I'm taller than you, your hair isn't
grey anymore and you turn away from me.
    oh mama. I look for you, my sister
has your deftness, my lover your sheltering arms.
    oh me. crying spreads in you like butter.
oh baby you don't have to worry, worry
is a bad mother. I spilled all over the
floor like a smashed jar
    of blackberry jam. I am embarrassed
broken glass   looking for my neat label.
    I can't need mothers! there is
such joy in setting whole foot after whole foot.
    he told me to breathe. It is that or
die. go away, everybody. he said just <u>breathe</u>!
    dogs answer each other across the <u>mallow</u>
mothers left them young.
my ears are left naked
I have put cruel rakes to myself.
    I cried,
and now I am diffuse.
    oh little self, you've gone far down the fence!
where are your shoes?
    jerked out from under you, but who did it?
Nobody to be seen.
    Quick and sharp, the wound
    I hold myself bleeding oh
    I'm bleeding,
    where am I?

Miscarriage? first menstrual flow? abortion? a combination
of the three? Akin risks sentimentality, yes. But her sense
of a poem as passion annealed via image saves her: the
hesitancies in her voice as she drifts in and out of conscious-
ness during the blood-trauma are poignant; and the final,
marvelous image of the shoes being jerked out from under
is, I feel, a stroke of genius. There is baby, or littlegirl-

talk, juxtaposed with sophisticated statement.   The rhythms
and cadences are complex and beautiful.   Akin's poems re-
mind me some of Ai's; but they have a compassion and ten-
derness lacking in Ai's.   Ai's seem like bars of cold steel
set up on a stage.   Akin's are warm, pulsing pieces of warm
fur.

Her "Patriotic Lovesong--To Joe" is a super tour de
force of the vagabond, on-the-road ballad.   And most of
Akin's poetry has been touched and enriched by the better
songs of Judy Collins, Joplin, Ronstadt, Arlo Guthrie.
The humor here is fine.   I'll quote the opening lines, omit
some thirty, and conclude with the last dozen lines.

> grope a continent
>
> squeeze Idaho's tits
>
> bite Oregon's ripeapple cheeks
> stroke with subuttered lascivious shudder
> California's bellywarm sand
>
> put it in texas, good and greasy
> fold a hot prick taco
> prick with hot sauce
> hands fumble breathless
> in Washington State forestry
> you got one knee
> in the ant pile of New Orleans
> blackpepper ants boogeying on your sweating skin....
>   oh my cowpoke
> my cowboy   my tonic   my lovemild ram,
> sheepstealer   horsethief   wetback and immigrant
>   alien
> and inbreeder and stealthy savourer of the lips of the
> flashflood wash!
>
> Dig deep your well, and drink, and deepfry in
>   petroleum,
> and fry your drumstick deep, and butter your sturdy
>   brown biscuits
> and honey your butter from your wildflower bees,
>   cows, cowslips--
> and make your longhorn cheese
>
> oh Joe, fuck America, fuck me!

A few words about the prose pieces, since they are
as adept as the poetry.   The first, "Rachel and Eurekie, "
is about the discovery of lesbian feelings.   There is real
joy--I've never read better bathtub-love.   The relationship
ends when the girls, discovered by the gross landlady, are
ejected from the rooming house.   Each goes her separate
way.   Yet, in a strange sense, goodby in Akin's writing is
never a real termination: one senses that all the experiences
she has had remain in her psyche with a vital living force.
"Gejeelde" is a tender presentation of a young woman who
accepts the peregrinations of her lover as part of her own
growth; her man wanders all over the west.   "A Trip to the
Desert" is my favorite of the three prose pieces.   The sen-
sory detail is fine, and Akin's love for the members of her
family on this reconstructed family trip, in an old van, into
the desert is unforgettable.   Here are some moments:

> Mama climbed into the back with us.   She hiked
> her jeans up on her hairy legs and stuck her hiking
> boots one by one over the back of the seat, giggling.
> She did love the desert too.   We were glad to see
> her.

Of her brother Alan:

> He wore a bandana and a hat from the Spanish-
> American war.   He had eaten raw porcupine, but
> never a girl.   To any food beside pinto beans and
> corn meal he sneered, 'Luxuries!'   To my moth-
> er's request to stop for coffee--'Luxuries!'   At my
> mother's terror in the VW's cross-country flounder-
> ing, he laughed shortly--'Let the old bitch walk. '
> ... His scalp flaked away with psoriasis.   I wish
> we had said all these things aloud.

> The Unitarian minister once said, 'Women feel
> about their houses the same way they feel about
> their cunts. '

> Squalor is not just a game the woman plays.   It is
> a whole pain.   Everybody in the family plays, very
> hard.

> I wore a padded brassiere which I stuffed with socks
> or toilet paper, and which I never changed or re-
> moved or washed: when the straps were eaten
> through with sweat and grime I would manage to buy
> another.

Akin's writing is a means, she says, of self-restoration.
Her menstrual flow, its inception, her abortions, her waver-
ing lust: "but madam / the cellar is filled with blood / even
the gopher holes are cheapened"--are triumphs of her spirit:
the family pieces, the whorehouse poems, the lovers' poems
enable her compassion to speak itself: "I am restored," she
writes, "the backyard visits my hands. I cup immense
places in warm fingers." Akin's is a talent of considerable
proportions. I hope that her life is her writing, and that
more work will reach us, spun from the incredible seams of
her special living.

THE POET AS PEREGRINATOR:

John Thomasson's White Hope White Saddhu White Trash*

This is a journal-poetry record of a young counter-culture man's peregrinations throughout the Mediterranean countries of Europe and North Africa, and India, Ceylon, and Nepal. It is the best book so far to treat that quest to the East that has become something of a cliché for disaffected WASP American youth. The models for the journey include Ty Power in The Razor's Edge, Gary Snyder, Allen Ginsberg, and John Lennon.

I must admit that I was put off by Thomasson's opening prose-piece which damns the Western (particularly American and French--Camus, Sartre) experience as sterile and intellectual; i.e., inimical to growth and learning, those vague concepts replacing the truth and the good of our grandfathers. Once again, a facile posing promised to entrap the writer who fails to comprehend that most typical American pose for the artist (Faulkner, Burroughs, Ginsberg, West, Berryman) is a non-intellectual, boozy high. Booze and dope are superior to philosophy and the sort of intellectual give-and-take one finds among European writers. But this is all an aside, since Thomasson's book transcends these limitations.

The first poem sets his intentions (stanzas two & three):

> I do not
> cease to be X
> but rather
> become not-X
> which not-X of course

*Reprinted by permission from Margins, No. 9 (Winter 1973/ 74) pp. 44-45; Copyright © 1974 by Margins.

```
    contains X
    or the idea of X
    all the same

    the trick is
    to transcend
    or reconcile
    or make
    a dialectic synthesis...
    or simply ignore
    such things
```

The passport-photo cover depicting first (and cancelled) the
writer in a suit, tie, shaved, short-haired and then without
suit and sporting a magnificent long beard suggests the poles
of Thomasson's quest, the beginning and end of the journey.

The first portion of the book is a journal of thoughts
and impressions of the speaker as he moved through various
Mediterranean countries.   The writing is direct, intelligent,
and often moving.   The style is projective, absolutely simple
in form and diction, and allusive (frequently in a finely cryp-
tic oriental way) in its best moments.   The genre is close
to Ginsberg's Indian Journals, and far less boring and pre-
tentious.   Perhaps a difference is that Ginsberg's travels
were determined by the locales of various gurus he hoped to
see and Thomasson's are not so programmed: his mind is
open to the impact of the day's events, without preconditions
or preconceptions.   The poetry is, hence, restrained and
deep; the ear fine and uncomplicated:

```
    a dandy
    is a cockpit
    shaped
    sedan chair
    four porter manned,
    a mazdoor
    methinks
    a pony driver,
    a pithoo
    god only knows

    a sannyasin
    is an orange clad
    renunciate,
    a saddhu
    a hairy holy man,
```

a naga
is content
with a loin cloth
and a blanket

a hippie
is a hairy honky
barefoot on the mountain,
some Indians think
that white men
are born
with shoes on,
and take no notice
of barefoot browns

up the hill together
Jai Amarath!
those coming down. . .

4300 plus
one tells the metric types
a mile or two over ice,
the grotto itself
anticlimax,
a cliche yes,
but getting there
is the thing
and how you get there
what you are

Thomasson meets various types on his peregrinations,
and he sees each with clarity, irony, and compassion: the
spaced-out flower child Scruff who begs her way through the
Orient; Larry, lover of bizarre occult drugged haze experi-
ence: "Larry is not at home in India / but neither is he at
home at home"; the clean, attractive WASP girl next door
who is actually an acid freak; the "sweet young Sunday Sup-
plement Hippie" whose mysticism and jargon are superficial
and entirely predictable. Enough of these people drift through
the poems to convey the sense of a world of wanderers pass-
ing by.

One complaint I have is that some moments come too
easily, particularly moments indicting contemporary America:
Reagan, Billy Graham, Popeism, the astronauts. The criti-
cisms are justified; my fuss is that Thomasson is obvious and
tinges his obviousness with self-pity:

Larry sits
at all hours indoors,
immersed in the occult,
the more bizarre the better

Not this, Not that
neither sleeping nor awake
now and then perhaps emerging
(unrecognized by himself or others)
from the drugged state
to hazy "normalcy"

Larry is not at home in India
but neither is he at home at home

To the sensitive it is given
to rot a la Rimbaud,
the ordinary go the Reagan route

The alternative for Thomasson is to observe, wander, share,
and to say little.   Few poets deal with the counterculture ex-
perience so maturely.   Efforts by these youngsters--and they
turn up in my writing workshops--are in general vapid, trite,
hokey imitations of the worst of the currently popular rock-
folk musicians.   Thomasson's mind is hardly that of a "Sun-
day Supplement Hippie. "   He proves what good writing has
proved for centuries--that our simplest experiences are often
our most profound, and that they transpire without intoxica-
tion or frenzy:

standing
ankle deep
in mud

unaware
I was feeding
leeches

my head
in the Himal
twenty thousand feet
above...

a rather
simplistic
state of man

Thomasson's wandering is its own reward. His routine was
to wander the foothills of Katmandu and Nepal, seeking
places where few if any whitemen had been. He eventually
becomes so much a part of his locale that beggars no longer
press him:

>   it never happened
>   last year--
>
>   maybe
>   I'm blending
>   too much

This poem reflects his state of mind well:

>   In different towns
>   at different times today
>
>   I've stopped
>   and sat
>   and seen
>   what seemed
>
>   the same ant
>   dragging the same feather
>
>   which could be true
>   of course
>   what with the wind
>
>   and thought
>   of Sisyphus
>   a ping-pong ball
>   in the ocean
>   and what to have
>   for dinner

Finally, Thomasson's return to the states brings its
pain, where he eventually gets a job popular with counter-
culture folks; yes, in the post office. He writes a poem in
a library, borrowing pen and paper from a librarian who
thinks that because he's hairy he's a thief. A driver tries
to run him down with his car on a smoggy street. He fears
that the plastic hippies of Los Angeles will suck him in.
The postal employees in the branch office where he works
christen him "Smith Brothers."

The wisdom of the book is in the illusion it creates
that each cell of Thomasson's body knows that the quest for
inner values is ancient, that all cultures are suspect and
corrupt, and that what matters finally is a strong individual
in his isolation.   Always he reserves his enthusiasm for an
inner strength and peace no religion or mystic can give him,
but which rather he has earned through sheer grit and a pain-
ful seeing, thinking, doing and feeling.   A poem ostensibly
about Timothy Leary states the position well:

> Dr. Leary
> merely
> crossed the line...
>
> between
> Maoist and Mystic
>
> a line thats
> clearly
> thin and fine
>
> between
> Maoist and Mystic
>
> even the words
> have much
> in common
> M-I-S-T
> a MIST
> in which
> many of us stand
> undecided
> blowing
> with the winds of change
> but what's so strange
> from peace and love
> to fire and brimstone
> what of
> the prophets
> jehad
> and christian anti-communism
> what of
> Shiva Himalaya
> come down
> to do the
> dance of death
>
> It's not a new trip

This is a fine book, and handsomely manufactured by Gary and Melissa Albers of Christopher's Books. It deserves a wide audience, especially of the young who are looking for alternatives to the various hazes they find themselves in. The book is authentic and unpretentious. I sense that Thomasson will probably not write much more: this book is a complete growth statement. I hope sincerely that my sense is wrong.

POETRY IS A FORM OF WALKING:

Paul Vangelisti*

Air is a book to notice. Vangelisti effectively has
made a European style of poem (particularly modern Italian)
his own. American poets pay much homage to European
poets, translate them, and revere even their bad poems.
My sense of this enthusiasm is that it remains largely on a
level of "outasight, man," or "this dude can really swing
with a line," or "dig the el crappo view of life done up in
these mad surreal images," or "there's delicacies here about
kitchen cupboards, fading flowers, and beaches like no Amer-
ican poet, man, can produce." It becomes fashionable to
toss about names like Zbigniew Hebert, Ahknatova, Goll,
and Pasolini. I'm not exactly knocking this energy, just
wondering why, if these poets are so splendid so little of
their influence tells in our writing. Is it that few poets we
read influence our work, really? Our absorption level is
not much different from a high-quality paper towel: it holds
in the discharge but fails to allow it to seep through to the
outside and reach the air again. Not only has Vangelisti
translated much Italian poetry, but, as Air shows, he has
understood that poetry sufficiently to employ it toward his
own poetic ends. Some examples:

"Style" in a fresh original way is about writing as
high heels, feet without shoes but wearing bobby socks,
bundles carried by old women. Vangelisti sees each line as
a depersonalized moment, in the sense that there is no writer
directly present; he conceals his emotions behind his texture
(which suggests cool) of sounds, cadences, and images.
There is, for example, no grammatical transition between
lines 1 and 2: yet they work visually--high heels twirl down
empty streets. This suggests the poem as concrete event.

*Reprinted by permission from Margins, No. 15 (Dec. 1974)
pp. 34, 71; Copyright © 1974 by Margins.

The next movement is to "cloud": "style" plunges into the
air and is "free of words"--which implies an esthetic purity
or distance removed from direct emotion.   It's as if Van-
gelisti wants his poem as art to breathe so sufficiently that
self/personae dies or is numbed.   A pure play of syllabic
motion ensues.   Then, other words (style) cut, slicing win-
dows for threat and for improved vision.   Still others fumble
and slouch with weight and age, as Shoeshine or Bicycle
Thief moments....   Realism.   Yet, the poem concludes mys-
teriously, someone (Vangelisti asks the question without using
punctuation) "enters the glass / and begins to eat."   Is the
devourer the poet?   Is he the reader?   I read the eater as a
poet who penetrates the "glass" of experience,   ravishes it
with his knife/words, and proceeds to feast.   The event of
the poem is cool, detached, depersonalized--qualities I see
in most of the Italian poets Vangelisti has published liberally,
in translation, in Invisible City (co-editor, John McBride).
Here is the poem:

Style

> of high heels
> twirl empty streets
> or cloud
> plunge into the air
> free of words
> of suitcases of words
> lift a knife how one
> slices the window
> no shoes but bobby socks
> bundles of old woman
> like sandbags
> scream who enters the glass
> and begins to eat

This manner of writing seems to me to fuse imagism with
surrealism; the blend produces a poem not very often seen
in American poetry.   Poets, as a commonplace device, elide
words for the sake of heightened tension within their lines;
Vangelisti elides tenses, agreement-structures, and thereby
constructs freshly.

Here is how he handles a simple love poem:

Poem for the Wind Poem for Margaret

> bush of hair
> girl's hair

> growing on mother's bone
> breathing
> your shallow navel
> drifts easily as if I
> turned away for a second
> it rises on a low wind
> ripple over you
> bush of a girl's hair
> and disappear

Certain moments here induce complexity. "Mother's bone"
is intriguing: what connection with Margaret? daughter to
mother? Is Margaret pregnant? Yes, the passage is inti-
mate ... pubic, near the navel. Speaker, watching the navel
move, is lyrically aroused. The passage: "drifts easily as
if I / turned away for a second" is subtle and delicate. The
movement of the girl's body is a "low wind," rippling, down,
until it disappears in the thighs. "Poem" is entirely eco-
nomical, precise, quietly rhythmic. The quiet, subtle motion
of the poem, its cadence, echoes the event of the girl's
breathing. Both motions fuse, creating a sense of wonder/
love/gentleness. I find the poem stunning and moving. Its
manner is like that of "Style"--crisp, clipped, depersonalized
until the rhythms of the lines accumulate towards the end.
The breath motion is the image, allusions to bone and wind
are quiet surreal devices.

"Derby" is a brief, precise, touching response to the
poet's father:

> that photo
> chin way out
> cradled in his arms
> first hat
> is the desperate father
> I carry on my back

"Deadline" incorporates and blends naturalism (wobbly
mattress, tenement setting, cough, glue pot, ashes) with
surreal/imagist effects. The compressions are stunning.
Poet as writer, poet as lover, poet learning to walk. Per-
haps Vangelisti says, finally, that learning to walk is what
poetry is all about. Vangelisti is finding his pace. I shall
close this notice with another of his poems.

Deadline

first the wobbly mattress
three flights up
into abstraction
heaved here sagging
of voice dog-tired
scissor cough like no cymbal
day in day out to objects
of the personal sit
glue pot and headline
ashes ashes
rumor don't fit
in the schoolyard of what was
windy as China
was promised the gust
of a woman in my arms
simply learning to walk

PLAYING IT WITHOUT NETS:

Lynn Sukenick*

Both for the quality of its poetry and its physical de-
sign Houdini has to be one of the finest chapbooks published
this year. The poet's collages supplement the poems and
support their tone without being illustrations of the poems;
or, rather, I read the series as a single work of 25 parts,
with collages. Moods vary from the playful to the profound:
Houdini deserves our affection because he superbly illuminated
our entrapments--we deal with our own better because of
strength we receive vicariously from him. And these entrap-
ments include those we set up for ourselves and those the
world throws around us. And this is why Houdini works so
well: Sukenick's intelligence behind the central figure is first-
rate and is able to transform the subject matter into so much
more than itself. She resists the temptation to produce old-
fashioned, coy daguerreotype poems. Nor does she try to ex-
plicate or define the powerful engravings Houdini, by Carol
Yeh, that inspired these poems. No. 4 illustrates Sukenick's
technique: the work is convincingly about the real man; but
it turns, and in its last part becomes much more:

> Houdini binds his body with chains
> and slowly struggles out of the chains;
> Houdini wraps his body with ropes
> and slowly he evades the ropes;
> Houdini secures his body with belts
> and suddenly he undoes the belts.
> This is a quiz.
>   Houdini wants to be
> more naked than he is.
> This is the answer.

*Reprinted by permission from Margins, No. 11 (April-May
1974) pp. 28-29; Copyright © 1974 by Margins.

No. 10 is marvelous in its interweavings of motifs:

> After we see him
> we see the chains
> of determination
> surrounding our friends;
> or the ropes of indolence --
> their auras.
> And
> the old dalmatian
> is held together by spots,
> the sky by its steep
> power poles.
>
> Rituals good
> for tottering pals.

No. 9 is a sort of cap-stone moment:

> Helpless.
> Never say helpless.

No. 19, one of my favorites, demonstrates Sukenick's ability to render the miniscule large:

> A green bug with fragile wings
> washing his face
> washing his whiskers,
> kissing the mirror.
> This is
> a parenthesis, an ant
> between two pillars,
> an interlude.
> Let's see if...

No. 24 is a playful dancing treatment of syllable-power, and sets the mood for No. 25 which begins as a sort of typing exercise and moves Houdini from the scene, into his final escape. I envy Sukenick's free play with language; these bravura moments convince me of her fine ear:

24

Hind Hound Undi Indio Hon Hun Ho Nido Din Don
Hod Nod

HID

25

In the din did Houdini nod.
Noise never made him feel he should.
Though even
they numbered in the hundreds
and did hound him
and descended,
this night of silence was what he needed,
and no nets under him.

I read Houdini and am less afraid of the fact that I have no
nets under me.

NAKED ANGELS:

Ginsberg, Kerouac, and Burroughs*

John Tytell's Naked Angels is the best book so far on the lives and writings of Allen Ginsberg, William Burroughs, and Jack Kerouac. It is crammed with biographical details; and the assessments of the various works by these men are generally swift and accurate. Each of the three lives is laid out in its essentials. Tytell is reverential; there is rarely a critical moment, or an adverse judgment levied against this trio of rather hairy writers. Tytell has combed the published interviews, and has visited the relevant folk, including the principals, with his taperecorder: Herbert Huncke, Carl Solomon, John Clellon Holmes. He has also spoken with Lucien Carr and Lionel Trilling, the latter that friendly professor-soul, now dead, who kept Ginsberg out of prison in the 'fifties. The book nicely feeds our greed for details of the lives of celebrities--and these writers are (except for Kerouac who, of course, is dead) celebrities. People, including those who don't read books, flock to Ginsberg's and Burroughs's readings; and Ginsberg particularly has managed (or produced) the sort of notoriety that makes headlines, and he has done it in the service of poetry, and certainly for himself.

In general, it is fair to say that if one is at all close to the contemporary literature scene in America, one feels surfeited with information about the lives and antics of these writers. There seems to be no other group of artists in American cultural history so widely publicized. And a lot of mediocre writing has gone down because of hype. When I received Tytell's book for review I didn't expect that it would be worth much. But there are several good things buried among facts already almost too-common knowledge.

*Reprinted by permission from Gay Sunshine, No. 29/30 (Fall 1976) pp. 30-31; Copyright © 1976 by Winston Leyland.

And Tytell's treatment of the subject is of the sort an ener-
getic, informed undergraduate college instructor would as-
semble for delivery to his classes.   In other words, there's
no particular sparkle or shine, and the pedantic moments
(there are several, especially in the latter half of the work,
devoted to the writing) do mar the whole.

        I find the chapter on Burrough's life the best in the
book.   Tytell has assembled all one needs, or cares, to know
about this brilliant man: the connections with his family; his
years at Harvard followed by years spent abroad on a trust
fund; his pursuit of medicine in Vienna; his deliberate slicing
off of his fingertip with a chicken (sic) shears; his graduate
work in anthropology; his immersion in the life of Chicago
where he was an exterminator, a bartender, and a private
detective; his tragic friendship with Joan Vollner Adams; the
friendships with Kerouac and Ginsberg; the role of the Times
Square hustler and drug user Robert Huncke in his life; Bur-
roughs as farmer in Texas; Burroughs as junkie; the friend-
ship with Neal Cassady; Burroughs in Mexico City studying
Aztec history and Mayan culture; his fascination with loaded
guns and his accidental shooting of his wife as they played
William Tell....

        And so with Kerouac: here, though, the details seem
at times transcended.   Tytell really tries to assess and un-
derstand this enigmatic figure; and he is entirely convinced
of Kerouac's major stature as a writer.   Kerouac, although
largely a loner, did bring people together, and was always
on the road until near the end, when stricken with phlebitis
he sat around his mother's pad drinking beer, watching tv,
and waiting for Mr. Death.

        Tytell expends most care and passion, I feel, on Gins-
berg.   And justifiably so; for, somehow, Ginsberg remains
the most accessible, copy-worthy, and congenial of the sur-
viving Beat figures.   Much already known about Ginsberg is
here: the disasters at Columbia; the connections with cheap
hoods; the mental hospital; the famous episode of Blake's
materializing during one of G's jack-off sessions; the friend-
ships with Carl Solomon and William Carlos Williams.   Ty-
tell's narrative ends with the appearance of "Howl" in 1956.
I wish the narrative had continued; for, certainly, Ginsberg's
life has been far from dull during the interval.

        Tytell's insights into Burrough's Naked Lunch are su-
perb.   "The Black Beauty of William Burroughs" should be

required reading for youngsters discovering the book for the
first time; and even the book's addicts will know better, after
reading Tytell, why this is one of a handful of major twenti-
eth-century novels. Tytell examines the book both thematical-
ly and stylistically, stressing its connections with Beat writ-
ing in general--the scatological, shocking aspects combined
with art, the amalgam so potent that it transformed judicial
thinking about the nature of pornography and culture. Naked
Lunch and "Howl" must be celebrated for freeing the human
spirit.

        Tytell is least convincing in his reading of Ginsberg's
poetry. When he says that Ginsberg "is feared in America
just as Whitman was feared: to believe in democracy is the
first step toward making it possible," he sweeps the strings
rather stridently. He proclaims Ginsberg a "saint." As
courageous and seminal as Ginsberg is, he is not a saint:
his obsessions with eastern philosophies, his guru-trips, his
fascination with drug cultures, his confusion of an oral tradi-
tion in poetry with the art of poetry, his apparent facile re-
jection of any kind of polishing and honing--viz., his penchant
for speaking endlessly into a tape recorder and publishing the
results--all suggests that this splendid man has feet of clay
and may not be the ultimate answer to the world's need for
poetry Tytell seems to think he is. Eclecticism does not
necessarily produce fine art. Stretches of The Fall of Amer-
ica, for example, I find bathetic, both as statement and as
style.

        Nor am I convinced when Tytell tells me that Gins-
berg's auto accident and his fall on the ice "are a synec-
doche of the general collapse he sees about him," a general
collapse of culture. This is silly. It's like thinking that a
poet's outrageous bowel-movement anticipates a new eruption
of Vesuvius (inverted, of course), or that a hefty wind-pass-
ing anticipates that momentous earthquake designed for blast-
ing California into the sea. What I'm saying is that Tytell,
in a generally fascinating, useful book, mars it seriously by
his ill-concealed hero-slavering. Nor does it help to excuse
the slackness in Ginsberg's verse by saying that his poems
"are meant to be sung; the singer uses them to see what is
there and what possibilities lie beyond." Maybe Ginsberg is
"headed in a folk and blues direction enriched by the disci-
pline of lengthy meditation and Eastern mantra"; but, folks,
I see it as an ACT, not necessarily as Art. Perhaps a
time-out is needed: old Walt Whitman, the father of us all,
invited his readers to loll with him on the grass. No need

to shake your genitals, or your hindu finger cymbals, to get attention. Ginsberg has written superb poetry; some of it, particularly "Howl" and "Kaddish," transformed the poetry of their time. Ginsberg doesn't need the sort of ribbon-waving, feet-licking, clamor-dancing that goes on in this book. And, yet, I repeat, Tytell's Naked Angels is valuable. My only regret is that it could have been much better.

POETRY-BIZ

or APR is Shot from Guns*

I was an early subscriber to The American Poetry
Review and read most of the early issues word for word.
With every number I experienced an unsettling blend of re-
vulsion and admiration. At first I thought my distaste was
a form of sour grapes--the editors of APR seemed to ignore
various poets who were favorites of mine. The editors
seemed largely East-coast focused, fostering a few "names":
Wright, Arrowsmith, Ashbery, Allen, Benedikt, Schwerner,
Williams, Zweig--all (with the exception of Ashbery) on their
prestigious "Contributing Editors" roster. This in itself sub-
stantiated my suspicion of the incestuousness of the APR en-
terprise--poetry-biz. At the request of the editor of Mar-
gins, I proceeded to review the July/August 1973 number of
The American Poetry Review.

First off, the Newton-Erikson, Baldwin-Giovanni fea-
tures bored me, which I admit may be my limitation. Nei-
ther feature delivers much fresh or exciting, and reads like
verbose, frequently pompous eructations about the "dialectical
process," "positive identity," the guilt of Oedipus's father,
the fact that a writer "cannot be told what to face," and oth-
er magnificent obsessions and break-through insights.

Contributing Editor Paul Zweig headlines a review of
a couple of books by Robert Desnos, one translated by Con-
tributing Editor William Kulik, the other translated by Con-
tributing Editor Michael Benedikt. Zweig appears in hip,
highly cropped frontal portrait, the frontality indicating he's
not afraid of nobody, the details of uncombed hair, a day's
growth of beard, mole over right eye, the beginnings of a
boil approximately one inch above left corner of left eyebrow

---

*Reprinted by permission from Margins, No. 8 (Oct. -Nov.
1973) pp. 38-39, 64; Copyright © 1973 by Margins.

--and that fixed, all-seeing gaze! In fact, the left eye is
lighted to look as if some thumb of the cruel universe has
pushed the eye a bit far back into the socket. The review
meanders around and ultimately lacks balls, probably because
CE (Contributing Editor) reviews books by CE and CE? Also,
it is hard to get very excited about Desnos' poetry, despite
the fact that there is a certain fashionableness about it these
days: according to Zweig, Desnos couldn't make up his mind
whether he was a true surrealist or not. In fact, Zweig
says: "let us call Desnos a magical realist, a poet of bril-
liant songs...." There follow a couple of Desnos' state-
ments on Silence and The Art of Poetry, in which this vast
illumination occurs: "The stillness which the poem sees,
even in our running, belongs to the great family of stillnesses.
The tree, the lover, the stone, the night sky, our own anxi-
ety, belong to each other. The poem knows this relationship,
and gives it shape." When will we stop perpetrating these
horrible clichés that pass for profundities in European writ-
ers? Are we so insecure as thinkers-poets-critics that we
allow these limpid statements to proliferate in compensation
for our failures as minds?

There follows next a page and a half of poems by
Contributing Editor Paul Zweig. "An ant lost on a sea of
pink trousers," "Me frozen still," "Meat-eaters are lonely,"
"When I share myself out to silence," "I plunge my penis in-
to every open flower" are lines chosen at random.

Next a page of Jane Cooper relaxed and casual sitting
in a classroom at Sarah Lawrence. I might be wrong ... but
the chair she's in doesn't seem the sort one would have in
one's living room. It's obvious that what I've heard of Ms.
Cooper, that she is "a nice person," radiates through the
picture. Her poems are "nice persons" too. Who can quar-
rel with the concluding sentiment of "Waiting": "Let com-
passion breathe in and out of you / filling you with poems"?
Or this conclusion for "Things": "Last night a voice called
me from outside my door. / It was no one's voice, perhaps
it came from the umbrella stand."

Then, Diane Wakoski's bi-monthly featurette, "A Col-
umn." Her thoughts are discursive and helpful: she deals
here with the problem of anthologies ... are they necessary?

Daniel Hughes writes a lengthy perceptive essay on
John Berryman, which makes this APR worth the price.
There's no picture of Hughes to condition me to accept him

because he's funky and hip.   There isn't even a picture of
Berryman!   There's intelligence throughout, and a particu-
larly helpful treatment of the problem of Berryman's self-
exposure in his last poems.   I expect soon that Hughes will
become a Contributing Editor.   Appropriately (?) an ad for
the Rosicrucians appears on the final page of the Berryman
piece.   The ad takes me back to my years as a kid when I
read Street and Smith Western magazines and fantasized over
the Rosicrucian ads.

The Contributing Editor who seems to get the most
mileage out of the fact that he is a Contributing Editor is
William Arrowsmith.   The Pavese translations ... 2 of them,
prose ... are prolix, dull, and cliché ridden.   I'd like to
see some of the space devoted to dreary pieces by foreign
writers given to journals, workbooks and diaries by im-
portant American writers, viz., Associate Editor David Igna-
tow's own splendid journals.   I blanch realizing that one of
the announced "Coming Attractions" for APR is yet "MORE
ESSAYS BY PAVESE TRANSLATED by WILLIAM ARROW-
SMITH. "   The caps are important, as part of the general
Hype.   W. A. is a marvel of prolificality (?):   how does he
manage to write so much and still manage to edit the Com-
plete Greek Tragedies, per announcement in APR?

Which takes us to the fold-out section, featuring an
essay by Bertrand Matthieu on Rimbaud's Illuminations (an-
nounced in orange ink) followed by Matthieu's translation of
the entire Illuminations.   To the Illuminations-o-phile the new
versions will undoubtedly induce considerable joy.   The vari-
ous versions I have read, including the French have all im-
pressed me as puerile and rambling.   I have suspected that
Illuminations turn on persons who are afraid to fantasize and
move towards madness, and who allow A. R. to do it for
them.   A friend and I read most of these new versions aloud,
thinking there must be some powerful thing going on, some
vision of Hell or Heaven we ought to have.   I bogged down,
kept going, and came within three poems of the end and
passed out.   I have a small complaint to make: Matthieu
illuminates the problem of dating and the sequence of Illu-
minations nicely, his photo--taken by his son--is subdued and
good, but of what moment is it to the reader that the trans-
lations were completed on Henry Miller's 81st Birthday, or
that they were completed in New Haven?

Poems by Contributing Editor Michael Brownstein fol-
low, complete with casual photo of young attractive wunderkind

poet looking up from a table, or the world, for the occasion.
"Outside" is a neat poem, although I don't much dig otter as
a rhyme for water.   The poem begins its parts casually and
in part 6, concluding, becomes fairly momentous: "bulls
come out and roll their marbles in the rain" whilst "tears
of God, etc. , water our garden. "

The Bourjaily piece on Tolstoy is an excellent cor-
rective to the image of Tolstoy as old fart.   A couple of
vintage James Wright poems, followed by an appreciation of
Wright by Contributing Editor Robert Coles, "the Pulitzer
Prize winning psychoanalyst and writer":   how neat to ferret
out psychoanalyst critics for poets! a nice, and free, exten-
sion of our sessions on the couch.   Coles likes Wright's
childhood sort of innocence: "And if a man doesn't stop
seeing what he did when he was a child, then he's got a spe-
cial kind of luck going for him. "   All of it's a spread of
mayonnaise for the Wright sandwich.

Donald Hall's plug for Allen Ginsberg's new book The
Fall of America is brief and misdirected: having absorbed
this book towards an extensive review of my own, I can't get
past the funkiness of the poetry, nor past the loquaciousness,
nor the self-indulgence.   Whatever, Hall's exposé of Howard
B. Gotlieb's attempts to corral a poet's manuscripts and pa-
pers, for free, for the Boston University Libraries is hilari-
ous and thorough.   Gotlieb should now start sending back the
papers he's already gathered.

Then a substantial section on a poet who while not a
Contributing Editor is a darling of the editors.   John Ash-
bery in "Lithuanian Dance Band" turns neat phrases; flicks
words ending in -y and -ing around with the skill of a ring-
master; gets into some embroidery with words like "little, "
"literature and life, " "struggle, " "exquisite, " "uncertainties, "
"delicacies, " "a nice place to live, " "pretty, " "lovely, "
"truth, " and speculates at the end Oharaesquely: "Yet we
are alone too and that's sad isn't it. "   There is a modest,
side-view smiling photo of the poet.   Then, Ashbery gets
critical treatment from W. S. Di Piero, who as a COMING
ATTRACTION, will write APR letters from Italy.   Di Piero's
essay is masterful, and does more to make sense of Ash-
bery's work than anything else I have read.   Di Piero knows
Ashbery's weaknesses, and knows his strengths.   Moreover,
he is a fine prose writer.   There's ease, intelligence, and
a lack of pomposity and strain.

Shirley Kaufman is the first (and only) poet repre-
sented from the West Coast; in general, APR is overloaded
with poets from the East Coast.   And it ain't true that that's
where all the poets are! I like Ms. K's no-nonsense poem,
and also her picture, which shows her from the neck (more
or less) down. I admire her reticence.   Then a page by
Cassia Berman, without picture, and with drawing, consisting
of a short poem, not much good, entitled "Evening Prayer" and
a long untitled work thoroughly Jewish and good.   The poem
is moving and deep.

Paul Eluard ... 2 pages of poems ... an essay on
him by John L. Brown.   At the risk of seeming a crank, I
just don't see the obsession American poets have with trans-
lations.   If an American poet wrote lines like:

Lying down like cinders beanth [sic] the flame
Have I surrendered can I designate nothing more
Pointing me out with a finger me so proud to be living

or

I throw myself forward I climb and I affirm my goal
I have at last emerged from my sleep I am alive

or

I know because I say it
That my desires are right
I do not want us to pass
Into the mire
I want the sun to bear upon
Our pains to quicken us
Vertiginiously
                    etc.

Same American poet, I bet, would never see them in PRINT!
What explains this obsession? Is it that we're afraid we've
overlooked somebody who might end up being great? Do we
prefer looking far away from home for the poet with that ul-
timate line, who will make any further poetry gratuitous? Is
this another facet of POETRY-BIZ, perpetuating the illusion
that Poetry MATTERS in the World?

Another eastern poet, billed as a farm woman from
New Hampshire, Maxine Kumin, has another of those hyper
frontal portrait views looking as if they were seeing a couple

of angels screwing. I do like poems though in which onions
breathe, beets wearing birthmarks wait to be operated on,
apples are "easy abutters" (this has to be a low), parsnips
are "rabbis, " potatoes produce "ten tentative erections, " and
the poet sees herself as "the tulip that slept" in God's navel.
Query: SHOULD CITY POETS BE TURNED LOOSE IN NEW
HAMPSHIRE ?

Not much happens in the rest of APR. A feeble piece
by Jack J. Leedy, MD, who does a lot of work with poetry
as therapy. Useful bit: if you suffer insomnia, try reading,
so Leedy suggests, "To Sleep" by John Keats; "Oft, in the
Stilly Night" by Thomas Moore; "A Ballad of Dreamland" by
Swinburne; a "Hymn to the Night" by Longfellow. Or, if
you were really depressed, how would you like to have John
Milton's "On His Blindness" shoved in your drooping face?
Or, if you are a drug addict, try getting "high on poetry":
"surely" Blake, Lewis Carroll, Dickinson, Thomas, Frost,
Whitaker, Spender, Stevenson, Burns, Whitman, Shakespeare
"are able to give our children bigger kicks than heroin, LSD,
marijuana, or glue. " O, addiction, where is thy sting?

Finally Richard Howard skips around among 5 books
published by the Cummington Press over the past 3 years;
and Donald D. Walsh replies quite convincingly to an attack
Robert Bly made earlier in APR on Walsh's translations of
Neruda. The issue closes with a pitch urging you to sub-
scribe to APR: THE MOST DARING OF THEM ALL ! with
the words increasing substantially in size as they scream
out at you. Yes, this is indeed a loud, loud review !

POETRY CHICAGO:

A Last Look*

Perhaps I meet the wrong poets these days; but, re-
peatedly, whenever that hoary rag Poetry comes up it is dis-
missed as a tedious bore, filled with the dullest professional
work being written today, an institution whose nether-parts
are closed with thick cheesy mold, whose skull is filled with
webs spun by somnolent spiders. Even poets who publish
there say pretty much the same thing. Yet, nobody seems
to want Poetry to go away. Perhaps because appearing in
those gray pages is still one of the best routes for ambitious
poets into the American poetry world? Perhaps it lives be-
cause of the little old ladies who caress it with their diamond-
studded triple names; or, because of the public school teach-
ers who send fledgling poets to it out of abysmal ignorance
of contemporary writing; or, because of the dozens of poets
who subscribe to it as a kind of jerking-off automatic response,
much as frogs twitch when you touch them with live wires.
Obviously, Poetry's sales must be sufficient for it to keep its
position as the most widely distributed and hence most widely
read poetry magazine in the U.S.A.

But how good is it? I propose to scrutinize the
March, 1975 number of Poetry to see for myself, and per-
haps to allay some of my prejudices against it, to determine
the drift of the journal, whether it indeed deserves the al-
most universal disapprobation it currently enjoys. I've just
assumed it's bad, hitherto, without ever giving it a close
reading. It's time to make amends. Poetry is like an old
antiseptic grandmother. You revere her and keep hoping
that she may pull something risqué, obscene, or outrageous
from beneath her skirts. I really have nothing against grand-
mothers; I merely want to find out how this one is behaving.

*Reprinted by permission from Kayak, No. 39 (July 1975)
pp. 62-67; Copyright © 1975 by Kayak Books.

I

Tony Towle opens up with a ten-page poem called
"Works on Paper." It's tedious, made to appear less tedi-
ous by a division into parts, and by the use of a three-line
stanza providing little suspiring places throughout. The
speaker is a Renaissance post-Brunelleschi architect who
really can't get it together. He is a dim reflection of Robert
Browning's human failure Andrea del Sarto, but without
Browning's energy, gusto, or intelligence. Tony Towle's
pallid aestheticism and lethargy register lukewarm on the
poetry thermometer. Towle's artist, like Browning's, has
wife-trouble (she prefers lovers). But, as wiped-out as del
Sarto is, he still has some balls.

As for the writing: in Towle's piece the clichés are
sweeping reforms, small army of workmen, strong beliefs,
the tools of their trades, toward the end of a long life, the
grandeur of the past and at the height of my popularity.
Also a preponderance of lugubrious phrases: in their realities,
irretrievable divided containers, with which to build, in my
contemplated youth, the impressive accoutrements of office,
in flashes of future visual effects, I aspire simultaneously,
in my last elaborated sketch, the so-called perfection of my
predecessors.... Further a sameness of phrase mars the
poem; Towle is greatly addicted to phrases beginning with in.
I count six of these on a single page. What draws my eye
(ear) to them is a recurring deadness. Whenever I hit one
of those clusters a little bell goes off, and I see that either
Towle's strategy betrays him, or he simply writes badly.
Assuming, generously, that he sought to convey the sensibil-
ity of a pompous man via this language, there is still, I feel,
an obligation for him (one that Robert Browning met superbly)
to write vitally while suggesting the grayness or dullness of
his central figure. He fails to do more than raise a little
bump on the biscuit.

What I'm really saying is that we used to call the
Fulbright Poem persists; and Poetry cottons repeatedly to it.
If we need a new label, let's call it the Civilizo-Historico
Poem. It's best to make occasional references backwards to
that decadent period of the Italian Renaissance exhausted by
the painter Raphael. Or to insert references to ancient
Greece, and particularly to Rome where the built-in parallels
with our own time seem more pronounced. Also, spread on
a veneer of philosophy. Towle obliges with "pondering the
meaning of it all." Then, write formally, as if you are

consciously writing lit'rachur, imitating or echoing the great
formal monument-poets of the past.

The trappings that give Towle's "Works on Paper" a
cultural glow makes us as poets/readers feel nice, washed,
and cultured, and cuts above our notoriously Philistine so-
ciety. These trappings are primarily (or rather exclusively)
from the Italian Renaissance. And for American poets and
academics Italy maintains something of a hazy Renaissance
hangover. So Towle drops Villa Giulia, Santa Maria della
Grazie, Palazzo Farnese, Bramante, Brunelleschi. Under-
stand that I am not against poets writing about the past, or
against name-dropping; what I discern in Poetry (and the ma-
jority of the poems in the March number reveal it) is a pat-
tern encouraging this culture-vulture writing. It can, of
course, work with a certain splendor--viz., Robert Lowell,
James Merrill. Generally, for me, these poems are a drag.
So, this mode did not die with the Fulbright poem; it flour-
ishes and is doing well somewhere east of Pasadena.

Dave Smith's "Dome Poem" is about poems. He
seems to wish to drive poets who, writing like Whitman, by
instinct and (by implication) carelessly, out of poetry land to
other borders. To the country of prose? Here, in the open-
ing stanza, Parian earns him points with Poetry's editor:

> Not, of course, the monster hunched downtown
> with its rigid paws coiled into purchase
> where it seems to take a quiet shit
> though it is certainly attractive enough,
> with Parian marble and stained glass slits ...

Smith seems to hold for simplicity in poetry; and his image
is the dome, housing all, yet in itself touching, unifying,
and metaphorically simple: "one drop of water" extended to
"its proto-shape, one wounded round atom smashing back in
vengeance. " The image receives its fullest development in
the final nine lines, an almost Arnoldian epic simile. My
point is that Smith's writing is not simple; his verse sen-
tences are fairly ornate, his diction, except for shit is for-
mal, traditional. And I've seen Smith's poems elsewhere:
he doesn't always write this way. Perhaps here he caught
the ambiance of Poetry, and decided to rub up against it.

Philip Kuepper's "A Coloring Fire," done up in a
series of five-line stanzas, has just the right platelets for
Poetry: it's another bookish poem reminiscent of Robert

Browning--this time of R. B.'s "house," about the interior
of a poet's domicile.   The details of "Fire" are Poetry-chic:
the Cote-d'Or, the Ile-et Vilaine, a mysterious ring (the poet
as Merlin?), a Chair of Forgetfulness (Edmund Spenser?),
croissants for breakfast (Winchell's doughnuts won't do), a
faience vase, an omphalos with a "secured knot," wood coiled
into "Pythian shape," Apollo, the Comtesse de Castiglione.
Curiously, Kuepper's trappings seem to work, and I like this
poem.

        Henry Petroski's "From the Observation Deck," is an
enjoyable, descriptive piece about a college campus, and,
hence, fits right in with the taste of many of Poetry's sub-
scribers.   I'd like to see his poem reprinted in the AAUP
Bulletin.   (This is not a slur; I've published poems there my-
self, and the readership is considerably larger than Poetry's.)

        Theodore Hars puts us right at ease in "Tocqueville's
America" with his allusions to the past and to books.   Obvi-
ously, if we haven't read de Tocqueville we'll miss something.
Also, we shortly read this plump basketful of grapes: Ovid,
penning his Pontic verse; O Maximus.   Didn't the old Romans
ever talk naturally?   Did they perpetually walk around de-
claiming O's at one another?   Were they all pompous orators,
speaking tacky blank verse lines, etc.?   I find many of Hars's
lines simply bad: "Waiting the annual advent of cranes"; "And
yet tonight when composed, attendant stars / spell out migra-
tion to the wintering geese" (this is pretty, in a way that
poor imitations of W. B. Yeats are pretty); "We thought the
continent our commonwealth" (Prose? Perhaps de Tocqueville's);
"the road disappearing behind us" (cliché); and "finitude con-
strains all creatures' wills"--this latter sung by a loon (lit-
erally) who has obviously either read his A. Pope or his
Lord Byron (of Don Juan fame).   I can't resist helping the
loon out by closing off his couplet:

        finitude constrains all creatures' wills
        whilst they demolish molluscs with their bills ...

        And I'm not being irreverent; I can't help feeling that
old Ovid, when not hung up on Pontic verse, would have en-
joyed this adaptation of his fable of the loon.

        Next, two poems by Greg Kuzma who writes a lot of
those skinny poems.   Here these poems interrupt Poetry's
Fulbrightesque flow, but do little to enhance the energy.
"The Brook" is a piece without urgency, filled with common-

places Frostian and childlike, and seems to have been writ-
ten by Kuzma simply to have another poem to send to the
numerous magazines clamoring for driblets from his pen.
The writing is almost always easy and predictable. And,
yet, the idea of the brook coming to life, seeping through the
landscape, is mildly interesting. Things pick up with an
image of "somber white" houses looking in "some weathers
in the fog" (I have trouble with this phrase) looking like eyes
or ears ("in order that the brook seem near"). Again, the
final line lacks verve. There's one good, fresh, exact im-
age: the brook comes out of the hills, drawing "its frag-
ments close" (this isn't too good); then it "drags through the
meadow where / the horses drag their feet / and mud it up."
"The Brook" concludes on a simple soft note: "the brook
exceeds its normal handsomeness / See how it shows itself
off." My guess is that if Martin Farquhar Tupper, Queen
Victoria's favorite poet, author of Proverbial Philosophy,
had written nature poetry, it would sound something like this.
But another Victorian poet, a real master, wrote a poem
called "The Brook." Kuzma might take a look at it. Tenny-
son's "The Brook" dances rings around his.

Suzanne Noguere's two poems I find entirely embar-
rassing. The first is a self-conscious, overwritten piece
about snakes lying "still as statues." The second is about
"organs and electric pulses through live protein" pleading for
"silk and tweeds to feel."

The best poems are at the end. A set of pieces by
Reg Saner is vital, despite a couple of Greeky touches. "The
useless is pure Greek" and "At last, Heraclitus, we two are
alone." And there are some questionable lines: "timberline
and the tundra still corny / with blossom"; "The typical
sublime of these glacial valleys" (Wordsworth at his best
would have made us feel this); "Goats in their high-heeled
shoes / nibble common prairie flowers, riding them / all
the way to the top." But good things transpire: there are
telling touches from mountain landscapes, a fine piece about
the body, and yet another poem on the theme of our dying as
we age--but this one is succinct and unpretentious.

Finally, Robin Magowan's "In Memory of Nancy Ling
(Perry)" is an entirely marvelous poem of slightly more than
four pages. No stanza breaks. I've read it to myself quiet-
ly and aloud; both experiences produce wonderful marbles,
fine sounds, spin-feelings. Magowan's touch throughout is
feeling alive. He's lived through something momentous; a

choice part of that bit of history called the Symbionese Lib-
eration Army.   Magowan writes vastly better than any poet
in this collection.   And I'm glad that Daryl Hine's strategy
led him to print Magowan last; grandma does have a surprise
up her skirts, after all.   And my patience, nervous little
shrew that it is, finds itself rewarded.   But is Poetry
(March, 1975) redeemed?

II

As for the prose in Poetry, David Bromwich's review
of Howard Blake's The Island Self succeeds in making Blake's
bad lines seem so good that when he (Bromwich) insists on
Blake's splendor, I perversely wish for more of his bad
lines.   And I am put off by an argumentum ad hominem fre-
quent in Poetry's reviews: The Seal of Approval guaranteeing
the worth of the product.   Here Austin Warren, "a constant
friend to the poet," and John Brooks Wheelwright "of Beacon
Street" are employed at good housekeeping, with Hart Crane
unwittingly hanging the livingroom curtains.   Blake, a vestige
from the thirties, deserves not to be forgotten; he strikes me
though--as I sense him through this review--as a periodpiece.

Richard Howard criticizes recent volumes by Philip
Levine and Daniel Hoffmann.   And he is surprisingly (for
Richard Howard) clear: hitherto he has hung suspended in
one of the major corners of contemporary criticism spinning
his dazzling webs full of glitter so obfuscatingly that he en-
traps himself, his reader, and the Poet (the meal).   No
critic of such renown has said so many entirely elusive, or-
nate things about poets.   Howard is to criticism what Gaudi
is to architecture.

The section on Levine's 1933 opens with rather mar-
velous Jamesian circumlocutions: I admire Howard's device
of supplying his own ellipses--the pacing of the breath hits
better that way.   Almost immediately, though, he obfuscates,
finding Levine's new book missing "just the conviction of
splendor, the just conviction which balances and ransoms the
conviction of ardor, the unjust conviction," present in They
Feed the Lion, Levine's earlier book.   Howard's wordplay,
repetitions, hesitations, leave me bewildered.   I feel as if
I've been rubbing my own sperm all over my body.   Yes,
Howard is the critic as narcissist.   He belongs in a tradition
of such critics--never dispassionate, usually flamboyant, and,
to paraphrase Samuel Johnson, never easy, vulgar, or there-

fore disgusting.   Among his forebears are Johnson, Swin-
burne, and D. H. Lawrence.   (I am not here writing of their
relative qualities.)

On Hoffman, Howard seems comfortable--perhaps be-
cause Hoffman is one of our known traditional poets.   How-
ard's opening sentences are quite masterful, if, perhaps, a
bit unfair:

> On the dust-jacket of this sixth book of verse,
> praise from a formalist master, a Zen master,
> and from a senior master of American letters
> would seem to settle Daniel Hoffman's hash into the
> kind of gruel which has something in it for every-
> one, but perhaps not much left over for the poet
> himself.   But no, it is just what is left over that
> enables Hoffman to be the poet he is--the leftovers
> of general and institutional approval are in fact the
> inception of his idiopathy, his self-disease.

Despite a certain amount of name-dropping this piece
represents Howard at his best: highly urbane, cutting and
incisive in subtle ways, and always fabricative.   He obvious-
ly regards criticism as an art; I wish that he were frequent-
ly less artful.

III

If Contributor's notes are a minor art form, which
they have become in a number of our small magazines,
Poetry's "Contributors" is about as useful and spicy as a
ten-year-old telephone book.   Here is a sampling: "Philip
Kuepper lives in New York City. "   "David Smith has pub-
lished two collections recently. "   "Theodore Hars is a gradu-
ate student in English at Stanford University. "   "Reg Saner
is currently on a year's leave from the English Department
at the University of Colorado.... "   "David Bromwich is a
graduate student at Yale. "   I fuss about the dullness of these
because I've become a Contributor's Notes addict, and gener-
ally turn to them first when I pick up a new magazine.
There's no reason why these shouldn't glisten and amuse,
and yet convey information.   Poetry's "News Notes" are lim-
ited pretty much to events in New York and to news of hand-
outs and prizes to such seminal writers as May Sarton, Con-
stance Urdang, Roger Pfingston, and Clarence Brown.   Yes,
and Daryl Hine supplies a couple of corrections: misspellings

in earlier issues.   The most interesting feature of "Books
Received" is the third category: "Verse and Prose Com-
bined. "

 Finally, the page facing the book cover is spread with
assorted goodies--testimonials from the greats: T. S. Eliot,
A. Macleish, W. C. Williams, St. John Perse ... most of
them, I'm sure, written while these venerable folk were still
alive, and preceding the reign of the current editor of Poetry.
A bit by Allen Tate closes the page--a testimonial I fear, no
longer true: "It's [Poetry's] vitality is as great, and its use-
fulness is greater than it has ever been.... "

IV

 At the suggestion of my editor, I decided to go back
and examine Poetry: A Magazine of Verse, I: 1, Oct. 1912.
The star of the number was Ezra Pound, with two fine pieces:
"To Whistler, American, " and "Middle-Aged: A Study in
Emotion. " There is also an eight-paged poem by the now-
forgotten Grace Conkling, which I find a distinctive, thorough-
ly enjoyable excursion into the aestheticism of the period.
Conkling's conception is Whistlerian and Pre-Raphaelite: sec-
tions are written to parallel classical music.   Emilia Lori-
mer and Helen Dudley write briefer pieces out of a similar
mode.   "I am the Woman, " by William Vaughan Moody blends
Swinburnian touches with programmatic material, and reflects
central interests of the time.   Harriet Monroe herself sup-
plies a brief parable about a Pre-Raphaelite king, to justify
poetry's existence.   Her intentions seem to have been un-
abashedly aesthetic; her prose trembles like a dew-drenched,
heavy-headed rose.

 Poetry I:1 reflected its time: and there are, I think,
between Ezra Pound, Swinburnian admirer that he was, and
aesthete in those late-century modes, necessary connections
with the more effete poets surrounding him.   Aestheticism
(and Decadence) was (were) the modes; and the focus supplied
by Harriet Monroe's magazine must have excited American
poets then.

 When I turn to Poetry, March 1975, I can't see any
evidence of new directions.   The magazine seems to be lan-
guishing in a backwater of American verse from which even
the skunks and tadpoles have long since absented themselves.
Occasionally, as with Saner and Magowan, the algae are dis-

turbed and clear water is revealed. However, this does not happen nearly often enough. Allen Tate's pronouncement is part of literary history.

GAB POETRY, OR DUCK VS. NIGHTINGALE MUSIC:

Charles Bukowski*

Last spring I witnessed a Charles Bukowski first: the debut of the great raunchy poet as actor. The vehicle, The Tenant, was a two actor drama written by Miss Linda King on her life with Charles Bukowski. Rumor had it that Bukowski inserted lines of his own ... to develop his own image in the play, so to speak. A pair of lines more or less to this effect were supposedly his additions, as delivered by Miss King: "You may be the greatest poet of the century, but you sure can't fuck." In a lively way The Tenant turns upon the problem of whether a super-poet should move in with his girlfriend, who would then, one would suppose, support him, buy him his beer, give him bj's, and let him torment her. The event that afternoon was choice. An actor scheduled to read Bukowski's part was unable to show, so Bukowski took over.

There were about twenty people in the well of the Pasadena Museum--sad, alas, because of the significance of the event: perhaps never again would Bukowski, script in hand, tread the boards. The props were few: a telephone-- used with nearly as much frequency as Barbara Stanwyck used it in Sorry, Wrong Number; a mattress upon which from time to time King and Bukowski, scripts in hand, fall down to enact their erotic comings together after dismal separations. The performance was pixie-ish and delightful and included a tender moment where Bukowski acted as W. C. Fields towards a child who had a brief moment of stage glory. Needless to say, the small audience laughed considerable, particularly over Bukowski's Bogartesque delivery, as foiled by the various stunning Bardotesqueries of Ms. King.

*Reprinted by permission from Margins, No. 16 (Jan. 1975) pp. 24-28; Copyright © 1975 by Margins.

The Tenant gave Bukowski a chance to say, under the guise of art and the protection of aesthetic distance, that he is a great poet of the age, perhaps of the century--or words to that effect.   There's never been any reticence about his declaring (and with some justification) the value of his literary achievements.   Certainly no poet in America as deserving of recognition was so long buried, ignored, and even despised by establishment critics, readers in droves, Rolling Stone, The Whole Earth Catalogue people, and granters of American Poetry Society Annual Awards.   I remember how jolted I was when I first read him: I was teaching at the University of California at Riverside and had been given a copy of Crucifix in a Deathhand.   I carried the book to a string quartet concert one night, began reading it before the concert began, experienced chills, elevations, charismatic flashes, barberpole exaltations, fevers in the groin.   I had not read such poems since discovering Dylan Thomas for myself in the fifties.   Christ, something awe-thentic at last, I exclaimed, nudging my companion who thought I had gone out of my mind.   No poet I was then teaching or reading marched so directly into the poignant grosseries of life, into the depths of soul-body-mind, painted it up quivering and wriggling on the wall, and let in drifts and wafts of compassion to sweeten the dregs.   Bukowski was unafraid of life's terror meat-slabs, and he made the angels sing.

I began to ask around about him--of other poets, of other profs.   If they had heard of him--yes, he was living in Hollywood in some dump, they said.   They dismissed him as a charlatan, snot and maidenkum-eating lecher, steeped in booze, flop-gutted, rancid-breathed.   What did he (all of that) have to do with poetry?   I gave up trying to explain how deeply he had moved me, and I didn't care whether he dug rolling around in his own puke, or feasting on maiden elixir kept in peanutbutter jars.   To me, he was a super-poet, the best I knew.   His example allowed me to loosen my own writing, which I was then beginning to engage in with professional seriousness.   He made Lowell, Snodgrass, Wilbur, Olson look like dilettantes.

Somewhat under the influence of Thomas Carlyle and his theories of hero-worship at the time, I (as other people were beginning to do) beat my way, carrying the gift of a six pack of Coors, to the poet's door one afternoon, four or five days before Christmas.   His little daughter was there, and they were trimming her Christmas tree.   There weren't many ornaments--some half dozen, which were hung eventually

on the lowest branches of the tree.   I found a man of terrific
charm--winsome almost.   Nothing at all of the retchable-hor-
rible I had been led to expect.   I have been an avid Bukow-
ski fan ever since, and pride myself on sensing his worth
long before he became a super-star of the far-out schools,
rock-a-groupie-by-babie scenes, celestial establishment quar-
terlies and anthologies, alcoholic (beer-drinkers largely)
freakout poets (LA and its environs are full of them) imitating
his special genre of poem, Gab Poetry.   And I don't hold Bu-
kowski responsible for the worst of imitators--a poet of his
stature drinks, shits, pisses, ejaculates and breathes breath
both fair and foul.   His imitators don't really know what he's
up to--and he slyly encourages them to believe that they
know, when in truth they fall in ordure all the while he sits
there waving his beer, all celestial brain-waving, smart-ass
and pooperoo poet that he is.   So, as he says, let the ef-
fluvium drift and fly!   Whoever lappeth it up, let him lappeth
away!

II

        The recent appearance of Bukowski's Burning in Water
Drowning in Flame: Selected Poems 1955-1973 allows me the
chance to say what in his first books reached me so tellingly,
and to describe what I find to be unfortunate drifts in his
more recent work.   I hope my remarks help cut through
some of the celebrity bullshit now seriously threatening his
reputation--and his work (since he seems finally to be be-
lieving a lot of it).

III

        Bukowski's It Catches My Heart in Its Hands (1963)
and Crucifix in a Deathhand (1965), two Loujon Press books,
are among the dozen or so most beautifully printed and de-
signed books of poetry ever.   It is not surprising that they
are collectors' items.   The earlier volume has been almost
inaccessible and the second almost equally so.   It is great,
therefore, to have these reprinted.   Bukowski has written
no better poetry than appears in these books.

        The very first poem, "the tragedy of the leaves," pro-
pels us into Bukowski's world: hangover, desertion by the
woman he has spent the night with, the landlady's threat-note
waiting to scream at him, a world that's failed him utterly.

Set up for the big blubbery whine? Self-indulgent, self-sorrow inflicting verse? No! There is a marvelous transmutation of the raunchy conditions via unusual images. The first line illustrates: "I awakened to dryness and the ferns were dead, / the potted plants yellow as corn...." Be academic: see how splendidly dryness in its syllable-time echoes awakened. Note how the idea of awakening implies grappling with a world, hopefully moving toward fresh insight. A fine compression follows:

> my woman was gone
> and the empty bottles like bled corpses
> surrounded me with their uselessness....

His ear is working: the long vowel sounds are well-spaced, dropping in at the right interval to keep the sound burgeoning. And the play of corpse and uselessness is fine. Bukowski avoids self-pity by sensing the positive in the sunlight as it brightens the landlady's note in its "fine and / undemanding yellowness." He must deal with his pain and says that the occasion demands "a good comedian, ancient style, a jester / with jokes upon absurd pain." A special wisdom leaps through with telling simplicity: "pain is absurd / because it exists, nothing more." He moves on to his own pain--not the result of his hangover, really, but rather caused by his tragic self-sensing that as a poet he is stagnant and dead: "that's the tragedy of the dead plants." His genius has not fulfilled itself. Here is the rest of the poem. Note the subtle rhyme-play between more and razor, both in end-stop positions. Note the effective repetitions of dead, dead, dark, stood accompanying their monosyllabic tough nouns. Note how execrating, waving, and screaming move together, as hall, final, hell, and failed weave end-of-line echoes. Note too his sympathy for the landlady as yet another victim. This kind of empathy almost disappears from Bukowski's current work:

> and I walked into a dark hall
> where the landlady stood
> execrating and final,
> sending me to hell,
> waving her fat, sweaty arms
> and screaming
> screaming for rent
> because the world had failed us
> both.

I dwell on these simple matters of technique because
I wish to stress the acuteness of Bukowski's ear.   These
early poems sing as you read them.   They possess superb
connections of cadence, rhyme, syllable.   A true authority.

Empathy is present in other poems.   "For marilyn
m." avoids the sentimental and locates a language suited for
the fey person Monroe was.   Bukowski seems to be address-
ing a fanciful child:

> ... and we will forget you, somewhat
> and it is not kind
> but real bodies are nearer
> and as the worms pant for your bones,
> I would so like to tell you
> that this happens to bears and elephants
> to tyrants and heroes and ants
> and frogs,
> still, you brought us something,
> some type of small victory,
> and for this I say: good
> and let us grieve no more....

"The life of Borodin," grandly empathetic, is a mas-
terpiece of its kind ... reportage ... the sad events of gen-
ius / Borodin's life ... wife-hounded ... sleeping only by
placing dark cloth over his eyes ... his wife lining cat boxes
and covering jars of sour milk with his compositions ...
house noises.   All of this is reported in taut free-verse
lines fitting the more rigorous dicta of the projective verse
theorists.   Nothing is overstated, everything hits its mark.
The comparisons and parallels between Bukowski's own life
and Borodin's remain implicit.

"The twins" provides another tremulous situation, one
that a lesser poet might easily have destroyed.   Here Bukow-
ski comes to terms with his hatred of his father, immediate-
ly after the father's death.   "A father is always your master
even when he's gone," declares the bereaved voice.   To make
an adjustment, the speaker moves through the house stunned,
then proceeds outside where he picks an orange and peels it.
Common day noises ... dogs, neighbors ... speak sanity.
The poet returns to the house and puts on his father's suit:

> I try on a light blue suit
> much better than anything I have ever worn
> and I flap the arms like a scarecrow in the wind

> but it's no good:
> I can't keep him alive
> no matter how much we hated each other.
>
> we looked exactly alike, we could have been twins
> the old man and I: that's what they
> said.   he had his bulbs on the screen
> ready for planting
> while I was lying with a whore from 3rd street.
>
> very well.   grant us this moment: standing before
>   a mirror
> in my dead father's suit
> waiting also
> to die.

The event is stark, human.   To try on another's clothes is, in a sense, to become that other person.   Bukowski's mimicry of death as scarecrow is a humorous / macabre touch and triggers the insight that despite the hate, the survivor can't keep the dead man alive, no matter how he may wish to.

"Old poet" derives from Bukowski's intense feeling of aging (he's 42 here) without feeling he has a public that respects his work.   He ages sexually, and finds himself reduced to dirty pictures instead of real bodies, in pleasure, he says, with "the fox in the ferns."   He's had too much beer, listened to Shostakovitch too often.   He takes a healthy swat at "a razzing fly" and "ho, I fall heavy as thunder...."   Downstairs, the tenants aren't upset; they'll assume "he's either drunk or dying" and let him alone.   Despite his depression and stagnation, every morning he packs off little envelopes of poems, hoping to place them in magazines.   Rejection slips get him down ... super-rejections.   But once again he sits at the typewriter, writing out his destiny.   The final few lines are a fine winding down of projective verse cadences and sounds:

> the editors wish to thank you for
> submitting but
> regret...
> down
>   down
>   down
>   the dark hall
>   into a womanless hall

> to peel a last egg
> and sit down to the keys:
> click click a click,
> over the television sounds
> over the sounds of springs,
> click click a clack:
> another old poet
> going off.

"View from the screen" might easily have dissolved into an existential self-pity; it has all the accoutrements. It shouldn't work, but it does, and deeply. The death-whisper of the heron, the bone-thoughts of sea creatures fill the universe on this final day. The poet crosses the room:

> to the last wall
> the last window
> the last pink sun
> with its arms around the world
> with its arms around me....

The sun seems benign and loving as it awards its pink attention. Perhaps the pinkness produces the pig-image, an unusual trope and one, I think, that saves the poem from turning maudlin. The Platonic cave motif is obvious:

> I hear the death-whisper of the heron
> the bone-thoughts of sea-things
> that are almost rock;
> this screen caved like a soul
> and scrawled with flies,
> my tensions and damnations
> are those of a pig,
> pink sun pink sun
> I hate your holiness
> crawling your gilded cross of life
> as my fingers and feet and face
> come down to this....

In these early poems, the act of writing is for Bukowski "to get ... feelings down." Now, that's not news, of course; it sounds like warmed-over Shelley and Keats. The crux is the nature of the feelings: are they surface, deep, sentimental, universal? In Bukowski's head, the urge to write, which for him (since he's done so much of it) must be as necessary as defecation, is prompted by his pain. The pain, somehow, is externalized by the writing; or, rather,

an image allows him to translate pain into a larger testimony
of the human spirit. And there is also, he says, "madness
and terror" along "agony way." Both are alleviated by the
act of the poem. There's something like a time-bomb ticking
inside his chest, and if it doesn't go off as a poem it will go
off in a fit of drunkenness, dope, sensuality, despair, vomit-
ing, rage. It's as if he's saying that as long as he writes
he leashes his terror in its cage. "Beans with garlic" is
exactly about this. A terrific idea, beans as loves! And
stirring them has to do with writing your poems--words as
beans, etc. The poem almost works. Here are the final
ten lines:

> but now
> there's a ticking under your shirt
> and you whirl the beans with a spoon,
> one love dead, one love departed
> another love...
> ah! as many loves as beans
> yes, count them now
> sad, sad
> your feelings boiling over flame,
> get this down.

The closing lines of "A nice day" deal with a knife the speak-
er carries inside him. A death of feeling: Bukowski can't
feel doom, so he goes outside "to absolutely nothing / a
square round of orange zero." A woman says goodmorning,
thereby twisting his knife:

> I do notice though the sun is shining
> that the flowers are pulled up on
> their strings
> and I on mine:
> belly, bellybutton, buttocks, bukowski
> waving walking
> teeth of ice with the taste of tar
> tear ducts propagandized
> shoes acting like shoes
> I arrive on time
> in the blazing midday of
> mourning.

This is a sizeable chunk of verse! Even the concluding pun
works well. The lines are well-made, non-derivative. Sel-
dom is Bukowski derivative. And to note the playful transla-
tion of E. E. Cummings in the final lines of one of Bukowski's

best poems, "Something for the touts, the nuns, the grocery
clerks and you, " is rare indeed.   The principal gesture is,
however, Bukowski's: foreign to Cummings would be a po-
etry created from the dirt on a windowsill.   At his best Bu-
kowski produces (invents) his own special rhetoric.   Then he
is never fatiguing, as he becomes in his later raconteur,
gab/barfly manner.   Too often his recent voice sounds like
one of his army (located primarily in southern California) of
inept imitators.   His best poems discharge themselves with
an Olsonesque energy.   One is touched by a vital creative
mind loving the creative act, prizing it, despite all the booze,
This special energy is what earns Bukowski a front rank
place among contemporary poets.   Call it originality if
you will; for, to paraphrase T. S. Eliot on Tennyson, Bu-
kowski has (had) originality in abundance.

                                    IV

     In At Terror Street and Agony Way (1968) a deteriora-
tion of Bukowski's talent sets in.   His paranoia, traceable in
earlier works, is heightened.   His temper grows discernibly
nasty.   His sympathies are now primarily with outrageous
folks, viz. , the guy who emasculates himself with a rusty tin
can and who wanders the freeway clutching himself; or "the
nice guy" who cuts up a woman and sends various parts of
her to various people.   It's as if B. wants to spit in your
face.

     The situations of the poems become more extreme.
It's as if Bukowski is aware that a sycophantic public ex-
pecting outrageous cartwheels and titillating obscenities ap-
plauds his showing off.   There is a discernible and regret-
table drifting from the superb humanity and tenderness of
the earlier poems.   And there is a troublesome, boring lo-
quaciousness; the finely turned work of the early manner is
usurped by rambling, grotty passages of prose masquerading
(cut into lengths) as poetry.   I continue to read Bukowski
nevertheless, because there are still surprises.   He remains
one of the most readable of poets; and the appearance of any
of his books is an event.   A core, primitive almost, resides
in first-rank poetry--a core of empathy, depth, wisdom-via-
suffering feelings.   This has shrunk almost away in Bukow-
ski's current work, replaced in part by a regrettable nasti-
ness.   I have in mind the vicious parody of Michael McClure
in this volume, and the tasteless piece on Jack Hirschman as
the narcissistic poet Victor Vania, written by Bukowski for

the delectation of his Free Press fans.   A man secure in his
fame and aware of his talent would not need to stoop to hack-
ing out bad jokes at the expense of other writers.

        One assumes that Bukowski is aware of his falling.
But is he?   Does he believe what the sycophants and third-
rate rock stars who seek him out tell him by way of flattery?
Is the celebrity status so heady that he joins the trained seals
and the poker-playing koi amazing the public with their tricks?
His boast that he is one of the great poets of the age is far
less true than it used to be.   I'd like to imagine that he
hungers for the funky anonymity he once enjoyed where some
of the personal pain became a pain heard--and produced the
splendid work.   Unsure of an audience, the voice in quest
gained its way through its humanity and compassion.   Per-
haps this, simply said, is what produces a writer's best
work.

        "Sunday before noon, " a wistful curse occasioned by
a whore, concludes with an impressive, almost funny piece
of hysteria.   But, the charm is deceptive; the poem is an
excursion into Bukowski's current narcissism:

> going down
> are the clocks cocks roosters?
> the roosters stand on the fence
> the roosters are peanutbutter crowing,
> the FLAME will be high, the flame will be big,
> kiss kiss kiss
> everything away,
> I hope it rains today, I hope
> the jets die, I hope
> the kitten finds a mouse, I hope
> I don't see it, I hope
> it rains, I hope
> anything away from here,
> I hope a bridge, a fish, a cactus somewhere
> strutting whiskers to the noon,
> I dream flowers and horses
> the branches break the birds fall the buildings
> burn, my whore walks across the room and
> smiles at me.

There's still some of the old originality here: juxtaposition
of peanutbutter and roosters, and the branches, birds, build-
ings open the poem as well as conclude it.   But the stance,
the narcissism of "going down" without resistance, the wish

to be wiped out, and to wipe out, is boring.   There isn't
much in life now (petulance) worth grappling with, or hanging
among the trophies you've so far acquired by drawing the
right beads on poetry-meaning, life-worth.   There is a nag-
ging, pissed-off tone now as Bukowski slips along towards
the next binge:

> and I got out of bed and yawned and scratched my belly
> and knew that soon   very soon   I would have to get
> very drunk   again.

His method of the scattered line (prose scattered across the
page) is an inferior imitation of those recent poems by James
Dickey written as bits arranged on the page.   Dickey has
handled the mode well, but here the mode is flabby, like a
white-fat flopping belly.   Separating soon and again, isolating
them to make them seem momentous merely emphasizes the
sterility of the passage.   Ditto, the repetition of very.

Now, too, Bukowski cracks wise with editors who re-
ject his poems.   He becomes a rhino-skinned poet s. o. b. :

> when a chicken
> catches its worm
> the chicken gets through
> and when the worm
> catches you
> (dead or alive)
> I'd have to say,
> even though its lack
> of sensibility,
> that it enjoys
> it.
>
> it's like when you
> send this poem
> back
> I'll figure
> it just didn't get
> through.
>
> either there were
> fatter worms
> or the chicken
> couldn't
> see.

                    the next time
                    I break an egg
                    I'll think of
                    you.
                    scramble with
                    fork

                    and then turn up
                    the flame
                    if I
                    have
                    one.

This poem has a certain attractive petulance, and the motif
of chicken, worm, egg, is original.   Also the Creeleyesque
lines work well as they drop themselves along.   But, for me,
the piece drifts into cuteness, and the possibilities of the ini-
tial images dissolve, smothered by a slight but real narcis-
sism.

        Particularly distasteful is Bukowski's obsession with
his fame.   In "The difference between a bad poet and a good
one is luck," he regales us with his life in Philadelphia,
broke and trying to write, waiting for the ultimate handout
to enable him to sit around "drinking wine on credit and
watching the hot pigeons suffer and fuck" on his "hot roof."
He hops a train to Texas, is busted for vagrancy, is dumped
off in the next big town where he lucks it by finding a local
broad who takes him in and gives him so many teethmarks he
thinks he'll have cancer.   But primarily the poem is about
Bukowski as great writer, and about his reputation--or the
way it waxes, as he feels it does.   In fine macho fashion,
he greets a bunch of his mistress' cowboy friends:

        I had on a pair of old bluejeans, and they said
        oh, you're a writer, eh?
        and I said: well, some think so.
        and some still think so...
        others, of course, haven't wised up yet.
        two weeks later they
        ran me out
        of town.

        He seems wistfully amused that trash men busy about
their work don't know that he, Great Poet, is alive--a thought
held, I would guess, by all great men who love the irony and
who snicker in their mush: "Oh, if they only knew how near

to greatness they are banging those trash cans down there
.... " If Bukowski seeks empathy here he doesn't find it.
The poem lacks any particularly fresh language, idiom, ca-
dence. It's all laid out there, much as you might find it in
The Enquirer.

　　　In "Lost" Bukowski waxes philosophical, much, sur-
prisingly, in the manner of a hip-Merwin. The Big Conclu-
sion is that "we can't win it. " Who's surprised? "Just for
awhile, " folks, "we thought we could. " But now we can't.
There's a spiffy Conclusion to follow Big Conclusion, a Big
Big Conclusion, one might say: "it is terrible to be de-
feated / in what seems to count. " This Life Significance
Statement serves up duck-music as distinct from nightingale-
music. Gabble rather than sweet bird-twitter. Is Bukowski
setting up here for a passel o' heads--who don't want their
freak brains taxed by truly heavy thought? The tiresome lo-
quaciousness here is typical of a feature marring much of
Bukowski's later poetry. I call this loquaciousness gab po-
etry.

　　　And gab poetry seems to be Bukowski's favorite genre
these days, particularly if one includes the numerous prose
pieces, stories and otherwise. The gab poem is related to
the old fabliaux of Chaucer and the medieval poets, a connec-
tion I'm sure Buk will (would) delight in. Obscenities in
those fabliaux, of a sexual sort: amusing moments--like the
husband shoving a hot iron rod up his wife's lover's anus,
whilst lover is taking a crap out the window; old husband's
young wife being swyved up in a tree just out of eye-shot of
old fart, trusting, standing amidst the flowers.... A trav-
elling narrative (with Chaucer at times presented in skillful
verse), garrulous, in which you feel nothing is left out, a
sort of gab accompanying spitoon sounds in some down and
out bar. Also, the illusion that the narrator, much in his
cups, is loading your ear as you lean beside him sniffing his
loaded breath and working up your own inebriation.

　　　"Hot" is a good example of Bukowski's gab poetry.
The speaker's been working at the post office, see, on the
night pickup run in an old truck. He knows Miriam the de-
licious whore is at home waiting for him, deadline 8 p. m.
At the last pickup the speaker's truck stalls and won't start.
Miriam waiting. Speaker arrives home late. Miriam has
split leaving a note addressed to "son of bitch" propped against
his pillow, the note held in place by her purple teddy bear.
Speaker gives the bear (heh heh) a drink, has one himself,

and climbs into a hot tub. (With or without cantaloupe?).
The poem all moves like narrative prose, cut up more or
less projectively, into boozy breath-groups. Nothing much
of interest (poetically) catches the ear--this is in a sense a
one-shot piece of work. It doesn't deserve much more than
a first reading.

Some of the other later poems, like "Burn and burn
and burn," are actually set in bars. Here is his new (I
think) sophomoric cynicism. It lacks all largeness of vision
and empathy, and comes off petulant amidst the "vomiting in-
to plugged toilets / in rented rooms full of roaches and mice."
Almost self-parody. Dreams and ideals are equal to poisons
--and since we can't cry (which would be our most legitimate
act) we can laugh and expel these dreams, ideals, poisons,
etc. Life alas (freshly said) "was a terrible joke." Con-
clusion?

> well, I suppose the days were made
> to be wasted
> the years and the loves were made
> to be wasted

This is bad contemporary Ernest Dowson. Instead of Dow-
son's roses and lilies Bukowski supplies vomit and plugged
toilets to stress his wasted days.

I have the feeling I should find the secret of life
tucked inside a little plastic envelope deep within a box of
Charles Bukowski Creepy-Crawly-Vomit-Sugar-Coated-Crunch-
Cereal. It has something to do with Disneyland and Head
Consciousness and Gab-Mouths Ripped and Bleeding. Jesus
Christ, Bukowski says, "should have laughed on the cross."
How do we know he didn't, Charles? There is a theory that
since Christ was so utterly mystical he felt no pain and joy-
ously (laughing even) welcomed his translation from life into
eternity. There's a secret hidden somewhere behind there.
But is it so hidden? For, in this passage Bukowski equates
himself with Christ, a risk of sorts for any poet to take.
The love theme is maudlin and sophomoric in its reaching
after profundity:

> out of the arms of one love
> and into the arms of another

> I have been saved from dying on the cross
> by a lady who smokes pot

writes songs and stories.
and is much kinder than the last,
much much kinder,
and the sex is just as good or better.

it isn't pleasant to be put on the cross and left there,
it is much more pleasant to forget a love which didn't
work
as all love
finally
doesn't work. . . .

"The beautiful," says Bukowski, "don't make it ... they die
in flame ... they commit suicide..., " they "can't endure, "
"the beautiful are found at the edge of a room / crumpled
into spiders and needles and silence ... they don't make it
... the beautiful die young / and leave the ugly to their ugly
lives...." This is all hardly above sentimental name-calling.
Who are the ugly? Who are the young and beautiful? Are
all the young beautiful? etc., etc. More Ernest Dowson in
modern drag dancing riotously with the throng!

One superb poem, "the catch," proves that Bukowski
can still bring off a masterful poem, as good as anything he
has ever written. The problem is to name whatever it is
one catches. In Bukowski's poem the catch is some sort of
fish; but the symbol is a good symbol and transcends itself,
as good symbols should. The guesses are that the creature
is a Hollow-Back June Whale, a Billow-Wind Sand-Groper,
a Fandango Escadrille with stripes. But the persons crowd-
ing around the catch can't agree. They pull it out of the
water and find it "grey and covered with hair / and fat and
it stank like old socks." Joyously the creature promenades
down the pier eating hot dogs, riding the merry-go-round,
and hopping on a pony. It falls off into the dust. "Grop,
grop," it says. Followed by a large crowd, it returns to
the pier, where it now has trouble breathing and falls back-
wards and begins thrashing about. Somebody obligingly pours
beer over its head. "Grop, grop," it goes. Then it dies.
The people roll it back into the ocean, argue over its name,
and then go home. Bukowski's fantasy is here beautifully
walled in by the tall tale. And the lines are spare, with lit-
tle of the loquaciousness of so many of the poems in this
volume. This poem will linger in my mind for a long time.

Charles Bukowski is an easy poet to love, fear, and/
or hate. He works at developing his own legend as loath-

some person, lush, and woman-devourer. And he has a win-
some, almost childlike, ingratiating side which various peo-
ple have experienced and enjoyed, frequently to their surprise.
He can be the best-behaved poet around, and one of immense
charm. Obviously, by discussing his personality I fall into
the trap of confusing the personality of the poet with the po-
etry. It shouldn't matter that Bukowski vomits 3 or 5 times
a week (if indeed he does), or that he gets laid as often
(sometimes getting it up, sometimes not), or that 77 of his
poems have appeared in little magazines this year, or that
Black Sparrow Press pushes him as a hot commodity. And
it doesn't matter--none of it--except for the work. My rea-
son for writing this piece is to cut through some of the or-
dure appearing about Bukowski--much of it sentimental and
unabashedly devoted to increasing his celebrity status. He
remains a considerable poet who has for the present moved
into something of a decline. Yes, say other readers, "but
as his poetry worsens his fiction grows better." Perhaps.
My own feeling is that poetry remains a more durable and
demanding art than fiction, that the depths of the human spir-
it declare themselves better in poetry than in prose, and that
the superior poet is equally the superior man. Buk, climb
back up on that fence, grab your beer and your paper and
pencil, gaze off over the landscape, and give us a fresh
stampede of tremendous poems.

THIS ROLLING STONE GATHERS MOSS:

Anne Waldman*

Better than any book I've seen for a long time, Wald-
man's Fast Speaking Woman convinces me that a writer by
becoming a celebrity can get work published and sold, and
earn a rather large reputation.   For years Anne Waldman has
functioned as the queen of the poetry hive at St. Mark's
Church, NYC.   They've been a busy, productive group, speck-
ling their territory with the right formic gyzm needed to keep
foreigners away, and to keep their area clear for smooth
swarming.   Ms. Waldman has labored well as Colony Queen;
the program at St. Mark's has been/is prestigious.   But
what will happen now that Ms. Waldman has become a celeb-
rity and is in demand away from the home community?   Will
a new Queen displace her?   Will she join the other expatri-
ates and move to Bolinas, California?   Will she live it up
at Trungpa-Time in Boulder?

I bought Fast Speaking Woman, delighted to see a sub-
stantial sampling of Waldman's work.   I had reports from
persons attending her readings, during which she reportedly
came on as a slinky, funky reciteress of her fast-speaking
chants.   Now, don't get me wrong--I'm not against perform-
ances.   I dig them.   But as a critic I try to keep a work
distinct from the public self of its author; the poem still has
to vitalize the page.   Fast Speaking Woman, I'm afraid,
would bore me as much live as it does in print.

Let me get down to specifics.   These are "chants, "
right?   So, in a sense Ms. Waldman excuses herself from
the rigors of writing Keatsian verse (but actually she bor-
rows a little honey from Keats, as a motto--sweetening--
blessing--for her book).   Yes, why shouldn't a good chant

*Reprinted by permission from Margins, No. 28-30 (Jan. -
March 1975) pp. 24-28, 69; Copyright © 1975 by Margins.

sustain interest? Why shouldn't the best qualities of a writ-
er's mind inform the chanting? I find Waldman's mind pre-
dictable, sentimental, self gratifying. A common device she
uses is to derive one word slickly from another; viz., mo-
bile derives from automobile; necklace derives from elastic;
abandoned dumps in from abalone; aborigine from gibberish;
demi-monde from demented, etc. These connections are
facile--that's my point. Wordplay is great when the inventive
or creative imagination of the writer is first-rate. Even
funky writing requires better than a comicbook level of in-
ventiveness. Hokey associationism. Think of G. Stein's
brilliance in yoking words deriving from similar sounds to-
gether. Old Boomlay boomlay boomlay boom wasn't too bad
at it. Nor was Patchen. Nor was Jeffers. In fairness, I
can see that before an audience of a couple of hundred fe-
males, the chant would hit everybody sooner or later: Wald-
man coming on as spokesperson for all downtrodden, sex-
object females from the beginning of time, through all cul-
tures, embodied in a slinky, pongee dress, wearing Carole
Lombardesque shoes, up there on stage, belting out "I'm a
jive ass woman / I'm the callous woman / I'm the callow
woman / I'm the clustered woman / I'm the dulcimer woman
/ I'm the dainty woman / I'm the murderous woman / I'm
the discerning woman / I'm the dissonant woman / I'm the
anarchist woman / I'm the Bantu woman / I'm the Buddha
woman / I'm the baritone woman / I'm the bedouin woman
...." I have a vision of all the women in America, stand-
ing up wherever they are, on a sort of Kate Smith American
relief-map; and all these women are chanting lines from
Waldman's poem, swaying in time, while the men retreat in-
to bank caverns, factory assembly-line shadows, the hills.
Then, altogether, in conclusion, and in upper-case, they
shout: "I KNOW HOW TO SHOUT / I KNOW HOW TO SING
/ I KNOW HOW TO LIE DOWN." And that's how Waldman's
"Fast Speaking Woman" ends: nicely ambiguous? lie down to
what? fuck? sleep? die? all three? or, none of the above?
I feel let down ... I wish there had been some pyrotechnics
there, of the sort that flashed off in that semi-porn flick of
not too many years ago, The Telephone. Set in New York
City--near St. Mark's Square probably--man wearing porky
pig mask can get it on only via telephone. He turns on this
broad who locates him in NY phone book (despite the fact
that his last name is Smith), and they spend a heavy date
yakking to one another in adjacent phone booths. But the
close of the flick is fantastic: comic strip routines called
in--the greatest female assertiveness comic strip animation
sequence I've ever seen. For animation-heroine uses whole

New York cityscape for dildos, saving World Trade Building and the Empire State Buildings for last: what she does is to pump up and down on them long enough to splinter them until they begin to crumble. Now, that's an ending! Fast Speaking Woman lacks a super-duper windup ending--Joan Blondell with callouses won't do.

Her other poems are marred by commonplace writing and sophomoric conclusions about life, love, and art: examples, from various poems--"I would be father I would be infant animal awesome / I would suffer / become extinct again / I would relight the earth with love...." "be insistent be an empire be a symphony / & in a moment's gentle passing / & in a moment's violent passing...." (Here, Waldman hits on the arresting idea of yoking together contraries--as Blake used to call them). Sometimes, as in "Pressure," the effect is of spreading stale peanutbutter over a half-mile long delicatessen roll--it's a waste of good paper to wipe these details over numerous pages, when, in actuality, all Waldman has going is a long series (hot shower, poolroom, bowling alley, bar, bathtub, restaurant, delicatessen, store, trolley, and the Alps) better assembled in prose. And, also, she's something of a culture-vulture, larding in a compliment or two, Waldman Seal of Approval: "Joan Sutherland's astounding voice"; "the cocktail party" and "the starry night"--compliments to T. S. Eliot and to Vincent Van Gogh; "Mozart's legacy / & Satie's"; "The Great Chain Of Being"--this one from a course at Hunter or somewhere, in Renaissance literature, for bright senior English majors; and these also hip-pretentious things she can't give up: "talking about Kerouac," "Louis Ferdinand Celine (all three names); Bach, Beethoven, Buddy Holly, Jelly Roll Morton. The most pretentious of these poems is "Light & Shadow," which allows the author to show off the various bits and pieces of books, things, philosophers, poets she's liked (including "the long shadow of Jesus," "Locke's reasoning light," "Homer's voyaging light & shadow," "Aristotle, dark & consuming," "Goethe's elective affinities," "Newton's arrogant light," "Calvin's stoic light," "poor Abelard suffering under prison's damp shadow," "Socrates' wise forehead," "Einstein's brain the speed of light," "Aquinas, Plato, Pasteur all light-bulbs in the brown study," etc. All of this I find entirely predictable. Moreover, the things I've quoted about Socrates, Einstein, Goethe are sentimental: they aren't felt. And that finally is my greatest fuss about these writings (I won't call them poems): there is too little feeling and there is a lot of showing off--or, perhaps, <u>showi-ness</u> is the word.

   One of Waldman's poems is called "Empty Speech."
Nuff said, ffffolks!

HOMAGE TO FRANK O'HARA*

The O'Hara cult continues. The most recent manifesta-
tion of it is this 224pp. assemblage of "messages" (as
the editors of Big Sky 11/12 call them) from people who
knew the poet, or "who otherwise feel some close connection
with him through either hearsay or his work or both." The
list includes former lovers, fellow-poets, painters, com-
posers, musicians, fiction writers, museum folk: Elmslie,
de Kooning, Waldman, Berrigan, Ciardi, Ashbery, Freilicher,
Koch, Rorem, Button, Duncan, Wieners, Whalen, Creeley,
Guest, Dubuffet, Schuyler, Neel, Katz, Guston, Brainard,
Southern, Southgate, Krauss, Padgett, Rivers, Schjeldahl,
MacAdams, Ginsberg, di Prima, Kaplan, Olson, Cage, and
Schuchat. There are lavish spreads of photographs and
paintings and drawings of O'Hara--the finest paintings, I
think, belong to Alice Neel. Few of these commemorative
messages (and they include several poems) are over four
pages long. All are as fascinating as fragments of a hip
novel, a saga of an elusive man dying tragically at age 40
(on July 25, 1966) after being run over by a dune buggy.
The story is well-known. What I shall do here is to con-
tinue the collage technique so effectively employed by Berk-
son-Le Sueur's messengers, and shall provide my own crit-
ic's collage made up of various actual statements appearing
in Homage to Frank O'Hara. What I hope to convey is a
sense of this complex man's appearance, personal behavior,
and art. Mine, then, is an arrangement from numerous
voices.

I

He seemed very sissy to me. He talked on the tele-
phone a lot. He drank a lot. He smoked a lot. And he

---

*Reprinted by permission from The American Book Review,
I:5 (Dec. -Jan. 1978-1979) p. 3; Copyright © 1978 by ABR.

ate in French restaurants a lot.   I think that almost every-
thing Frank did he did a lot.

Clothes liked Frank.   His jeans fit him as if they wanted to
go to bed with him.   When he walked down the street, Frank
held his head tipped up as if he had perfect confidence in the
clothes underneath his chin.   I remember Frank's walk.
Light and sassy.

He wasn't handsome, but he had a kind of beauty: the taut
Irish fairness and freckles, the high brow and profile like a
Roman coin with an elegant thug's broken nose, the delicate
curving mouth.   We talked about opera or movies or both.

Frank was very well put together physically.   The scale of
his body reminded somewhat of the drawings of ideal male
proportion by Dürer.   He was very pleasing to look at.
Frank's nose rose above those early disasters to resolve
itself into a mature hump of bone that divided his face into
its two profiles like a mountain ridge.   In shape and forma-
tion, though, it was an Adirondack, not an Alp--it was an
old nose.

When he came in the door he looked beat.   I started with
the mouth, with those teeth that looked like tombstones and
then included the lilacs that had faded.   I began doing por-
traits of Frank in the fall of '52.   That was after I'd slit
my wrists over something.   He had blazing blue eyes, so if
you were stuck you could always put in a little blue to make
the picture more interesting.   The long neck, the high cheek
bones, the bridged nose and flaring nostrils reminded me of
an over-bred polo pony.   His lips were pushing into the fu-
ture to taste what it was like there.

Frank was very polite and also very competitive.   Sometimes
he gave other people his own best ideas, but he was quick
and resourceful enough to use them himself.   Frank's normal
expression was a tough aggressive one.

He was a born talker.   He loved giving advice.   He could
be a tough customer in an argument.   His tongue could be
sharp, and after a few drinks, more than that.   He loved a
fight, he loved drama, he enjoyed being a star.

He was attracted to "stars."   In the early years Frank was
under suspicion as a gifted amateur.   After seeing Judy Gar-
land's first big show at the Palace Theater, Frank said,

"Well, I guess she's better than Picasso. " He wanted every-
thing to be noble.

He had a lovely sardonic sense of fun.   Frank's kisses were
soft and fierce.

II

Frank.   Frank and the dance.   Frank and Me.   It's all in
his poems.   I think his whole life is.

He seemed to dance from canvas to canvas, from party to
party, from poem to poem.   The whole art community was
his Ginger Rogers.   He didn't make distinctions: he mixed
everything up: life and art, friends and lovers.   Frank
needed a job, and he was in love with the Museum and
brooked no criticism of it.   He liked coming to my gallery.
I saw him a good deal.   I can't remember a word of what
was said.   Yet the less we saw of each other, the more we
got on each other's nerves.   We both thought of suicide as
the final resolution of our desire as we stood again below
deck by the hectic Atlantic.

III

His homosexuality was not a barrier, but it was not a sub-
ject we discussed.   Frank plunged into bed with a number of
handsome young men.   But three of his profoundly engaged
love affairs [with men] were platonic.

I reached down to touch his cock, which was big and erect.
I had glimpsed that Frank had a big cock and had loved the
idea.   I crawled down under the sheets and kissed it.   Per-
haps inside the heart of a woman lurks the desire to convert
a homosexual ... but I do not think this was what made me
want to go to bed with Frank.

That summer, Frank's bathing suit had been a rather unre-
liable blue canvas triangle, a French number, I believe, that
sort of floated above his personal parts.   Rats, I thought,
not knowing whether to laugh or cry.

Frank said, "The cockroach and the ginko tree are the old-
est things on earth, " as though that made everything all
right.

IV

As important as art was to him, it was after all only part
of life and not separate from it so that he had to shift into
high gear to get ready for an esthetic experience. He was
in high all the time. Frank O'Hara smelled rats. And from
the common rats about the house he made his poetry, as
Auden had. Poets are no better at elucidating a work of art
or poetry than anyone else. They are often the worst crit-
ics--worse than having no poet at all. Frank loved virtuosity,
the pyrotechnics of it.

Secreted in O'Hara's thought is the possibility that we create
only as dead men. His talent was obvious even when he was
a freshman.

His startling ability to write a poem when other people were
talking, or even get up in the middle of a conversation, get
his typewriter, and write a poem, sometimes participating
in a conversation while doing so. Poetry flowed out of him
·as easily as breath.

He wrote quickly, revised little, but his manuscripts show,
brilliantly. You are getting the language first-hand, from
where it gets put together in the mind. Part of his method
had to do with Surrealism. But he never "did" Surrealism.
Any particle of experience quick enough to get fixed in his
busy consciousness earned its point of relevance. The poet
does not deduce, but he is thinking.

He never sought to influence the young. He wasn't particu-
larly interested in his career. Frank's fame came to him
unlooked for.

V

        --the sand is treacherous
didn't it take Creeley's daughter? and cars
took Pollock, took Betty Olson

Linda says at the funeral friends stood in clumps,
like people in galleries who know each other.

He was purple wherever his skin showed through the white
hospital gown. He was a quarter larger than usual. Every
few inches there was some sewing composed of dark blue
thread.

"Have you seen
Frank? I heard
he's in town tonight. "

THE WHITE ROCK MAIDEN TRIES TO GET INTO

THE KAYAK WITH WHITMAN'S ESKIMO:

Howard McCord*

Howard McCord is a good poet. I've seen his poems in various places, have reviewed one of his chapbooks favorably, and have had work of my own in his excellent magazine Measure. I've even enjoyed his hospitality on one of my trans-American trips. He is a man of immense energies, an indefatigable walker, a peregrinator who seems to move around looking for that one navel-place of the earth where profound energies will overwhelm him and finally bring him peace. He's tried Iceland, the Himalayas, the American deserts and mountains. Thomas McGrath calls him "a kind of ecologist of the spirit" whose quest is for "the numinous element in landscape." Now, granted that McGrath's observations are window dressing, they still make good sense; my notion of McCord is, though, that his desire to merge with the numinous outdistances his perceptions; he's a latter-day Wordsworthian receptive to great earth-throbbings of the spirit but lacking Wordsworth's focus and tact. The whole world becomes McCord's Lake District; impulses from a vernal wood do not suffice, complete with sleeping bag, dried apricots, and Tang. The poet meanders over the lost and forgotten depths and lows of the universe, with Whitmanesque conductors stuck all over him--charged B-batteries of the spirit set to receive Mother Nature's Good News.

The publication of his Selected Poems allows us to see the sixteen-year drift of his talent. In some ways, this talent is impressive. He seldom writes badly--he senses well how line-breaks best occur, and his ear for rhymes and tonalities within lines is competent. My complaint,

*Reprinted by permission from Margins, No. 21-22 (June-July 1975) pp. 74-76; Copyright © 1975 by Margins.

though, is one I have with contemporary myth-poets who see
poetry as a tribal act, and who end up finding commonplace
sermons in stones, streams, and Smokey Bear.   First,
throw a string of shell beads (include a couple of grizzly
bear claws) around your neck; second, let your hair grow
long; third, buy a faded pair of jeans at the local Goodwill
or Salvation Army store; fourth.... My theory is that
you can't be a nice guy and feel large; in order to assimilate
the gigantic heights of Nature, you must have experienced
the depths.   A poet who hasn't known deep despair, tragedy,
pain will satisfy himself with the trivia of his life--the details
of what he had to eat on his climb to the mountaintop, what
his wife and kids wore sitting beside a pine tree, the most
abstruse place names, some of them impossible to find in
any but the most complete World Gazeteer.   Perhaps my
theory is wrong; but I don't think so.   Suffering has the pow-
er of enlarging a writer's empathies; and a first-rate writer
(rather than a dabbler) must have experienced pain.   The
Throb of the Universe encompasses an entire range of hu-
man feelings ... and the poet of magnitude, one capable of
receiving potent impulses from the world, without shattering
his body or mind, has had to experience much, and profound-
ly.   Otherwise, it seems to me, he remains a sort of White
Rock Maiden, kneeling beside the limpid forest/mountain pool,
twitching gossamer wings, sexless and fairly bloodless.   The
White Rock Maiden is a creature of culture; she'd dissolve
into a mist if Whitman's "greasy" eskimo got out of his kay-
ak and came up to her.   What I'm saying is that much of
contemporary myth-writing seems sanitized, deriving from
literature rather than life.   I allow that there is a legitimate
cerebral fusing with myth--Olson is responsible for much of
it, and Duncan, Robert Kelly, and Clayton Eshleman are
living proponents of it--that I can accept easier than I can
the look-I'm-no-stranger-to-the-woods-bearshit-raspberry-
eating-type of poet.   There's intellectual integrity in Duncan's
work, and some in Snyder's even when he's rejecting intel-
lectuality for a polished-bone-in-the-nose stance.   The prob-
lem with McCord's nativism is that it lacks the depth of
Snyder's, who, incidentally, is one of McCord's totem-poet
tribe figures.   (See McCord's poem to Snyder's son Kai.)
The difference is essential--say, the difference between The
National Geographic on the one hand and Io on the other.

        Here is an instance of McCord's attempt to elevate
the trivial:

        At Salt Lake, rock climbing in the Wasatch,

> Sanskrit, Matthew Arnold, and I turned
> Catholic and stopped getting falling-down
> drunk.   Bought a . 44 Magnum and a . 303 Enfield
> but I haven't been able to kill anything
> since I was seventeen, before I bought the boots.

The allusions to hip-reading, pacifism, religion, and alco-
holism aren't very intersting.   The compressed writing is in-
sufficient to make the details pulse and glow.   And a line
like this, verifiable no doubt, but dull, is characteristic of
the chatty nature of much of this book:

> I had never met anyone I had not invented
> until Dora.

These passages are from "All Hallows' Eve, " a lengthy poem
with philosophical-religious pretensions, which I'm afraid does
little more than bring McCord off as a nice guy who gave his
"foul weather jacket to a beggar man, " "helped dig a base-
ment, " studied Anglo-Saxon, Old Spanish, and Chaucer's dirty
words, responds patiently to his sons' questions about sunsets
and dash lights and who feels very married.   After three
pages of surface feelings and journalese information, Mc-
Cord winds up with a direct adaptation of a not particularly
good passage from Dylan Thomas: McCord concludes--

> and so Dora and I hum a bit, on our
> sweet and swinging way to death.

And when he writes a poem unabashedly religious and mo-
mentous, he spins out the baldest clichés--these appear in
the culminating section of "A Letter of Saint Andrew the
Dancer":

> The Risen Christ ... the dualities / in great sanity ...
> the divine madness that is the power ... a stately,
> measureless blur of light ... the oppositions ... the
> immense dance purified by light ... infinitely ex-
>   panding ...
> all existence ... infinitely extending in time ... the
> absolute present ... beyond the firmament ... the
> silent peace of the white and motionless light ... etc.

One hungers here for Yeats and Eliot whose abstractions
emerged from potent, original images.   To read a passel of
the world's theological/metaphysical writers doesn't guaran-
tee that your own poetic statements deriving from them will

make it as poetry; your own intelligence needs to have been
seared, preferably before you started working on your college
degrees and reading all those culture-folk.   I feel little ur-
gency behind McCord's religious poems ... numinosity, yes;
pain and transcendence, no.

        Nor does his naming of friends assume any talismanic
force.   I find this passage from "Fables & Transfigurations"
excessive:

                ... I try and chart
        the True Hesperides, with
        old service numbers (mine 425-94-25,
        Dora's 989-20-95W), empty coordinates
        that never found either of us,
        two saints: Jude of the impossible,
        Dympna of the mad, sons
        Robert and Colman.
        All of the tribe--maniac shamans
        wise in their wounds--Bob, Lafe
        Gordon, Gus, Sam Pendergrast,
        the five-two ghost of Fraenkel
        I met in the desert
        sucking on a rock.

Does all of this detail really matter?   Isn't it material for a
private journal, the raw origins of poetry rather than the
poems themselves?   Doesn't the naming of friends (known al-
most exclusively by you alone), and the dedication of poems
to private friends derive from the Poet as Nice Guy syn-
drome?   Isn't the need to demonstrate in print what a fine
and faithful person you are, evidence of a lessened poetic
power and a need to garner in approval from the world of
poetry readers?   Hopefully, we all know lots of nice guys
and gals--they make our world comfortable and caring; yet,
isn't it the people (writers) we know who risk the outrageous,
who aren't afraid to be vigorous bastards, and who disdain
a genteel energy who drive us into depth / joy / hurt dimen-
sions of life?

        I find McCord's best poems to be those unabashedly
mythic.   When he tries to be Bear or to move within an
American Indian's psyche, he adopts voices generally more
interesting than his own voice.   Even here, though, he falls
into what I call The Culture Trap.   McCord's primitive (in-
cluding Bear with his primitive consciousness) regards the
mountains, life, and art and sees their relevance through

Culture. In "Walking to the Far Sea: A Suite for Bear,"
for example, there are fine moments of metamorphosis:

> I am becoming a bear.   I roll in a bed of sage
> at noon, and wrap my paws in the smell.
> Hair is growing from the center of my palms.
> The road is sliding down the hill.

The poem is about McCord's forest/night fears, and as he
moves down the forest roads, protected by his car, his
thoughts seem to move in and out of bear-consciousness.
But he trims: this observation with its literary image shows
his human psyche at work: "The forest is a language of long
green tongues / more ancient than bears, and skillful."   The
next line is too obvious for the human consciousness, and
suggests a sort of primary wisdom one might associate with
a bear of some verbal prowess: "Beyond the forest is the
sea."   The suite moves between these two consciousnesses;
the result is a pastiche decorated with images that don't quite
make it:

> A serpent hangs from the sky
> with his head over the sea.
> He is swaying his head to and fro
> and singing.

In "IV" Bear becomes something of a good Christian, a very
literate, contemplative Christian, who takes most of the blame
for his "dispossession":

> Father, the agility of our wrath
> ends intelligence, and what I do--
> ill, fevered, head full of broken words,
> my paws burning and wet,
> is made wholly my own by our dispossession.

My point is that Bear or Massassoit or Urff the Paleolithic
Man regarding a tree or the distant horizon would not speak
introspective lines out of the English Romantic poets; and this
integrity of the primitive voice seems to me when violated a
regrettable travesty.   Too many contemporary American poets
are hung up on roots and myth; they succeed at best in cre-
ating mildly interesting postcard views of life; such poems
are the equivalents for all the beaded bags and the jewelry
hawked at "authentic" Native American stands throughout the
western United States.   It appears that the guise of the primi-
tive means either (1) that the poet using the guise has ex-

perienced life insufficiently to create deep poetry out of him-
self or (2) that he is timorous about laying himself on the
line.

I sincerely hope that I have not been too severe on
McCord.   I admire his energy, and his commitments to his
art.   I might have selected another poet to raise these same
problems; and I have wanted to discuss them in print for
some time--as an antidote, or, at least, to stir poets up,
particularly those who venerate this type of writing.   I hope
for dialogue rather than injury.

POEMS WRITTEN WITH ONE HAND CLAPPING

OR, BLOWING AWAY IN THE WIND

Gerard Malanga*

I first heard of Gerard Malanga during the late 50's when he was one of the beautiful people attached to Andy Warhol's Factory crowd. Malanga was into making and being (as distinct from acting) in movies produced by A. W. In one movie, I recall Malanga dancing, badly filmed, as some lithe Pan, accompanied by Viva or somebody, freaked out in psychedelic light and bad sound. I didn't then think of Malanga as a poet, but rather as a well-beaded, super-trendy person, one of the bees hovering about the Warholian honeypot. He was into brilliant sequined and silver-studded leather outfits. Now he seems to wear white a lot--but I'm getting too far ahead.

The first time I noticed Malanga as a dude with pretensions to poetry happened when I picked up some poetry mag, mimeographed, based in New York, which had a certain underground celebratiousness by featuring a naked poet: the issue I saw featured Malanga (naked frontally as well as backally), an exceptional stunt for those days when pretty men hardly revealed the dew lapping their groins, usually well-jockstrapped and/or underweared. And Malanga was pretty. No fat, nice face, nice genitals, not too much body-hair, etc. Lotsa poet-soul, so it seemed. Thereafter, I seemed rubbed against Malanga's poems everywhere. Warhol's blessing helped his various careers a lot, it would appear. Because, let's face it, Malanga seems to be a poet who moves because of hype and connections. Now, I gather, Malanga is more or less on his own, and seems to have transcended the chintz aestheticism of the early years, to a

*Reprinted by permission from Margins, No. 28-30 (Jan. - March 1976) pp. 81-82; Copyright © 1976 by Margins.

mystical poetry which typically writes itself off the page and
quietly self-destructs. He's writing poems inspired by the
sound of one hand clapping.

Gerard Malanga's latest book is Rosebud: Poems by
Gerard Malanga, published most handsomely by the Penmaen
Press. A handsome woodcut on the cover features romantic,
nearly nude figure of slim poet lying on floor or bed with
book open, Chopin-type top hat above him resting on a slanted
board, moon and bare tree outside window, naked faceless
woman, a little pregnant, threatening to enter via a door to
disturb poet's reveries. Mystic sun worked out on floor.
Mystical plant. So Chopinesque! So George Sand!

But what of the poems? Easy phrases abound in near-
ly all of them: "frozen with silence," clouds crossing moons,
"in the distance," "the invisible wind," death in the dream,
waking from the dream, earth silenced, "the life of the one
real dream...." There's no point continuing to list all the
vague goodies. I'm told that Malanga recently experienced
his white night of the soul period. Dressed in mystic white
he seems to wish to appear as pure non-body meditator who
delivers whitening mystical poems, finger-snapping good.
I've heard Malanga read some of these poems. He's a poet
caught up in his own whiteness.

Now, if we want to fantasize about the sources of po-
etic inspiration: let's oppose bloodred beef filets dripping
and glistening with saliva-inducing juices ... a sort of won-
derful "sillion," to use G. M. Hopkins' word, shiny with pro-
tein. Let's oppose these bloodred beef filets with white daisy
petals, or with nitre scraped from the ceilings of a guru's
damp cave. White can't stir us up much. The only poet
I recall who worked a brilliant poem as white was Robert
Frost with "Design," a tour de force describing the visual
(and deeper thematic) materials of: a white spider, a white
moth, and a white heal-all flower. To lack redness, I am
saying, or to lack tint, is to come off as pallid, precious,
ineffectual. Chintz curtains, not beef on the hoof.

Apparently one of the current Munchkin poet-folk
Malanga admires is W. S. Merwin. And Malanga has all
along liked to present nice greeting-poems and special poem-
notes to people he knows, likes, and admires. Also, if you
are famous he'll take your picture. My own estimate is that
he's a much better photographer than he is a poet. Merwin's
influence, alas, is the sort that drives Malanga deeper into

his own ephemerality, into Billie Burke-esqueries. The last
poem in Rosebud, dedicated to Merwin, is facile: nor should
the sentimentality (existentialism via Cap'n Crunch) be over-
looked. Poet watches lights go out in a valley and thinks of
a dark tree losing its leaves. This is a view from a "lost"
mountain. And, gorgeous Apollo, lift your wand and strike
"that is" from this short poem!

Another aspect of Malanga's poetry is self-obsession.
Again, pallor and whiteness are clues. If Malanga's world
were more substantial he'd fill the landscape with limpid
glassy pools, Pre-Raphaelite, surrounded by jonquils, nar-
cissi, roses, forgetmenots, asters, devoted to casting up the
poet's image for his own delectation. I don't feel ever that
Malanga's self-obsession is masturbatory. There's a win-
some purity about it all; I feel that a lovely angel with some-
what bedraggled, though still iridescent, wings has tumbled
from the sky, can't return, and is locked on earth with snow,
stones, and gentle regrets.

Now, before Malanga-admirers grab their scented
rapiers intent on disembowelling me, let me say that I do
not quarrel with Malanga's fondness for cultivating a Maha-
reshi-center calm: certainly there is a wellspring of silence
below silence, as Roethke thought of it, where we are re-
stored. And when Malanga works best he presents images
of that center as a philosophical position sought after and
felt. I have to say, though, partially felt, because the im-
agery he uses remains too pallid, not much above the level
of a chant offered up at your local yoga class. In his poem
"snow voices swirling," the title is the most vital moment of
this ephemeral poem. The words, essentially sentimental,
flag where a telling image might have convinced me that Ma-
langa was capable of profound feeling: "inside," "a silence
is hiding," "all i need / its here in this silence." Mia Far-
rowesque. I want to be dazzled, sun-spun, head-whirled,
spirit-whirled. And I'm not.

The master of this genre was Wallace Stevens. All
one has to do is read "The Poems of our Climate" (image
of white bowl: "cold, a cold porcelain, low and round, /
With nothing more than the carnations there"), "On the Man-
ner of Addressing Clouds," "On the Surfaces of Things,"
"The Curtains in the House of the Metaphysician," to
realize the immense range between two talents with similar
responses to the world. None of the backpage hype, no mat-
ter how prestigious the mouths from which it drops, can con-

vince me of Malanga's achievement.   Lowell apparently called
him "probably the most promising and abundant of the younger
poets"; Rexroth unhedgingly declared him "indisputably the
most important young poet under 40 writing anything of inter-
est in America today"; Eberhart saw him as a "torrential
writer with true verbal gifts"; and, Harold Norse, with a
gram of hedging, saw him as "probably the most gifted poet
of his generation." I am sorry to have to file so strong a
minority report.   I'll take Keats's musings on that urn any
day.

THE POET AS PUSHER

James Tate*

Most of James Tate's poems in Absences, for me at least, reach little peaks of awareness before they slide down into some disconnected mood, latching in again to another, sometimes impressive, peak image. It's as if some portions of the tape are missing. Continuity within the poem is too often adventitious, unless, of course, one feels that separate lines happening within the same "poem" generate an aura, something like that the mystic claims to see around every living thing, including persons. Perhaps the ideal reader of such poems (and Tate is one of the best-known of several writers who write them) first takes a few hits, settles back, and lets the lines swim in his head ... systole, dystole. After the immense promise of The Lost Pilot (supported by The Oblivion Ha-Ha), I had hoped for better. Tate has the maturity, the fine sense of language well-directed (or shafted), and the passion of the first-rank poet. But, I don't know what's happening--and this essay is an attempt to define my reservations. My remarks should be read as belonging to a reader in a quandary, not to a reader who sets out to damage a fine talent who has already contributed glorious breath to contemporary verse. I shall begin with a definition.

What I call the Snigger (or Comic Book poem) has become a legitimate genre with numerous practitioners throughout the country. New York City imitators of Frank O'Hara lead the pack. The Snigger, I feel, derives from self-pity concealed thinly behind irrationally contrived images (surreal) and humor. The grubby chore of pushing that boulder of existence back up the mountain takes sinew and will. The sniggerers, at their worst, lassitudinously allow their muscles to slacken, laughing gently and sexually all the way to the

*Reprinted by permission from Margins, No. 13 (Aug. -Sept. 1974) pp. 34-35, 88; Copyright © 1974 by Margins.

grave ... or, to be more accurate, laughing gently and sex-
ually on the spot of chosen ground from which they will not
move (symbolically, or symbiotically--Iowa City) until
rigor mortis freezes their lips into that final smirk.   Their
muscularity dissolves in favor of a consciousness giggling at
destiny.   It still taketh guts to stand up, to watcheth your
guts fall out, to make some effort to pusheth them back in-
side the body cavity, and thereafter to judgeth the experience.
When these poems work they produce the effect of that hor-
rible snigger, a background sound for a fearsome contem-
porary danse macabre.   They remind me of those crowds of
skeletons enjoying themselves in Janes Ensor's paintings ...
they participate in a final, grim mardi gras.   And Ensor's
paintings are among my favorites in twentieth century art.
Bizarre fun, jolting us into spirituality.   When such poems
(paintings) work, great!   Whey they don't....

        In one of Tate's poems seeing-eye people (heh heh)
take over and give the dogs a break by leading them around
for awhile.   People harness themselves and lumber over
a mountainside, their heads aching from buzz saws.   These
are "see-through people" with only enough depth "to fall more/
or less forever."   They have sad little dogs for friends, dogs
born blind, unable to tell a swinging door from a snowcapped
mountain.   Tate's people lead these pathetic dogs:

                    We led them by
                    dragging them through
                    terror then beauty
                    turn about with
                    the off chance that
                    we The Seeing-Eye
                    People might know
                    one from the other

                    And lend them
                    the courage as their
                    kind has so often
                    lent us to awaken
                    each day to the
                    impenetrable darkness
                    and still to find
                    an excuse to jump

                    from one grave into
                    another.

The stance of the miserable doomed human waiting for Dog (<u>God</u> spelled backwards) is fairly typical of the universal complaints scattered throughout <u>Absences</u>. Here is a random sampling; most of them are from different poems:

1. I don't know if I'll bother to get up.
2. I am not responding to anything.
3. I should be / just about awake now.
4. I want to lay myself down on a large platter / of innocence. . . .
5. I who have no home have no destination either
6. O yes, our lives are going on without us.
7. I'm in the birdbath don't come in.
8. I play everything backwards.
9. I'm late now.
10. How can I fear anything. / I can drive with my lights off.
11. We should all be behind bars.
12. I failed everyone.
13. I was alive.
14. I don't know what I'm going to do.
15. I was confused / then I got used to it
16. I'll never go that far again.
17. Why do I bother to speak?

Strung out this way, these statements of soul/mind/experience sound groovily solipsistic; and they occur with sufficient frequency to color the entire book with astigmatic hues.   At their best, Tate's cryptograms are reminiscent of those wisely cynical remarks Oscar Wilde tossed off with such prodigality and such success in the 1890's.   Wilde's barbs set themselves securely in the necks of their victims, and his humor was urbane, outrageous, but seldom solipsistic.

Tate's poems frequently develop as a fleshing out of some telling opening lines of a cryptic sort.   Usually, the fleshing out fails to match the bite or originality of the beginning ... too much oyster-flesh flab surrounds the pearl, and the pearl is too often of doubtful price.   Here are a couple of good beginnings:

The eye wants to sleep
but the head is no mattress.   ("Absences" 3)

People behaving like molecular structures
with pins in them   ("Absences" 5)

The poems that follow, in both cases, are inferior to these openings. My feeling is that such pairs of lines would be better alone, unless they can be developed integrally into a poem as good from the neck down as it was in the head. Tate has an enviable facility for apothegms, and this facility, I think, is a real threat to his excellence as a poet. He seems too easily satisfied with flashing his lines; and he assumes that the existence of a nice glare in an otherwise fairly miasmic poem saves the poem. Dictum: the marshlight is not the marsh!

Perhaps the most telling way to describe the Tatorial method is to look at one poem in some detail. "Absences 14" has nearly all of the faults and virtues of its brothers (or, are poems, like angels, sexless?). Tate's speaker dashes from room to room, charged by "life wrapped up in a shoestring." Well, right off that's not much life, unless you develop a paramecian humor to ease the intake-outtake of your bivalvular emotions. He needs a few Alps, but can't see any. He drives himself inward "like a rat" hating what it loves, or, continuing to be cool, loving what it hates. His hatred prompts a life-comment in the form of a riddle-joke: if you hate life (which you love), or, if you love life (which you hate) would you kill yourself (burn down a forest) to kill one bear (whatever causes your hate)? This a conundrum worthy of Nelson Eddy trying to find Jeanette in the Rockies. The playing around provides Tate with an illusion of profundity: we are driven inward also with the rats of life-- meaning? Is life a big cheese? a big cheese on a shoestring?

The next few lines are excessive. Tate can't let his own cleverness lie quiet; it keeps playing with itself under the covers. A luxury of blips and bloats, plus one fine phrase: "days like ragas." That's good, isn't it? Tate's listened to his Ravi Shankar. Then, an Alpless world sort sums up and moves the poem mystically forward. The image is yet another variation on the desert, wasteland, T. S. Eliotesquerie motif. Implication: since the world is flat, the appropriate posture for me to take is also flat. No mountain exists to push that blasted Rolling Stone up, even if I wanted to. But Sartre, I can't take it to heart. At best I'm a whimper/limper, a tart/fart, pretty full of, yet feeling little pain.

Then a quartet of lines grammatically fuzzed (the like is hip) and lyrically not much above the level of a Crosby-

Stills-Nash ditty. What was it we wanted to do? fuck? cut
our throats? dance? pick our noses? jerk off? build imita-
tion Alps out of sand? The poems come down to the kitsch
language of CSN lyrics: "Rife with rising roses / hosanna
savanna." The first line might have been written by a little
old lady poet proud of her three names; the "hosanna savan-
na" is a form of pleasant burbling, inducing comfort-feelings,
and warmth towards the writer's sense of play: there's no
magnetism or threat here--he'd be an easy guy to be around
to know. It exudes a sort of stoned religiosity. A passel
of heads would find the phrase funny, outasight. The poem
ends with an image of "air crawling out of the tires." For
me, this doesn't work, and seems introduced merely to make
a handspring seem momentous. Again, poet as handspring
artist: life (air) crawls out of tires. Yes, we're all doomed
to deflate; the human race is screwed. The sound of escap-
ing air (crawling is lethargic) is whimpering. And, I sub-
mit, whimpering is not enough.

In Absences Tate is often betrayed by a fondness for
automatic writing. Cleverness prevails, and he burdens the
reader who cares for his work (as I do) with the chore of
sorting out the good from the bad. No poet, obviously, can
be consistently interesting; no mind is ever always that alert
and fertile. Tate risks much, as most good poets do, sur-
real, or otherwise. Often these poets fall victim to their
own cleverness and assume that whatever spins from their
minds, no matter how adventitious and automatic, must be
good. It's sad to see a fine talent putting manacles on his
legs and stumbling through the pallid landscape of his imag-
ination pretending he's Nureyev. The devices become tricks,
the statements solipsisms. Poems that take the limits of
the poet's shell as the limits of the universe do little to in-
spirit or move us. And I'm old-fashioned enough to expect
a poem to grab and move me.

There is yet another side to Tate's work: the play
that he engages in with his reader. The effect is like that
managed by a speaker who belittles what he's just said. He
takes us into some serious statement then undercuts it, and,
I think, merely undercuts (undercutes?) our confidence in
him. "End of a Semester," for example has some fine mo-
ments. Stanza 1 concludes: "Nobody remembers / what
came out of the sea." This is a fresh comment on the trag-
ic distance we have moved from our origins. The stanza
break allows us time to reflect before we proceed. And we
do move; it's Venus we have forgotten:

> her nose broken;
> nobody cared about the green diffused light
> across her wrist.
> Now, ten thousand Americans
> die every minute

Momentous! but is he really talking about the blindness of
men to the beauty of Venus at the time of her birth, or at
the time of the invention of her myth? I'm confused.   And
the leap into 10,000 Americans dying every minute?   Be-
cause they can't remember the green light (green = go?) on
Venus' wrist?   Because of the Vietnam War?   Because of
overeating?   Because of what?   The new stanza makes it
clear; and we have a perfect example of Tate's mockery: all
these Americans die

> from an overdose of cough drops.

What else is new? I can't respond because I have not been
swept along by the poem.   Whether or not Tate gets "through
history," as he says he won't, leaves me entirely beached.
I can always smoke my own dope; I need a little help with
my spirit.   Tate, in this book, at least, lets me down.   I
hope that it is but a lesser moment in an important career.
He's too gifted to settle for anything but his best.

THE FÜHRER BUNKER:

W. D. Snodgrass*

W. D. Snodgrass' The Führer Bunker is a rare ex-
ample of ambitious, on-going verse sculpture. The mono-
logue is the medium, the event unifying the projected work
(now over half-completed) is the suicide of Hitler and a clus-
tering of followers: Goebbels, his wife, his five children,
Eva Braun. Voices of survivors include Speer, Heinrici,
Weidling, Bormann, and Fegelein. The focus is on the
bunker in Berlin chosen by Hitler as his final refuge. The
duration of time is one month, the final month culminating
in the suicides. There are twenty monologues. They con-
stitute, as Snodgrass calls them, "a cycle of poems in pro-
gress." I gather that he is not exactly certain of the final
count--there are already nearly a dozen completed mono-
logues not appearing in this collection. I admire Snodgrass's
courage in presenting an incomplete work for public scrutiny.
Since he is a poet of stature (Heart's Needle remains one of
the handful of fine books of its decade) he will be widely re-
viewed; and there is a danger, I should think, that the re-
views may discourage or dissuade him from further writing
in this mode. The Führer Bunker is gargantuan: few poets
have the energy or the daring to attempt work on this scale.
The scope reminds one of Robert Browning's The Ring and
the Book, that multifaceted slant on domestic murder, ex-
amined through the various voices of the principals involved
--and of Tennyson's Idylls of the King. In a real sense,
Snodgrass seems to be working at what seems possible for
him as an almost epic form. And despite the flaws in The
Führer Bunker, it will be around for a long time to inspire
writers who've come to realize the sad limitations of the
locked-in, private, first person, obsessional poem.

*Reprinted by permission from The American Book Review,
Vol. 1 (Dec. 1977) p. 14; Copyright © 1977 by The American
Book Review.

The problems raised by the poems are these: There
is a general sameness of voice. The monologues are usually
long (the best--the Hermann Fegelein, for example--are
short). The cadences of succeeding lines border on the mo-
notonous, a monotony the frequent end-rhymes, well-turned
rondeau (spoken by Magda Goebbels) don't quite modify. After
reading the poems to myself, and then hearing them read by
De this past summer at Yaddo, I've concluded that the fault
is primarily one of voice: Snodgrass' technical skills are as
much in evidence as ever, but I rarely feel in these Bunker
poems that the master's voice has a real chance to be heard.
He seems to strive for the manner and presence of a stage-
able work; as a result the voice is too often in language and
timing Shakespearean. There's considerable fustian; viz., in
this passage from Hitler's first monologue:

> Who else sold out? Bremen? Magdeburg?
> They would go on in this pisswallow, in
> Disgrace, shame.   Who could we send to
>   make
> Their lives worth less to them?   In our
>   camps,
> You gas them, shoot, club, strangle them,
> Tramp them down into trenches, thick as
>   leaves.
> Out of the ground, at night, they squirm
>   up
> Through the tangled bodies, crawl off in
>   the woods.
> Every side now, traitors, our deserters,
>   native
> Populations, they rise up like vomit, flies
> Out of bad meat, sewers backing up.   Up
> There, now, in the bombed-out gardens,
> That sickly, faint film coming over
> The trees again. . . .

Or, this moment from the last of Hitler's monologues, de-
pends, I feel, for its effect on a peculiar staginess of tone,
cadence, and diction:

> Tell me I have to die, then.   Tell me.
> What have I counted on?   Tell me
> The Odds against me.   You can't be
> Sure enough.   My name.   My name on
> Every calendar.   Relentless, each year,
> Your birth comes around.   My death:

> My lackey; my lickass general. My Will
> Scrubs it all out, all of you, all gone....

Yet, despite my quibbles over a sameness of tone and
a stagey language, the sequence is complex in brilliant forms.
I've already mentioned Snodgrass' achievement in sustaining
the rondeau form, one of the most demanding, playful forms
in poetry. Magda Goebbels is enamored of the rondeau; con-
fronted with her tragedy (she's about to poison herself and
her five children) she sings on in this form. Her monologue
(19 April 1945) turns on 28 three-line stanzas, all arranged
in four parts, each embroidered around two (and only two)
end-rhymes per section; and, as a further bravura stroke,
true (and rhymings thereon) dominate three of the sections.
Here is how Section I begins:

> How can you do the things you know
>   you'll do?--
> One last act to bring back integrity.
> I've got just one desire left: to be true.

> You can't pick how you'll live. Our times
>   will screw
> Your poor last virtues from you,
>   ruthlessly.
> How can you do the things you know
>   you'll do?

> My mother drove me on: get married to
> Quandt. Rich. Kind enough. If elderly.
> I've got just one desire left: to be true.

Speer's stanzas, in the initial poem by him, is arranged to
reflect the incredible sense of order in Speer's architect
mind: his pattern is of a pyramid dissected from top to bot-
tom; later, as Hitler's fate moves to its consummation,
Speer's order is greatly jostled--the pyramidal form is now
vestigial, is of fewer lines, and is broken with more con-
ventional lines carrying disaster news. Speer's first mono-
logue concludes with this moment of self-realization:

> Why let
> Me live? Time
> For one cigarette.
> He has forbidden us all
> To smoke, then sends us all
> Up the chimney. Up the chimney?

Idiot.   Use your eyes: if he gets his way,
We won't have a chimney standing.   No
    doubt
He knows that I will not obey.   Perhaps
    he knows
That I am going to betray him.   And no
    doubt he knows
That I am faithful.   That I evade my
    better self.   That I
Neglect my knowing.

Goebbels, Hitler's Propaganda Chief, usually favors the tacky
tetrameter couplet:

The rest is silence.   Left like sperm
In a stranger's gut, waiting its term,
Each thought, each step lies; the roots
    spread.
They'll believe us when we're dead.

And, less seriously perhaps:

Our little Doctor, Joe the Gimp
Comes back to Limpness and his limp;
Hephaistos, Vulcan the lame smith
Whose net of lies caught one true myth:
His wife, the famous beauty, whored
By numbskull Mars, the dull warlord.

Goebbels achieves a zingy, at times almost Gilbert-and-Sul-
livanesque lilt, fraught with a marvellous irony.   During his
first appearance, though, Goebbels, occupied burning his per-
sonal papers before moving into the bunker to die, employs
a collage form made up of newspaper headlines in bold-face
print (BERLIN'S DEFENDER / STRIPS FOR ACTION.   NAZIS
DUMP STRASSER / ESCAPES TO ITALY); mottos rendered
in a form of Gothic script (Give all thy worldly goods / Unto
the poor and follow me.); and his ubiquitous rhymed couplets,
here primarily reviewing his numerous love affairs as he
tosses photographs into the flames.   The couplets eerily
emphasize his cynicism:

You can't help start
Hankering to keep some small part
Of this world.   You wear satins, ermine,
Rouge and rings, gross as Fat Hermann.

> .... Now we can get down to what
> Counts--cleaning out the whole vile lot
> Ernst Roehm was right: only a man
> Who has no possessions can
> Afford ideals. We learn once more
> To do without. Where but in war--
> The leveler--do all things meet?
> Rich and poor, now, dig in the street
> Together; walls bombed out, in flame,
> Bury weak men and strong the same.

Goebbels moves from the fireplace to his piano.   Headline:
EDUCATION MINISTER PLAYS GERMAN SONGS.   The tune
he renders first is a sentimental war song: The glowing sky
behind him (Berlin is burning) is "the blood of soldiers flow-
ing / Lord have mercy on our souls." Clubfoot Joe, as he
calls himself, waxes Hesse-esque, with one of those senti-
mental little home, bucolic-nature ditties so engaging to the
German soul:

> Within my father's garden,
>   Two little saplings grow;
> The one of them bears nutmegs,
>   The other one bears cloves.
>
> The nutmeg's fresh and lovely;
>   The cloves are sharp and sweet.
> Now comes the time of parting
> Never again to meet.
>
> The winter's snows are melting;
>   Far off these streams will flow.
> Now out of my sight you vanish;
> Out of my thoughts you go.

Eva Braun's brother-in-law, Hermann Fegelein, a
lecher, was caught trying to flee Berlin, was jailed, ques-
tioned, and finally shot. His is the most scatalogical con-
science of the lot; there's little subtlety in his mind as he
juxtaposes his sexual exploits with his own impending assas-
sination:

> spreadeagled in
> the hall with her pants off   radio girl
> I could have had her anytime I wanted
> shit
> three days ago when I said shit

> they squat   say this was a test
> at the last minute the reprieve

> no

Bormann apparently betrayed him to Himmler, or so he believes:

> martin came in
> to finger me   said I was with himmler
>   in some sellout to the west   I wish
>   to sweet shit Id of known

>   but I screwed them
> every one   shit not that blackhaired slut
> on the sofa   margaret cocktease
> turned me down

His bitter consolation is that he foresees the Russian avengers:

>   oh you'll just pray for vaseline
> sweet jesus no   they cant just
> can they
>   shit   shit   shit

Having devoted the past four years myself to reworking historical material into possibly new poetic forms (Ann Lee, founder of the Shakers; King Ludwig II of Bavaria; Elisha Kent Kane, the American Arctic explorer), I do see some of the enormous problems Snodgrass confronts, and I empathize with him, and greatly admire his achievement, despite my reservations. I am sure these poems (and the completed version when it appears) will be widely read, discussed, and imitated. They deserve much attention. In converting these slabs of marble into sculpture, Snodgrass may not be Rodin or Giacometti; but he is a St. Gaudens, and that is no mean achievement.

THE DOGGED POET, OR, THE POET AS DOG:

William Wantling*

      William Wantling was forty-one when he died on May 2, 1974 of a heart attack brought on by codeine and wine. He was introduced to heavy dope, he said, through the military; when he was hospitalized in Korea he was given morphine. "It was beautiful," he said. "Five years later I was in San Quentin on narcotics."

      I first heard of Wantling via Marvin Malone's Wormwood Review, and remember being struck by his potency. I heard little else of him until recently when I received a copy of his last book 7 On Style from his publisher A. D. Winans of Second Coming. I was amazed to find that Wantling had published over ten books of poetry in his brief life--and all of it from small and almost inaccessible presses. In fact, Peter Finch, of second aeon, Cardiff, Wales, emerges as the publisher who more than anyone else has published Wantling. The second aeon press, in collaboration with Caveman Press, Dunedin, New Zealand, published San Quentin's Stranger, the only selection of Wantling's work, edited by Trevor Reeves. At the recent Small Press bookfair in San Francisco, I had a chance to talk with Winans, Fulton, and Blazek about Wantling. The tragedy of Wantling's death struck me, as did the irony of his being ignored in poetry circles. To assist in making him better-known, I shall present a personal assessment of his poetry, of the bits and pieces of it I've been able to assemble. Two of his books I already owned. Three more were kindly loaned to me by Paul Mariah, no stranger himself to Wantling's experiences.

---

*Reprinted by permission from Margins, No. 27 (Winter 1975) pp. 8-13; Copyright © 1975 by Margins.

I

Wantling's energy attracts me. There are photos of
him in his books: a handsome, burly fellow of sensitive
mein and an aura of the rambunctious. His passions were
obviously huge: dope, alcohol, sex, poetry--a sort of Ken
Keseyesque figure who would have been right at home up
front in the Merry Prankster Kool-Aid Acid bus. But what
did he know of poetry? Surprisingly, perhaps, he knew a
good deal, much of it learned from whatever scroungy an-
thologies the San Quentin prison library contains. For
throughout his work--even those poems most Bukowskiesque
and loquacious and formless, there is a fascination with tradi-
tional forms and diction. And this polarity between the liter-
ary and the realistic (his own word) is useful for understand-
ing Wantling's entire work. Rarely, though, did he allow
formal matters to dominate his personal energy: his poems
normally have unique urgencies. He was seldom that tatty
poet who writes for the sake of writing, as an equivalent for
a good private jerk-off--the Muse sniggering into your ear
from the other end of the obscene telephone.

It is easy to pin Wantling as a minority poet. And
these days minority voices are in. Hooray, I say. It's
about time. And one of the minorities being heard from are
prisoners. Often, the kind folk on the outside of the walls--
the mother-hen editors and anthologists--are sentimentally ad-
dicted to the plight of these men; and as a result much pub-
lished prison writing leaves much to be desired. Wantling
is an exception. His prison poems transcend their material.
It doesn't matter ultimately that they were written in prison;
like most good poems they transcend what another writer
would have dished out as a snivel, or as a cliché. And
every life, including prison life, has its clichés.

What I propose to do is to characterize a few of
Wantling's books, and in the process suggest the man's con-
siderable range and power. Hopefully, some publisher will
get the message and publish a full Collected Poems. A com-
plete assessment of his work would, of course, examine all
of his published work, including that in magazines, and in-
cluding the few critical pieces on him. John Bennett's Vaga-
bond recently devoted space to Wantling, and makes a fine
start towards pulling the strands of Wantling's career to-
gether. I sincerely hope I am able in some small way to
stimulate further interest in Wantling.

II

I begin with the earliest of Wantling's books I have at hand: The Source, published by Len Fulton, as a Dustbook, in 1966. Len tells me, incidentally, that copies of this book are still available from him. Fulton introduces The Source with a few essential and perceptive comments about Wantling. He compares him to Dostoevsky, another writer who wrote from "the utter crush of the Cave," as Fulton puts it, rather than from a pinnacle of weeping narcissism. Wantling's arrogance is never pained. He is, says Fulton, "a tiger, raucous." He is imperfect and "springs with a certain prodigious elusiveness from the page; he needs discipline and yet, as for Dostoevsky, that achieved will almost certainly mark Bill Wantling's decline." Len needn't have worried, since Wantling himself resolved the issue by dying. But, back to The Source.

The title poem is a fairly conventional poem to a Venus/Atlanta-in-Calydon/Diana figure. But with differences; and I am glad the book begins with so traditionally inspired and wrought poem. Wantling spins a panegyric to mythic woman, muse of poetry, love, and life. His capitalizations of pronouns is entirely old-fashioned, Swinburnian. And one hears behind his cadences that marvellous lyric by Swinburne, "When the hounds of spring are on winter's traces," anthologized in nearly all anthologies of English literature. Phrases like "wild imagining," "rose to light," "mare-white thighs," "hounds of destiny," are reminiscent of Swinburne. So is "Her love about Her like a field of frozen fire" a direct imitation of Swinburne's lines from his great "Laus Veneris." Wantling's treatment of conventional cadences is masterly; he is never enslaved by his models. His ear is his own, liquid and singing. An auspicious start. For it is from such a point that Wantling moved out to incorporate as his own an incredible range of themes and styles. Here is "The Source";

> and She we know yet have but seldom seen
> rose from the sea where all paths lead
> rose in Her robes of lucid silver light
> Her cornflower eyes of wild imagining
> rose to light all the cities of this earth
>   with Her mare-white thighs
> Her love about Her like a field of frozen fire
> Her whimpering hounds of destiny straining
>   at the leash

The second poem, "Heroin," is in quite another mode.
Reportage, perhaps, projective, colloquial:

> High, once I ate 3 scoops of icecream
> high it was the greatest
> greater than the Eiffel tower
> greater than warm sex, sleepy
> early on a morning. . . .

A well-tooled Shakespearean sonnet follows. Despite the
quaint, conventional language and period turns in the verse
lines, the drift is modern--an easy Existentialism:

> How is it, though the mind extend
> few plans that Time may not erase
> when we have wandered to our barren end
> and left no trail upon the sands of space,
> How is that we, cut to life's bare bone
> and protesting our unjust fate as Man
> fearing emptiness and O alone, alone
> outlines against the emptiness we scan,
> How is that we hold our heads so high
> and explain the emptiness away
> and fill with myths the empty sky
> that endless cipher which we wander day to day?
>
> Yet we are only puzzled by the myths we spin.
> Why not deny The Myth and face the Emptiness
>   again?

"How to Make a Molotov Cocktail" is a tautly woven
political poem, curiously artful in its cross-echoes of sound
and cadence:

> the Bitch-ridden cliché that tightly
> turns the hidden twitch of truth re-
> mains the same--only Quick of Death
> is prone to know the new--& seldom
> bidden change seldom does it change
> --the same today as when the Bolsheviki
> bullets flew & all the gutters flooded
> crimson with the Czarist blood. . . .

Moments here read like parodies of Swinburnian assonantal
verse, the consonantal repetitions twisting back on themselves
humorous-wise, as Swinburne would have said. Also, the
"as when the . . ." is faded old Pre-Raphaelite mannered

writing. I have the feeling here, as I do throughout most of
Wantling's work, that he is deliciously engaged with the pas-
tiche he's up to; it remains, therefore, his own--he's the
master in charge, he holds the whip.

       Towards the close of "it's cold for August," Wantling's
rampant energy emerges. He releases his rage against soci-
ety, its wars, pollutions, sterilities: but with minimal suc-
cess:

                    & what if the dam should
                            suddenly burst
                    if suddenly I should run
                    headlong, frothing, haphazardly
                    hurling shrapnel grenades
                    into high-noon crowds?
                    if suddenly tossing aside the
                            dead ugly ache of it
                    all, I equalled the senseless
                    with my brute senseless act?

                    O My, wouldn't I
                    shine?   wouldn't
                    I shine then?
                    wouldn't it be I then who
                    had created God
                    at last.

This is not particularly successful. The literary writing of
the first part ("brute senseless act," the periodicity of "if
suddenly...," the Swinburnian locutions of "dead ugly ache
ache of it / all," "if suddenly I should run ... ") isn't fully
controlled. And the illusion of freshness in the last stanza
drifts off into sophomoric statements and questions. Yet,
the tonal shift in the last section is a welcome change from
the preceding lines.

       "The Dog as Poet" is a superbly realized poem. It's
raunchy energy breaks through in a way no poem in The
Source so far does. "The Dog" is essentially a skip-through
of the poet's life, and has good humor and much good writ-
ing. Poet's birth was easy:

                    as a pup
                    I was popped forth
                    like a clean new cork
                    from a poisonous suppurating bottle

> no hard & angry birth here
> an easy lay
> begot an easy liar
> dreamer, scoundrel....

Fucking bitches became Dog's preoccupation, his "raison
d'etre." "Servicing Bitches in Heat" might be an appropri-
ate subtitle for the whole poem. Bitches steal energy from
his writing; and yet bitches inspire him. His first bitch
was

> blue & easy
> she thought me hers, said
> I could cure the melancholy of
>   her timid soul
> spur on to glory the timorous genes
>   that were her lot in life

He sensed the blue bitch entrapping him, killing his cre-
ative juices; so he loped off, hunched, "wild and free," the
soft wind "running" in his fur. In a fine tour de force patch
of writing he becomes Dog as Don Juan:

> Is there one the insolent pup
>   won't lay?!
> the whispers went:
>   his mother was a bitch's bitch...
>   his father was unknown...

> Yet which of us would itch of this
> when bitches free & easy, hot-tail
> cool-tail, slim or overblown
> lay before us every night
> begging us to cork their bottles
> & cork them stiff & tight
> & so many bitches, be it known
> that spending night upon spent night
> would never know them all, their pretty ways
>   their tortured groans
> the way they spread without a fight?

> & after many an exciting night
> I filled my belly in their kitchens
>   & slipped away
> before the dawn advanced to burn the dark
>   & turn it into day
> before the sun exposed my bitchings

> & gave the target for a shotgun blast
> before my days of happy rut & ditching
> were put to end at last....

Yet, clever dogs grow old--as Dog does.   Now he writes his
verse this way:

> before I start my singing I ensure
> my spot is where the sun is warm
> yes, in the sun is where I lay
> only in the sun, day on endless day

III

Sick Fly (second aeon, 1970) takes its title from a
passage by H. L. Mencken: "The Cosmos is a gigantic Fly-
wheel making 10,000 revolutions a minute.   Man is a sick
fly taking a dizzy ride on it."   The advance Wantling makes
here is towards what I would call disquisitional poetry; i.e.,
poetry in journal form, written almost as a letter home--
snatches of private autobiography written in plain, non-poetic
language.   He seems now to have abandoned his earlier
literary pretensions.   Here is how the poem begins:

> It was Tuesday morning
> I was flunking out of school
> The February sun was hazy
> I went to bed with 2 jugs of white port
> to drink myself asleep
> but I kept flashing back to the day before
> ... I kept letting my dog off her chain
> & she kept running out in the road to
> chase the gasoline tanker
> & she kept clipping under the rear wheels
> & she kept yelping with surprise as she
> sat in the road with her guts hanging out
> between her back legs & her eyes
> never stopped looking at me with shamed surprise
> as if she'd got caught shitting on the rug
> & then the sun was bouncing off her eyes
> like a handball off the blank concrete wall
> flicker   /   flicker
> death
> flicker....

The impact of the violent death leads him to pills.   He takes

numerous ones, old pills he's stashed, not sure what they
are. He swallows "half a handful, all colors." Sweat runs
down his "back legs." He resists puking until the pills be-
gin to work. His trip is a bummer: "things" come out of
the corners towards him. There's a black hole in his wrist.

       His artery jumps out and gushes blood two feet in the
air. The blood turns to pus. Incredible noise: 10,000 steel-
heeled boots stomping. Two days later his wife finds him
under his bed, curled up in a ball, covered with shit and
vomit. In the concluding lines Wantling places himself on a
pinnacle far above the cave and assumes the delicious gran-
deur of his pain. When he complains that the gods have
forced him into poetry, he loses some of the potency of this
otherwise magnificent poem:

> But here I am now fairly calm
> full of tranquilizers & group therapy
> It evidently wasn't my turn afterall
> What I wonder is, why all the hassle?
> Why all the bullshit?
> I never wanted to be a poet anyway
> I'd carry a lunchbox like everybody else
> if only the muttering would stop

Dope drifts through these poems, implicit in the disjunctive
forms themselves. And perhaps that's the best that dope-
poems can do, give a sense of the mind's jumping, flashing
chaos. There are really few successful dope poems around,
written under the influence, that is; a couple by Ginsberg,
perhaps, or by Snyder, and a few ravings by lesser folk.
Perhaps, finally, it is the rational, whether fucked, surreal,
or normal that interests us; wild drug-induced ravings belong
to madness--even Artaud's ravings in their final stages, at
least those available in print, make surface sense. But, to
return to Wantling: his dope poems work mainly because he
gives us the exteriors of the experiences; in other words, he
doesn't smart it up for us with invented hallucinations, nor
does he pretend that he's writing whilst spinning. We see
what he does before, during, and after a trip; he's even fun-
ny--read his poems describing his riding a bicycle stoned.
I hurt for him, but I laugh too. My feeling is that in this
volume the exploded lines come from his dope experiences,
and not from reading William Carlos Williams, or Charles
Olson, or Robert Duncan, or Robert Creeley. A disrupted
life angles through these lines, determining their shape. A
good poem to James Dean, an elegy, works because Dean too
merits the fractured line; it suits his fractured life:

                    parts of your torn jacket
            are still offered for sale

                                and
            a boy just pimping into
        pictures
                    keeps your twisted
        body steering wheel

                                on his
        L. A. wall

                    and still we hear
            your muted icy hipster snarl
        ... see the soft smile breaking / and guess your rage and
                                        wonder at it all

The concluding poem, brief, almost a colophon, is startling:

                        actually
                        to sum up 35 years
                        Billie Holiday
                        is the only sane person
                        I ever met
                        & shooting heroin
                        the only sane thing
                        I ever did

                                IV

        San Quentin's Stranger is a fine job of bookmaking, and
is easily the best of the perfect-bound Wantlings I have seen.
Len Fulton has assembled what is so far the essential Want-
ling, incorporating poems from The Awakening (Rapp and
Whiting), Obscene & Other Poems (Caveman Press), Sick
Fly (second aeon), and 10,000 r.p.m. & Digging it, Yeah!
(second aeon and the nola express).   Stranger is distributed
in this country by Second Coming, PO Box 31246, San Fran-
cisco 94131.

        "Poetry" presents Wantling's conflict between his al-
legiance, on the one hand, to "good word music and rhyme"
in poetry; and, on the other hand, to the guts material of
prison life (extend this to mean all non-slick life).   So, he
did not after all abandon the problem of literary writing.
"Poetry" is a touch poem, and as a poetics deserves a place

among the more seminal poem-statements written by contem-
porary poets. He writes in non-rhyming couplets, giving a
sense of Wantling under the strictures of self-imposed form.
But, even when he appears formal his voice resists the form;
or, rather, with the form he allows his slack, midwestern
voice to have its way--almost as if he's writing home to
good old Mom. Because of the importance of the poem I am
quoting it in its entirety:

Poetry

I've got to be honest, I can
make good word music and rhyme

at the right times and fit words
together to give people pleasure

and even sometimes take their
breath away--but it always

somehow turns out kind of phoney.
Consonance and assonance and inner

rhyme won't make up for the fact
that I can't figure out how to get

down on paper the real or the true
which we call life. Like the other

day. The other day I was walking
in the lower exercise yard here

at San Quentin and this cat called
Turk came up to a friend of mine

and said Ernie, I hear You're
shooting on my kid. And Ernie

told him So what, Punk? And Turk
pulled out his stuff and shanked

Ernie in the gut only Ernie had a
metal tray in his shirt. Turk's

shank bounced off Ernie and
Ernie pulled his stuff out and of

course Turk didn't have a tray and
he caught it dead in the chest, a bad

one, and the blood that came to his
lips was a bright pink, lung blood,

and he just laid down in the grass
and said Shit.   Fuck it.   Sheeit.

Fuck it.   And he laughed a soft long
laugh, 5 minutes, then died.   Now

what could consonance or assonance or
even rhyme do with something like that?

"The Cold War" employs a bizarre image to suggest
America and Russia at odds with one another.   The image is
total; Wantling leaves all the connections up to our imagina-
tions--the way a good poet should:

The Cold War

today i saw a strange sight
i saw a set of mutant ugly siamese twins
joined from hip to shoulder--
they were hissing, snarling, sneering
each mouth spoke hate for the other
and the one with a right hand
waved a dagger at the one with a left hand, who
also waved a dagger...

they were duelling

The prison poems ring true because a great human being
emerges from the pain and the shit.   Wantling was gifted
with a braggadocio that kept him sane.   Perhaps calling this
quality a crazy gusto might be more accurate.   He sensed
somehow that his best chance of maintaining balance, con-
fronted by shock treatments and other prison brutalities, was
through an ironic detachment.   This he expresses superbly
in "Who's Bitter?":

when Judge Lynch
denied probation
& crammed that 1-14
up my ass
for a First offence
I giggled

            when Dr God
            stuck 7 shocktreatments
            to me
            for giving my chick
            in Camarillo
            2 joints
            I laughed aloud

            now when the State of Illness
            caught me bending over
            2 jugs of Codeine
            cough medicine
            & charged me w/ Possession
            and Conspiracy
            I shrieked
            in idiot joy

            a bit worried
            they all inquired
            --What are you Wantling?
            --A goddam Masochist?
            I, between hilarious gasps
            O howled--No,
            --I'm a Poet!
            --Fuck me again!

        His Dionysian joy in life is paradoxically real in "Di-
onysus in Summer." Here he shouts out his earth-intoxica-
tion, his joy in being alive--this despite the paradox that as
Dionysus he dooms summer and mangles the innocent hare.
The poem, finely cryptic, is one of my favorites.

        In "Obscene" he is at his most original, writing what
he feels is the poem that will surely get him busted. The
poem, then, as threat; the poem as grenade. Note with what
relish he bites out his conclusion. He has come a long way
from the traditional poems of his early books. Here is a
mature poet finally at home in his own voice and style:

                        Obscene

            her sweat mingling with mine
            I slowly slide along & down
            find her navel with my tongue
            & her only eye of love
                form a tiny pool
            her mindless legs fly open

I tongue her cunt, her
    musk a pungent funk
        part flower
        part rutting beast, & I
a wolf involved with winter moon
    howl soundlessly
a serpent
            climbs my spinal tree
rooted in my balls
flowered in my skull
I know the Unicorn
some itching prick of its
ivory spiralled horn & mount
that mythic beast, am one with it
surge deep   into her cave
pouring through her center
    her abandon
        approaching adoration
the look of love about her
like a field of frozen fire
the ecstasy of Spring
damping down her thighs
&
a documentary
on deep-sea fishermen
who, angry at their luck
come upon a herd of Sea-lions
& their highpowered rifles
firing into the herd
& the carcasses
    float
        useless
        undisturbed
their heads bobbing the waves
    like footballs
their dead eyes staring
    the horizon
            their sea
            their skies
their
        "spindrift gaze toward paradise"
            their dead eyes
as the camera pans
to the Captain
at the rail
& his rifle
& his shining teeth

& the mirth of his tightlipped
grin
        the obscene abandon
in his eyes
        & the local
public prosecutor
who reads this poem & wishes
"it had been published so I
could take you to court, Boy
on charges of Obscenity !"

V

    7 On Style was Wantling's last book.   According to Al
Winans he was writing it just before he died, after a long
creative drought.   Wantling apparently felt that his poem on
Neruda was the best he'd ever written.   How appropriate that
his final book should treat problems of style.   How rare that
a poet of such immense disasters should consider style at
all.   (Walter Lowenfels, a personal friend of Wantling's, says
that Wantling's work has important affinities with Artaud's).
Wantling's excursions into other men's styles move from
Samuel Beckett, to Charles Bukowski, to Neruda.   Each is
a stunning exercise in affection, in the mode of the other
writer, and all fun.   There is an amazing piece, too, on
stream of consciousness writing, done so well Wantling takes
us in completely.   In the Beckett piece he says:

                    That sentence has
a wonderful
        SHAPE   It is
the   SHAPE
          that matters.

This dictum Wantling believed only some of the time.

    "Style 2" is the most ambitious of this series.   It is
straightforward, outrageous, obscene, funny, intense.   Want-
ling adopts the voice of a professor lecturing his students on
style.   The central problem is this (and we've seen it before
in other guises):   how can a traditional style (Wantling says:
"Poetry is Style") serve events.   To make the point that
Poetry and Style "can be found anywhere," he incorporates a
letter from a woman written to the editor of the local paper.
Wantling provides only line breaks for emphasis, in this, his
found poem:

I want to tell you
what happened to your cat
after you dropped her off--the
first few days
she stayed just about where you
dropped her
waiting for you to come back
then hunger
drove her on along the road
searching for food & shelter
by now
she eats anything she can find, rotten
wormy, disease-laden ...
dogs & other animals
chase her, &
she is almost hit by passing cars
exposure to freezing nights
almost kills her
but your cat is tough ...
I found her today
she was beside my mailbox
right where you wanted her to go
that nice farmhouse in the country
only trouble was
your cat couldn't see me
her eyes were pasted shut
with infection
                    every bone
showing through her dirty hide
her stomach distended
with worms & starvation
too weak to stand
she made a little noise at me
but it was for you
to hear ... she is dead now

this, indeed, is poetry, not because it speaks
of random, terror, abandon, of
Quick too quickly cut, but
because it speaks of it with Style
because of concrete, sensory detail, stark
outline of emotionally charged events
extreme economy and, woven through it all
a strand of universal raging wonder at
the savage god called Death....

The episode, Wantling concludes, is "Reality imbued with

Style. " The poem was successful, for it made Wantling cry.
Then he develops his rationale further, moving into the very
heart of his poetics. He is ultimately traditional: Poetry
as Style (Art) is reminiscent of ancient Greek and Roman
writers: there is a savage god called Death, there are the
quick and wiry shadows of our lives, and there is the ran-
dom terror we must triumph over. Style becomes the Style
of the State--the State gasses creatures in Cyklon B cham-
bers. Wantling reduces his rage:

                              & I have
        dulled in 40 years
                        previously
        I raged & snarled &   pissed & moaned
        fuck you, Universe! Shithead!
                              fuck you I howled
        you Punk! I'll rip you off
                              instead!
                                    yes
        once I tried to outrage
        the random quirks of quick
        the way they outraged me
        but now I write of perverse curious things
        without a curiosity; I inscribe
        these ugly Random lines
        with only random anger; I've achieved
        a certain academic detachment & aplomb
        my colleagues, now, are
        more impressed
                        the Universe
                              much less ...
        Oh
        before you leave
        you may wish to prepare
        for next week's lesson:
        Style 3! please
        read the entire works
        of Chas Bukowski. never
        mind the
                Man...

Despite its faults, Bill Wantling's poetry deserves to be heard,
and heard aloud! He is not the poet on the pinnacle, holding
his prize scroll in one hand, his newest book in the other,
screaming for recognition. I think it was his friend Winans
who said that Wantling had given up on an audience in Amer-
ica, and the fact of his diminishing reputation (it was never

much to begin with) here was as much his fault as anyone
else.   American poetry is poorer by his disappearance; for,
there is a savage god called Death.   Wantling has met him.
He leaves us with remorse, and much human beauty in a
body of splendid work.

CATATONIC SURREALISM:

Victor Contoski*

Victor Contoski is a master of a kind of poem popular these days. Simic, Tate, Knott, Codrescu, and Hitchcock, among others, write them. Their mode is what I call <u>catatonic surrealism</u>. Catalepsy, says the dictionary, is "a condition of suspended animation and loss of voluntary motion in which the limbs remain in whatever position they are placed." I find this definition useful, except that for limbs I would substitute brain or mind. I have written these kinds of poems too, and the process goes something like this: dissociate your head from the rest of your body; i.e., suspend head, remove as much furniture from it as you can--in other words, remove the tables and chairs from the ballroom. Then, let appear whatever figures, images, symbols want to dance and play. Invent a narrative to go along with these movements. Keep the narrative accessible; keep the framework possible logically. The scrim against which these figures behave often contains a landscape ready-made for you to incorporate into your poem. Use it. And be entertaining, surprising, humorous, jesting. Your cataleptic state originates your poem, which you twist and work for optimum effect. The narrative line is more available than purer surrealistic poems are apt to be. The narrative is less association and meandering, less flashy. I prefer catatonic surrealism to other surrealisms.

These poems are generally of three kinds: 1) the threat or paranoia poem; 2) the fairy-tale poem; and 3) the recipe or information or imperative poem. Sometimes the kinds blend into a single poem; and, of course, the reader will find several good poems in <u>Broken Treaties</u> that defy this Caesarian division.

---

*Reprinted by permission from <u>Margins</u>, No. 11 (April-May 1974) pp. 30-32; Copyright © 1974 by <u>Margins</u>.

I prefer Contoski's threat/paranoia poems to his others. They have more depth--which is not surprising, since the conditions of our lives, simply because we're human, are fired with threat: the imbalance happens when we begin to suspect hostilities that aren't there. Then, our feelings turn paranoid and we are more or less immobilized by our fears. Contoski seems to take the state of cataleptic suspension (which I use positively) as a way of dealing with hostilities. A fine presentation of the problem is "The Mailman." Here is the poem in its entirety:

> In the dark of night
> he has opened what is mine
> looking for money
> and copying excerpts
> for his novel.
>
> For years he has
> burned my mail in secret
> trying to make me believe
> my friends have forgotten me.

If this poem lacked humor we'd suspect the speaker of being ill. But it works. We've all suspected the mailman of withdrawing our mail; and, if he does it in "the dark of night" he is that much more threatening, devious and hostile. The poem has charm.

In "Hunting Poem" mysterious tracks appear in the snow. "During the night / something / crossed my path. Its footprints / cannot be found in any book." The speaker, as if to forestall or prevent the perpetrations of the mysterious, begins to follow the tracks through the snow. There is a certain attractive courage here; threat paranoia does not immobilize the speaker.

"Homecoming" is less successful. It skirts self-pity and sentimentality, and picks up bits of clay. The geniality of the voice does not quite work; it's too casual, too simplistic for so heavy an encounter. The fault is in these pairs of lines, I think. They are at some distance from one another in the poem and determine the tone and thematic drift:

> And my old master, Pain,
> greeted me with open arms.
>   . . .
> Welcome home,
>   said the old master, Pain.

"Morning Moon" is another poem that doesn't quite
make it.   Contoski's vision is insufficiently complete: the
cataleptic vision failed to provide him with a well-realized
scene.   It is simply too easy to see "ghosts of Indians ...
reeling through darkness ... drinking their courage, / their
faces smeared with grief. "   The "barbarians in the hills"
busy "sharpening their weapons" is also facile.   The threat
is too vague; although there is a fine driving in towards the
close:

> The full moon hangs low
> over Madison, Wisconsin,
>
> like a chip from a statue
> of an ancient civilization.
>
> Yellow as from age.
> Red as from fire.

One of the most blatant and original poems of threat
is "Teeth. "   Ostensibly a love poem, it begins with the im-
perative: "kiss the one you love. "   And when you do, what
do you find: teeth waiting behind the lips.   Not particularly
informative, nor newsworthy.   And, Contoski nods when he
mars the poem with a detestable hip locution: the teeth
wait "like a man with a weapon / waits in a dark alley. "
The image isn't particularly fresh in the first place, and the
dislocated language doesn't help.   But this is a minor fuss.
The remainder of the poem is good.   The scrim of Contoski's
brain is agile and alive.   The chess-set motif is especially
horrible and telling:

> 1.
> Kiss the one you love.
> Behind the lips
> teeth are waiting
>
> like a man with a weapon
> waits in a dark alley.
>
> 2.
> They are not knives
> but clubs.
>
> They come down on meat
> like a lead pipe
> on the head of a woman.

3.
Sometimes in dreams
they wither and turn soft
like rotten cactus.

They curl up and fall out
like men refusing to fight
an unpopular war.

4.
If you are beaten long enough and hard enough
your teeth will be knocked out.

Then you can use them as chessmen:
front teeth, pawns;
back teeth, pieces.

5.
They line up in the mouth
like soldiers for inspection.

Ever since I can remember
they have surrounded the tongue,

reminding what is soft
of what is hard.

"Dictionary Poem" is one of the most successful of
Contoski's fairy-tale poems.   It borrows the vague temporal-
ity of genre--"many many years ago"; the motif of the lover
--although here they are bored with one another; the inven-
tion of a monster--the Dictionary; the projection against a
backdrop of national upheaval--war is waged over the Dic-
tionary; magical events--the dictionary flies like a kite; and
resurrection--the dictionary returns as a vampire from the
dead and must finally be killed with a stake through its heart.

Obviously fairy-tales are fables, and "Dictionary
Poem" can be read as an intriguing indictment of the ossi-
fication (or entombment) of language for political and social
power.   Establishments fight over the sanctity of their words.
This seems a bit heavy, perhaps, and we should take care
not to damage the delicacy of this work.   Because it has
sheer fantasy too.   Briefly, the dictionary frees itself and
becomes a figure of vengeance, sucking blood from volumes
of poetry--which originally sucked words from it.   Here is
the whole Poem:

Dictionary Poem

1.

Many many years ago
a man and a woman
both naked
got into bed
and found they had nothing
at all to say to each other.

Still naked they arose
went to their desks
and began writing a dictionary.

2.

It began with a.
By the time it reached
the middle of the alphabet,
it was already jaded.

Yet what could it do but go on?

3.

When Mary Sue used the dictionary
it wanted to close on her breasts.
But she wanted the meaning of egregious.

4.

When the state waged war
in its name
it marched in protest
shouting: lies, lies!

But nobody recognized it.

5.

As it grew older the dictionary
envied the leaves of the walnut.
It envied the distance of the stars.
It grew bitter at its own altruism.

6.

One March day a man tied a string
to each corner of the dictionary.
He took it to an open field,
let out ten feet of string,
and ran as fast as he could.

The dictionary rose in the wind.
It lifted him above the clouds;
it fell on his head and killed him.

7.
The man and the dictionary
were buried together.
From his grave grew a red, red rose
and from its grave a briar.

8.
But the dictionary did not die.

It rose from its grave at the full moon,
entered the library through an open window
and settled in the poetry section.

Each night it lay on a different book
kissing it and sucking its blood
until the librarian found out.

He buried the dictionary in the reference room
with a stake through its heart.

Despite its illogicalities and fantasies, "Dictionary
Poem" is highly accessible. Its references are known myths
and legends and not irrationalities. The sequential develop-
ment, I think, shares something with comic strip method;
the parts could just as easily be frames.

"Money" is a fine example of the imperative poem.
The form is rarely unalloyed, since it is frequently mixed
with a special reportage through which the poet communicates
bits of information, almost as if he had culled it from ency-
clopedias. Here is what I mean: Contoski begins "Money"
by informing us how money behaves:

At first it will seem tame,
willing to be domesticated.

It will nest
in your pocket
or curl up in a corner
reciting softly to itself
the names of the presidents.

It will delight your friends,

> shake hands with men
> like a dog and lick
> the legs of women.
>
> But like an amoeba
> it makes love
> in secret
> only to itself.

Then, in an imperative portion we are told what to do with money:

> Fold it frequently;
> it needs exercise.
>
> Water it every three days
> and it will repay you
> with displays of affection.
>
> Then one day when you think
> you are its master
> it will turn its head
> as if for a kiss
> and bite you gently
> on the hand.

The conclusion is a turn towards horror. The idea is obvious--an obsession for money poisons; but Contoski brings it off:

> There will be no pain
> but in thirty seconds
> the poison will reach your heart.

"Salt" is my favorite of Contoski's poems. It combines the cataleptic dream-vision with the fairy-tale and the imperative-informative motifs. Contoski's imagination is at its best here. Salt spilled on a wooden table enters the grains of the wood and "will never bloom again." A butcher dries his bloody clothes in the sun: "Salt turns them white." People in a park are "honoring salt." A princess works for a witch and makes "salt with her tears." Each day she fills a pail. Imperative: "Put the tears of a princess / on your mashed potatoes." Then we are informed that "salt lies deep underground" and must be dug out by "dirty men" who "stand amazed by its beauty." Religious statues are carved from it, and left for the centuries. And, this profound, cryptic, personal conclusion:

> My first communion:
> far down under the earth
> someone placed on my tongue
> a pinch of salt.

My least favorite of these "Broken Treaties" are the hand-
ful of overtly political ones towards the end of the book.
Contoski's efforts to symbolize his disillusion about tradition-
al American idealism as a dead poker hand is admirable and
works when he moves away from this commonplace political
statement:

> Someone has been lying about America
> all these years--saying it is the land
> of justice, idealism, and freedom;
> that it is the land of opportunity
> where any boy can grow up to be president.

> Lies: all of them.
> They come from the mouth of the dealer
> who has just given you the four of hearts.

The best of these is "War Poem." Generals look at the
stars and dream of women, while their wives bravely die
of cancer and their sons are massacred. Congressmen weep
over their unfaithful wives. Mathematicians count the enemy
dead. Late at night the president, in the White House,
writes poetry, scanning the night skies for an adjective. T.
Jefferson's ghost fucks a virgin in Nebraska. In Warren,
Ohio "the streetlights stagger like drunken soldiers." The
town sleeps:

> Protestants breathe in.
> As Catholics breathe out. Nobody snores.

> Only an evil old lady lies awake
> hoping her only son will die.

I admire this book. I enjoyed reading it. Contoski's
talent is impressive. The risk he takes is of continuing to
repeat the handful of formulas (fairy-tale, information poem,
etc.) he finds congenial. I sense that he can do much more
varied work.

A small fuss: Erik Rudans' drawings, scattered lib-
erally throughout, despite their skill, are distractions. Oth-
erwise, the book is handsomely produced.

THE GIFT TO BE SIMPLE: THE SHAKER (ANN LEE) POEMS:

An Interview with Robert Peters*

Matthews: What most intrigued you about the Shakers when you first ran across them? When was that, and how did it happen?

Peters: I found the Shakers through serendipity. Last summer, driving cross-country to fellowships at Yaddo and the MacDowell Colony, I got lost near Albany--the only time, I might say, on the entire huge jaunt that this happened. Trying to find the freeway, I saw a sign that said "Shaker Museum: 3 miles." We (I was travelling with my friend and companion Paul Trachtenberg) were near Old Chatham, NY. We drove to the Museum ... and spent three hours there. An incredible experience! While the Museum is not in actual Shaker buildings, it does contain an amazing range of Shaker cultural and industrial artifacts--and agrarian ones as well. We left there with a thorough sense of what Shaker life must have been like. I bought a history of the Shakers--Marguerite Melcher's The Shaker Adventure.

When I arrived at MacDowell, we had to camp at a state park north of Peterborough, New Hampshire. I spent two days sitting on a hill overlooking a lake reading The Shaker Adventure. Increasingly, Mother Ann Lee, the female Christ and founder of the religion, absorbed me, until by the time I was settled in my studio at MacDowell I knew I would try to write about her. I had driven east, from southern California, with nothing particular in my head to write about. I was tired of writing about my own pains, undergoings, obsessions, etc., and hoped to locate a subject larger than anything I had so far written. In a sense, I feel the subject of Ann Lee was a fantastic gift.

*Robert Peters interviewed by William Matthews 1/74. Reprinted by permission from Granite, No. 9-10 (Winter 1974/75) pp. 2-12; Copyright © 1975 by Granite Books.

You asked what interests or intrigues me about the
Shakers. Well, a number of things. The visionary element:
in a way these remarkable people were like an assortment of
William Blakes or Swedenborgs. Angels were as real and
as present to them as living folk. Curiously, too, their
time, the late eighteenth century, coincided with Blake per-
fectly. I haven't looked into it, but I would guess that
Swedenborg and other philosophers/religionists had somehow
conditioned the time for visions ... perhaps in reaction to
the deism of the eighteenth century ... the rationalism. It
does take some imagining to see oneself as the female Christ.

The simplicity of their lives intrigued me also ...
and the sleek wonderful machines they invented. A Shaker
woman invented the circular saw. Other Shaker inventions:
the snap clothespin, and the industrial washing-machine.
And, of course, everybody knows about Shaker furniture.
Not everyone knows though that the Shakers are largely gone.
There are about 8 elderly ladies left, 3 in Canterbury, New
Hampshire, the rest at Sabbathday Lake, Maine. I'll be
visiting the Maine ladies this coming August to read my
poems to them, as part of a Shaker Bicentennial Commemora-
tion. I'm quite thrilled about this.

Well, the passing of this tremendous two-hundred year
energy from, at least, this physical plane also intrigues me.
At one time, just before the mid-nineteenth century, there
were nearly 9,000 Shakers, living in some twenty communities
scattered around New England, as far west as Ohio, and as
far south as Kentucky. Of course, their belief in celibacy
didn't help their growth much.

The fact of celibacy was in itself perplexing ... what
in Mother Ann Lee's psyche led her to adopt this position (it
does seem needlessly extreme) for herself and her followers?
The more I looked into the causes, the more taken I was with
Mother Ann. She had four children ... they all died in child-
hood. These deaths she took as the judgment of God against
her for her carnality. Also, during one of her imprison-
ments, in a madhouse dungeon in Manchester, England, in
the 1770's, she had a vision of Adam and Eve getting it on
in the Garden of Eden, a vision so horrible it convinced her
that she must reject her carnality. One of my longest poems
is an attempt to convey the shock of her experience. Yes,
I did have a little help from Hieronymous Bosch! So, her
psyche seemed freaked to me ... understandably so. She
has to be one of the most incredible women who've ever

lived ... courage ... gentleness in the face of severe beat-
ings and manhandlings.... In fact, her early death (she was
in her forties) was the result of beatings she incurred trav-
elling around New England trying to inspirit struggling Shaker
communities. But, I'm sorry, Bill, I'm rushing way ahead
here. It's a subject I'm still crammed full of....

Matthews: I suppose this female Christ who started
the sect heard voices. Do you hear hers?

Peters: Yes, I have heard her voice. Once I got
going at MacDowell I literally felt possessed by her. Let
me say though that I never once saw her in an actual vision
... more a felt presence ... of energy supplying me with
poems and for ideas for poems. I wrote frenziedly for three
weeks, and, finally, once I had typed up the initial set, found
there were actually an even hundred poems. This freaked
me ... I took it as a good sign ... that Mother Ann was
with me, and that the poems were good. I've never had so
prolific a writing period in my life. And, as you know, the
poems are varied ... lyrical, narrative, simple, complex,
formal, free. Whenever I was stymied I'd take a long walk
through the New Hampshire woods and almost always, by the
time I had returned to my studio, I had broken through. I'd
feel Mother Ann's presence, as energy. I'd talk to her, too,
grateful for her directions.

I suppose, in a sense, that any ambitious writing we
do is the result of our being taken over by some force ...
I won't say mystical or religious. You've experienced this
too. I guess it's just another way of saying that the creative
act itself, despite all the theorizing, remains an utter,
splendid mystery. I like it that way. I am Mother Ann's
creature (beautiful, I hope) ... and in that sense I am a
Shaker ... one thinks of the classic case of Milton ... as
Blake said: Milton was of the Devil's party without knowing
it. So, to answer your question: I did hear her voice quiet-
ly moving through me and into my poems. I thought particu-
larly that she liked my gentler song-type poems ... the short
things. And, since my own career as a poet began because
of the death of my five year old son Richard from a one-day
meningitis, I shared with Ann who had lost 4 infant children.
So, psychically, writing the portion of the book dealing with
the loss of her children, I felt she was making statements
through me, assuaging her own timeless griefs, if you will,
from her reach beyond, in the spirit world. Nothing heavy
here--a fantasy in my own head ... yes, working out my own

loss as well. I wish I had the splendid facility Ann had of moving over into visions ... perhaps that's what superb writing is all about ... having, somehow, the ability to perceive this way. Does that make sense to you?

Matthews: Yes, it does. It's as if there were no seam--and I don't think there is--between the material and the spiritual.

Peters: I'm bothered though by my own unwillingness to go all the way. I hedge and qualify on these matters. That's my old 'forties liberal scepticism showing through ... to be mystical isn't intellectually sound. Respectable is perhaps the better word.

Matthews: You do though believe in Ann's belief that she was Christ returned. And you write poems in her voice.

Peters: Yes. I believe in her belief. Hedging?

Matthews: Well, the Shakers believed in abstinence from sex. The theme of androgyny permeates these poems. Do you associate androgyny with religious experience in general, or creativity in general? I hate questions in general, and I know you're interested by the Shakers in specifics; but maybe this is a good place to begin talking. And of course the Shakers are interested in sex, in the larger sense of the word: hasn't the sect become a matriarchy?

Peters: You're questions aren't easy, friend. Yes, the sect was a matriarchy ... but since the Shakers believed in the absolute equality of the sexes that idea had to be modified. They were balancing things off: Jesus was the male Christ. Christ they saw as a spirit. Ann was the female Christ. That balanced things off. She insisted on the balance, consciously writing nothing down herself, since Jesus hadn't, and insisting also on there being nothing written about her until she had been dead some thirty or forty years ... which made for problems, since there are few accounts in the Shaker archives by people who actually knew her. There are some though ... but it is difficult to get a real sense of what she looked like. The duality she carried further into the idea of Father Power and Mother Wisdom, a dual, sexual godhead, with Jesus and Ann as their immediately lesser counterparts. The Christian Scientist belief in Mother/Father God clearly derives from the Shakers.

Shakerdom, once it was organized by Mother Ann's
followers after her death, was entirely communal and had
safeguards against sexuality built in.   For example, men and
women were entirely segregated.   Visitations between men
and women were ritualized, with, say, five men going of an
evening to visit five women.   The exact distance the row of
men, seated in chairs, was to be from the row of women
was carefully measured.   Also, the dress, particularly of
the women, was designed to conceal body contours ... the
famous scarf effect crossed over the women's breasts is an
example.   Also, the pattern of dormitory living: 3 or 4
men in a single small room ... beds near one another and
open to view discouraged any flamboyant sexuality.

Then, too, the frenzy of the shaking during religious
rites was an equivalent for sexual frenzy ... getting it off
spiritually, so to speak, shaking, moaning, yelling, falling
finally to the floor or ground, shaking off carnality for the
sake of visions ... calm ... release ... orgasmic, yes.
A great idea.   It strikes me though that it would have been
much easier to fuck some.   I don't know of any fucks though
that produced visions.   Do you?

Matthews: No.   Usually the effect is a kind of benign
blackness and blurriness, rather than the clarity visionaries
describe.

Peters: And the Shakers not only generated individual
visions, but had mass visions as well.   And this fascinates
me, too.   During their highly ritualized, patterned dances,
before the individual shaking and trembling occurred, they
(same sex though) freely touched and kissed one another.
No homosexuality implied ... a sort of purity, rather ...
sexlessness, I suppose.

Matthews: Yes, but what of their androgyny?

Peters: Bill, I truly don't see much androgyny be-
hind Shaker rituals.   I'd like to.   Most religions seem to
idealize the androgynous person.   Sentimental Christian pic-
tures of Jesus confuse his sexuality ... he's usually too
pretty to be a man and not pretty enough to be a woman.
Antinous-worship with the Romans.   Greek gods and god-
desses.   Ever dig one of the biceps on those ancient Sibyls?
Minerva worked out some, too.   No, I think that the Shakers
maintained absolute differences between male and female, and
prohibited sexual congress between them for the sake of a

heightened spiritual awareness. If they had been more an-
drogynous, of course, they would not have so severely segre-
gated males and females. I think this makes sense ... I'm
playing with ideas now.

Matthews: But what do you feel writing poems in her
voice ... isn't your own sexuality involved?

Peters: Sure. I've wondered why I so easily slipped
into Ann's person while writing these poems. My own ex-
periences have been bisexual, as you know, and I'd have to
say that most of the time while I'm writing I feel neither
male nor female ... both kinds of responses feel at home in
my psyche. The assuming of masks, or roles, by poets is
not particularly mysterious.

Matthews: But, as I see it, most poets don't range
much outside their own psychic ground. They try to stay
male, if male, and female, if female.

Peters: I think you're right. And I don't see myself
as a unisex poet, but rather as one who can slip as easily
into a female psyche as into a male. My Byron poems--that
chapbook Byron Exhumed published by the Windless Orchard
Press last year--allowed me to drift in and out of male and
female personae, including Byron's wife and a young Harrow
student (male) who commits a sort of feminine suicide on
hearing of Byron's death. Also, one of my most successful
poems, "Gauguin's Chair," spoken by Van Gogh, was an at-
tempt by me to feel both VG's male and female natures.

Matthews: What I hear you saying is that the poet,
finally, has to be ready for whatever voice male or female
takes over.

Peters: Yes. If his hangups prevent this happening,
to me he's a crippled writer. D. H. Lawrence has always
struck me as a superb male writer who could slip effortlessly
into the female psyche and make that sensibility live. I hope
that my Ann Lee poems convince women that I've felt her
psyche. So far I've had conflicting responses from women
who've heard me read the poems. One says, "Yes, your
capturing of the female psyche is amazing." Another says,
"You remain a man writing about a woman." In my own
head, Ann exists as completely female. Part of her vitality
for me is a feminine vitality. I can't imagine her otherwise
... as a sort of Bella Abzug bouncing her boobies? Never!

Also, to maintain a Shaker balance Ann would have
seen herself as thoroughly feminine. In a universe directed
by Mother/Father God, their Spirit--Christ--would be care-
fully divided according to gender: Ann female, Jesus male.
The Camizards, that French sect who actually persuaded
Ann Lee that she was the Female Christ, I'm sure were
struck by her femininity. Camizards--a pair of them, fled
France for Manchester, England, believing that Christ's Sec-
ond Coming was immanent, and that he would come as a
woman. Through a Quaker couple she was close to, Ann
was gradually convinced that she was the incarnated spirit
the Camizards had sought.

Matthews: What criteria do you suppose a spirit uses
to choose a medium, or a historical figure to choose a living
writer? I've always found looking for a place to live was a
very dense and risky thing to do.

Peters: I love this question. Because in a sense it's
not real. Ann Lee did not choose me. I felt her inspiriting
me once I had gotten underway. This is how it happened ...
and I think this is a fairly universal way for poets to write:
I conditioned my head by reading Shaker history, songs, fan-
tasizing about Ann Lee and the few facts we actually know of
her life--and they are few. I walked a lot, releasing various
interfering tensions that had nothing to do with writing these
poems. Finally, my brain became an active Ann Lee scrim/
chamber/world, and scenes/sounds/colors/events began to hap-
pen there. It was scary but neat ... I thought at any mo-
ment the inspiration-energy would dissolve before I had done
all I wanted to. So I began subconsciously to invite (even to
expect and to demand) her help. I found myself talking to
her, with her. I sat evenings expecting her to materialize
out of the studio shadows, or on my walks in the MacDowell
woods to see her coming towards me. I liked to imagine
that she lingered somewhere in the woods in front of Edward
MacDowell's log studio. So, she didn't choose me. I cre-
ated her as a presence, to help me with the poems. And
she didn't let me down.

Later--a month later--at Yaddo (Saratoga Springs) I
discovered that she was buried fifteen minutes away, at
Niskeyuna (near Albany), in the old Shaker cemetery adjoin-
ing the Albany airport which is on old Shaker land. I clear-
ly remember the excitement of going there that first time.
The day was gray, chilly. Paul Trachtenberg was with me.
We moved all over the cemetery until we found her headstone,

in the center of the cemetery, and larger than the other
simple stones. I was afraid she would not be there.

Matthews: What were your feelings then?

Peters: I found it, adjoining her brother's plot. He
died the year preceding her (1777) from a cracked skull he
received at the hands of a mob. He lived almost nine months
in pain before he died. But as I stood there no great flam-
boyant spiritual moment ensued ... a gradually intensifying
high, rather, which lasted for hours after I left the cemetery.
I tried to revisit the grave weekly, as an energy source.
Every time it worked. Don't get me wrong ... I never be-
lieved I'd conjure her up from beneath the sod. Only once
did I feel an actual almost protoplasmic energy come towards
me and envelop me. The reverential act ... yes ... that's
what it was that gave me energy. I dug up dirt samples
from the grave finally. I'd like to think that the fact that I
put some up in a small plastic sack and sent it to Ned Arn-
old of Liveright explains the fact that he is publishing the
book. I have enough soil to grow something in here at home
... but I haven't found an appropriate plant. It should prob-
ably be some herb, since they were famous for their herb
culture and sent their herbs throughout the world. And I
feel her energy now, talking this, and I dig the feeling.

Matthews: Religious experience so often seems "be-
yond words." And yet a poet is always among words. It
must be spooky. A classicist works with a "dead language,"
but a poet touched by a sect whose members will not propa-
gate works with a dead, or a dying, culture. Or does it
feel at all like that?

Peters: No, it doesn't feel like that. In fact, the
Shaker experience seems entirely vital, immanent, alive, to
me. I talked with a couple of the old surviving Shaker ladies
in the village at Canterbury, NH. Eldress Bertha Livesay
said that none of the Shakers is dead ... they are alive in
the spirit realm ... and that is the important one. I should
have expected such a belief, obviously, since there was no
sadness in these splendid old women. Also, she said that
their ideals do survive today in various communal societies,
especially in the so-called "counter-culture" groups. In my
own life I've been sorting our sexuality ... and the idea of
celibacy intrigues me. In the past, I've assumed that living
a celibate life was impossible without being odd or deranged
or denying. I don't feel that way any more, after exposure

to the Shakers: I can see how a vibrant beauty and an im-
mense productivity can result from celibacy. If you don't
allow yourself time to burn over sexual fantasies, your en-
ergy can be directed elsewhere ... a far-out idea for this
sex-ridden culture we are in. If you choose not to get it
up for either male or female you're as good as dead! I'm
not saying I shall end up celibate. But the hassle of sex,
especially homo or bisexual sex is so head-and-time-con-
suming it seems a dismal waste of emotional energy, anx-
iety. I want to know the possibilities of a rich, productive,
loving life without the sexual burn. It may not be possible
... because I don't think of myself as a mystic ... which I
would have to be, I think, in order to translate my heavy
sexual energy into higher thoughts, or my poetry, or what-
ever.

     Matthews: Is that the only way?

     Peters: I don't know. I've come to respect the celi-
bate though in a way I never have. It (celibacy) doesn't have
to be a denial of life at all ... a celebration rather. Shoot-
ing sperm into an orifice isn't on its way whatsoever
towards eternity-orgasms. I guess what I'm hoping for is to
be less sexually driven than I've been; and I hope Mother
Ann will help me find a balance. That's the practical side
of my fascination with Mother Ann ... that's what I've just
tried to describe. So, alive in one's consciousness. I don't
see any of the vast expension of Shaker energies over the
last two hundred years as in any sense lost. It's around,
waiting to be tapped.

     Matthews: You wrote most of the Shaker poems when
you were sequestered, at the MacDowell Colony, and Yaddo,
right?

     Peters: Yes. And the sequestration was great! No
phones, visitors, interruptions! It's a great place (or both
places are, Yaddo and MacDowell) for allowing yourself to
be taken over by phantasms and spirits.

     Matthews: I was thinking earlier of readers who con-
sider persona poems to be insincere because they're not in
the poet's own voice. Whatever that is. I imagine one of
the pleasures of writing poems is ventriloquism. You've
written in a number of voices; what do you think?

     Peters: I've always thought that term persona was a

fashion-word cooked up by critics who wouldn't recognize a
real poem if it came up and bit them on the glans.   I don't
think we pretend in any superficial way when we slip into the
presences of other persons ... living or dead.   Do you?

Matthews: No.   I think the prejudice against persona
poems comes from a sentimental idea of "sincerity," and it
annoys me.   It must annoy you, too, since you've written so
many persona poems.

Peters: These persona are all facets of ourselves ...
if we are into them in any feeling way.   A good piece of
writing of this sort ... mask, persona or whatever, has to
be felt, if it is to be good.   I love writing in voices: yet
they are my voice.   A voice enables one to confront his own
problems, ones he might for various reasons have to keep
private.   When I pretend I am the young Harrow undergradu-
ate cutting his wrists over Byron I become that youth and
feel a fascinating physical love for Byron.   When I am his
wife I feel her feeling him.   When I'm Van Gogh I feel male
and sexual--towards Gauguin.   I like to take various roles
when I teach, too.   Keeps people awake.

Matthews: How much are you part of the "larger
world" when you write?   Everyone writes to please and in-
struct himself; but the "self" includes a vast and particular
experience of "the world."

Peters: I feel that I am always part of the "larger
world," and that all of my poetry is evidence of that.   I
love the paradox of needing to be sequestered in order to
demonstrate the ways you are of this larger world.   There
is, in my mind, no world smaller than the sense we carry
about with us as poets, of our connections with a total world
of energy, imagination, history, presences.   Your own work
is rich evidence of these connections.   I guess I'm really
saying that the microcosm always implies the macrocosm.
With The Gift to Be Simple I feel I'm into dimensions new to
me, with important ramifications.

Note: The Gift to Be Simple was published by Liveright,
Inc. in 1975.

MUD WOMEN, MUD MEN:

Peter Wild*

A couple of reviewers have assumed that Cochise is
either a brand of Indian blanket, or the name of an old Ari-
zonian sitting on his haunches beside the road smoking his
pipe, waiting for tourists to stop so he can tell interminable
stories--a sort of brown ancient mariner.   Actually, Cochise
is a county in Arizona, a name derived from the primitive
Americans whose earliest legacy of some flattened stones and
a complete absence of weapons showed them to be a pacific
folk.   In later ages, they apparently moved from being seed-
growing people to hunters.

Peter Wild's Cochise is a place in Arizona, but it is
also primarily a spirit caught by Wild as it drifts through his
imagination and latches in his pre-occupations, hurts and
joys.   There is little artifactual or anthropological about Co-
chise.

The poem "Cochise" illustrates what I mean.   First,
the poem is non-antiquarian.   Wild's ancient culture is
maimed, tortured, and diseased by contemporary white culture.
His Indians, Mexicans, Spanish-Americans, and Americans
(typified by himself and a few friends and acquaintances) are
all somewhat passive, full of experience, and immobilized in
the present except in their fantasies.   "Cochise" is vague; the
surrealism keeps the reader unsure of exactly where he is.
The speaker is visited by a woman, possibly a descendant of
the Cochise primitives: "a mud woman rearing from the land-
scape / dissolving in her own salt lake. "   The speaker doesn't
welcome her: "You are the last person in the world I want to
see today. "   But she makes herself comfortable in his leather
chair, and he puts his arm around her, lights her cigar, and

*Reprinted by permission from Margins, No. 14 (Oct. -Nov.
1974) pp. 57-58, 72; Copyright © 1974 by Margins.

fetches her some liquor and canapes from his refrigerator.
She is a vision-figure who touches the speaker's mist-seeing
of his own "troubles, with family, friends, and church. "
She tells him about her one-legged lover who has nothing but
love to give her, and she wants to know who the speaker
keeps sane. "Being experienced, " he says, "I know what to
say. " This seems to give her courage, and as he settles
back in his dentist's chair, and begins to dream, she is
erotically aroused:

> ... while your breasts slump beneath the sweater,
> the nipples looking around my room like baby birds
> expecting food. they start to eye me. they want
> to bite me on the face.

He escapes her lust via fantasy, and tracks Cochise "our
stronghold" stalking a lion, "taking strength from the beast. "
He becomes Cochise--the figure symbolic of the ancient tribe,
laboring up the mountain, his own hands "veins climbing over
the labyrinth. "   Cochise shows him how to "win. "   The track-
ing of the lion (an anachronism in the American Southwest)
becomes in a curious way the tracking of the woman who is
so far out on the mudflats she dissolves in her own salt lake.
Across the sky, a boy ("the person we fear most") drives a
flock of sheep: "they stumble, sparks fly from their hooves,
their curly heads. "   Stars "dive down" to eat the woman's
hair.   The speaker's lips are coated with "powdered gold. "
The boy, smiling, opens his magical pouch, takes the speak-
er's arm and they begin to dance, rejecting the woman.   But
the speaker has a pact with the woman--there have been
promises and an exchange, and he says that he does wait for
her.   Yet, dancing, he says: "We swear never to go back. "

The poem is even more cryptic at the end than at the
beginning.   Since it is the title poem, it deserves close read-
ing, and is, I think, the key poem for the entire volume, one
of the most closely-worked and unified books of verse I have
read for a long time--the whole reads like a single poem of
fascinating, rich parts.

Myth informs "Cochise" in almost every line: the odd
old cigar-smoking Indian/Mexican woman who seems to sym-
bolize the ancient past brought forward to the age of refrig-
erators and dental chairs.   She is also physical/earth/sex.
The speaker (I assume he's a persona for Wild) escapes,
fantasizing that he perform the Jessie-Westonesque act of
stalking the ancient primitive hero stalking the golden lion

stalking himself.   Lion in Arizona?   Wild fuses European
and American hunter-figures.

    Transformations of the literal into the interpretable
happen easily in Wild's poems; it is a simple matter, there-
fore, to see the Cochise figure of the lion-stalker trans-
formed into the Apollonian boy stalking his sheep across the
sky.   Also, the dance they perform is ritualized, ancient.
The decision never to return to the mudflats and the woman
(the past?) asserts the reality of the present--one can't go
back from it.   The woman must come from her place in
dream/reality to the speaker's house, leather chair, refrig-
erator.   The dilemma is obvious: the fantasy life when we
become most man/woman is never wholly real: our heroic
acts (stalking beasts, enjoying primal sex, inhabiting the
skies) happen only in the mind:

        you scream as the stars dive down
        to eat your hair, powdered gold coats my lips.
        and he smiling opens his pouch,
        takes my arm.   we begin to dance,
        and though I wait for you
        he knows about the promises, the exchange--
        we swear never to go back.

The facts of the poem are equally real for the modern brown
man with Cochise blood in his veins and the modern white
man who, like Wild, compassionately shares the Indian/Mexi-
can/Spanish experience.   Few writers have ever conveyed
such empathy so convincingly.

    "Sins of the Tongue" is another fine poem.   It's
framework is mythic and reveals Wild's skill in maintaining
the tensions and originality demanded by the opening lines.
Too many poets writing in the surrealist mode settle for a
clever opening and ride out the rest of the poems irrelevant-
ly.   In this volume Wild doesn't falter.

    "Sins of the Tongue" begins: "The tongue is bit be-
tween the teeth."   Assertive, poignant.   The whole body fol-
lows the tongue, and is, in a sense, its straining, guided
horse.   When the tongue speaks the mist shoots droplets,
rainbows, clouds.   A burning pillar (the ubiquitous myth-
touch) beckons you to keep talking and moving.   The pillar
itself is transformed, "a phantasmagoria with legs and fin-
gers" looming before your face.   Like the tongue, the skies
sprinkle rain.   You may choose though to keep the tongue's

rain within your mouth, the tongue folded within, "a snake
swirling in a barrel, / a snake finding a place among leaves. "
Then Wild brings off a characteristic feat--he introduces an
image (of a bulldozer) so extravagant it should not work.
But it does.   The tongue trying to speak, locked inside the
mouth, its jaws "curled around it, " is a bulldozer with its
"rudder" jammed.   During the daylight, trying to extricate
itself, the bulldozer/tongue overheats; at night, quiet, it en-
joys auroras of calm.   The strain and tension contrasting
with the peace of night cause the tongue to grow brittle

> until it shoots from the head
>   all muscle,
> until like the swelling Phoenix
> you stand skin clothed in flame and words,
> eyes empty.

This ending is swift and kaleidoscopic.   The pain and striv-
ing of the tongue locked inside the mouth explode with an al-
most orgasmic force.   Like the Phoenix reincarnated from
its own ashes, the man/tongue stands clothed heroically in
flame and words.   His eyes are "empty, " i. e. , he has be-
come his own vision and, hence, has no need for vision.   I
find this resolution a rare and inventive symbolizing of sex-
ual/religious ecstasy.   The quest for the burning pillar, pres-
ent in men's physical minds from the beginning, leads to in-
tense physical clamor; one must rape his landscape (bulldoze
it, even if the rudder is jammed) in order to achieve ecstasy/
vision.

      "Pulling Weeds" is also about moving through pain to-
wards vision.   The first stanza is incredibly original in its
cryptic motions: for example, the speaker need not actually
be the man killing snakes and pigs; yet he may be.   The
juxtaposition of the first two lines juxtaposes the events of
the lines:

> My hands grow stiff from the slaughter
> a man killing snakes and pigs.
> in knee-pants I wade through the yellow flood
>   filling the yard, not clinging
> but like ink slipping,
>   angel faces, bodies twisting

The leap back to childhood (knee-pants) intimates that Wild
has shared the guilt of slaughter all his life: that the fact
of his birth, almost, is an immersion in death, "the yellow

flood / filling the year." And in this flood he slips and en-
visions benign angel faces and tragic bodies twisting. A literal
image of sunflowers skillfully concretizes the poem before flash-
ing out surrealistically--the sunflower heads are human heads,
and have shared human misery and blood; the clouds nightmar-
ishly "tainted" float in and lick and feed:

> already sunflowers shut their eyes,
>   freeze against the gore on their cheeks,
> and the clouds float in through the trees.
>   tainted, to lick and feed.

Kites fly (note: Wild is a superb kite-maker, a purist in
the art who begins with the cutting of reeds for the frames).
They are "venomous girls undressing to paper." The sexual
fantasy becomes his own pain/guilt experience, forcing him
to go into his house, into its "bowels" where he waits as the

> sweat dries tattoos
> of my cooling sins over me.

This line: "my hand falls through the puddle of my chest"
is the only one that fails me in the poem--it seems unfelt;
too self-consciously Magrittesque. A minor complaint, for
the poem concludes with a splendid mythic image of three
kings who initially suggest Christianity, but because of their
bark teeth are Indian/primitive. They are benign, though,
and the result is a sense of quiet ecstasy worked through by
the speaker in his struggle with lust:

> three tall kings walk through the street,
>   rolled snow and weeds,
>   bowing, waving their arms slowly,
>   humming through their bark teeth.

Since the theme of suppressed or re-directed lust as a means
to vision is common in Cochise, I read it as Wild's acknowl-
edgement of the heavy Roman Catholic imposition of sexual
guilt over the once-primitive Indians, Mexicans, and Spanish-
Americans, a guilt shared by whites as well, especially those
living near or involved closely with those multi-cultures, as
Wild is. Of course, Wild writes other sorts of poems that
are non-ethnic, non-mythic, in the way these poems are. His
talent is diverse, and almost always he's able to invest his
work with feeling and depth.

His poems here have the flavor of the story-teller re-
citing parables. Wild holds up his sometimes horrible ex-

amples as a means of jolting us into changing our lives.
Even his humorous, entertaining poems have some of this
reforming intention.   He does it all without being didactic:
The morals are not too stringently drawn.   Behind his
surrealist method is a strong narrative sense, located most
often in a natural primitive world of elemental forces, birds,
and animals: geese, dogs, mountains, oaks, knives, eagles,
sandstone cliffs, lightning, thorn bush, wolves, moving clouds,
deer, spiders, and butterflies.

        In "The Candidate" the narrative sense is strong, al-
though the story itself is entirely unconventional.   An aging
man who "spits out a few / rotten teeth with the toothpaste /
and a little green blood" each morning, who defecates "gold
doubloons" (he's hung up on money), and with a crust of
toast in his mouth "begins running through the day / in his
rubber suit," passes through landscapes, pursued by brown
smoke and shadows, witnesses death as corpses and sex as
girls lunging from bushes, becomes a destruction-death fig-
ure who feasts on leather and tendons, locks himself in his
home, goes to bed, unaware that the "wolf-eared moon"--a
superb image--will eventually get him.   The man is primi-
tive, modern.   His rat-race is thoroughly contemporary; his
rubber suit is metaphorically a business suit which conven-
tion dictates he wear as Rubber Man.   He's obsessed with
money and haste.   Sexual harassment dominates him, as
death of spirit and of body wait everywhere to ambuscade
him.

        The prevalence of anapests and heavy spondees in
Wild's poems have the effect of making the poems sound like
translations; they seem delivered by Indians who know Eng-
lish well but keep a flavor of their aborigine tongue.   Wild's
use of simple active verbs also conveys this sense; his verbs
seldom perform their expected actions though; and in their
turning toward the unexpected and the surreal, Wild emerges
as a master of sophisticated style.   His use of stark color
also suggests the primitive: "blood drips from the faucet,"
"cats stick like nuggets of gold / in the trees," "the flowers
/ hold out their white and gold funnels."   The final poem
concludes this way:

                    the heat is pouring up from the
                        hard calcareous ground;
                    the clouds float like heavy ink spots
                        above the piny Catalinas.

Wild's poems make attempts by other white poets to rub against American Indian, Mexican, or Spanish-American culture seem superficial. Wild's voice is authentic, unforced, in a way that tripping followers of Castenada and his Don Juan are not. Castenada advises that you find yourself a place on top of a nearby mountain, strip, cover yourself with brush and lie there for 24 hours while the spirit of the place does you to a fine turn. Obviously, any such radical exposure to vegetation and the elements would induce exceptional feelings, of a solipsistic sort--no matter how tied in they are with a universal consciousness, time-spirit, or Yaqui-godwisdom. Wild's vision non-solipsistically encompasses various cultures.

Here is how he treats a sense of place. In "The Abstractionist," a painter, growing fat, sets up his one great exhibition and watches the cultured folk flock to view it. He is amused; and he maintains his own identity, projecting it against a vision of landscape, humanscape, paintscape. His (and Wild's) vision is, as I read it, entirely broad, human, engaging, free. The self is in its place (Castenada's Sitio). The place is in the self. The self is in the whirling peace of a vast human engagement. This is the issue, it seems to me, of Wild's Cochise.

THE GREAT AMERICAN POETRY BAKE-OFF

or, Why W. S. Merwin Wins All Those Prizes*

It's always easy to deal with persons who aren't offensive in any way; and if those persons are poets who write unerringly and weave a superb style around clichés that don't sound stale, you have a poet it is easy to honor. In fact, judges nearly tumble over themselves to decorate poets of this kind. What one might call the boy-explorer ethic prevails: poets clean in heart, clean in hand, clean in mind, clean in the hearts of their countrymen....

I have been an avid follower of W. S. Merwin's writing for years, and he has foraged me with splendid work when I desperately needed foraging. His translations are consistently first-rate; and his several volumes of original work contain a number of both large and small masterpieces. Only now, however, after intensive readings of Writings to an Unfinished Accompaniment, do I understand what have apparently come to be his formulae for success. He seems increasingly to be settling for less than his best; and my essay is meant to be constructive--a warning as well as a description of some of the facile and suspect devices in the work of this considerable poet.

I had--and quite rightly--responded to the intense purity of Merwin's diction; everything is clean, no obscenities, no words from science or technology, no words smeared or bleared with trade or toil. His language is basically conceptual. A Puvis de Chavannes world we might say, as distinct from a Van Gogh. Also, his music lulls me into believing that such exquisitely-manipulated sounds have depth. In a real sense, Merwin is a modern free-verse Swinburne--his

*Reprinted by permission from Northeast Rising Sun, No. 8 & 9 (1977) pp. 3-6; 11; Copyright © 1977 by Cherry Valley Editions.

techniques are so fluent and polished you forget what he is
saying, marvelling at the technical brilliance.   And the tone
is always somewhat formal, grave (in a French sense), sel-
dom humorous, never offensive.   But when you take a good
close look at this new work behind its flawless surface, and
divorce his ideas from his craft, you find a series of pos-
tures.   This essay I shall devote to describing what I feel
are some of Merwin's recipes for whipping up prize-winning
delectables for the great American bake-off.

The Merwinesque landscape: comparisons with paintings don't
help, since there is almost no color in these poems; and
when you look closely there are hardly any details, except
for vaguely present bandages, clouds, asters, worn-brick
surfaces, a paw print, smoke, gold, a doorstep, a crack in
a wall, etc.   If paintings don't work, perhaps parallels to
drawings or etchings will.   But here too the scenes they en-
shroud (Merwin's dominant tone is empty, stoned, elegiac)
are so uncluttered they would hardly keep our attention long.
Here is how one such drawing might look: a flat foreground
landscape with a hint of a mountain in the background.   Near
the mountain(s) a light, possibly from a lantern, shedding
some beams of a sufficient thrust to suggest divinity, or the
light up the road, etc.   In the foreground a nice big stone
with the initials W. S. M., or your initials, on it, and pos-
sibly a quick scribble of a wolf chasing some pale sheep, or
a flea carrying a basket of little diseases.   To paraphrase
Richard Howard's illuminating back-cover blurb, Merwin's
landscapes are not, therefore they are; and since they are
not we may justifiably call them visionary.   They have, says
Howard, "a quality of life ... which must be characterized
by its negatives, by," he helpfully explains, "what it is not,
for what it is not cannot be spoken."

Merwin's landscapes, to me, reflect his versions of
what the French poets he translates and reads are like.   I
find it helpful to call them Beckettian, a Samuel Beckett land-
scape reduced to even fewer essentials than Beckett's have, a
space with vague bits of this and that appearing here and
there.   Here the doomed of the earth, or the gently betrayed,
wander searching for the light which must be there and must
be meant for them, or for the voice they feel calls them with
news of chance/fate loose against them.   There are, as I
said earlier, no dramatics in Merwin's land of the lost.

Merwin's images: At least 15 poems have mountains; almost

as many have clouds, lights, doors and windows (both shut
and open).   There are quite a few clouds, almost no rain,
dogs (they seem to be his favorite animal), sounds we can't
quite decipher, numerous stones going like flames, meant to
speak in some mysterious, mystical way to us.   I'm
not against a poet's objects: I merely try to indicate by
means of a list what Merwin's are like.   None is clearly
seen.   He gives us cloud, say, and leaves it up to us to de-
termine its special nature--cumulus, sagging-with-rain, cir-
rus, etc.   An important facet of poetry is the image-making
process.   An image suggests something concrete, a thing
seen: and the conditioning of most readers, for better or
worse, is that an image translates itself into an object al-
most as soon as we come upon it in a poem.   Obviously an
image carries one or more concepts with it, just as an egg
in a basket represents more than breakfast.   Merwin's image
leaves the visual possibilities almost entirely open.

Merwin's counting: He loves to count, as a means, I sup-
pose, of giving the illusion of concreteness.   Counting re-
quires little of the senses.   Also, counting has something
Orphic about it, cabbalistic: there's magic in numbers, etc.
And you needn't ever find a person behind the numbers.
Desolate.   For whatever reasons, Merwin loves numbers:
1 window, 17 men with shovels, 70 tongues, 1 star, 10
changes. 1 cloud, thousands of languages, 1 or 2 eyes, most
of my tongues, 1 leaf, etc.   At one point in Writings Merwin
apparently sensed the pointlessness of counting, especially if
your landscape is devoid of meaning.   "Exercise" is an ad-
monition for us to stop counting, as a means of forgetting
other things like fire, earth, and water that are apt to be dis-
turbing and even, if one is enervated enough, tormenting.

     A "list" passage suggests a talismanic medieval super-
stition riddle telling you how to get rid of warts, acquire a
healthy mind, or minimize the pains of childbirth.

Merwin's metaphysical paranoia: If we don't forget fire, that
means we can continue to experience pain, doesn't it?
Through pain (the immersion of our parts in fire) we possibly
purify ourselves, poor suffering bastards that we are, for-
gotten and despised by the gods.   The universal whine is
born of an injured sense of betrayal by forces larger than
ourselves, viz., the gods.   The whine is as old as Merwin's
hills, Noahesque.   I had assumed that the hydrogen bombs

had blown it forever out of existence.   Its pallid cry sounds
anachronistic.

"Habits" is the most explicitly hunted/haunted of these
poems.   They (are they gods? other people? demons?) keep
handing him around: they cling to his memory, they use his
eyes for their own sockets, they borrow his tongues so they
can tell him back that they are he, they loan him his ears
so that he can hear them.

I feel comfortable with this, and admire its suggestions
of the mythic and the antique: Oedipus losing his eyes, the
slaughters in Titus Andronicus, Billy the Kid going down on
Jean Harlow ... it's comforting to see the self pursued by
the Eumenides.   A sow loves her mud.   And the gods have
always had it in for us.   Hubris.   And, since Merwin's
theme does date from Orestes and Job (and who knows how
far earlier still) Merwin is profound: his hamstrings have
those unarguable ancient latching points.   Merwin becomes
then a quasi-religious poet, a sort of lemonade mystic (a
little sweet, a little sour, milky-hued on the gray side).
And it's neat to talk about his ideas.   It makes him eminent-
ly teachable and reviewable.

So was Wallace Stevens religious, mystical, concep-
tual.   But when Stevens borrowed a Platonic or a Shake-
spearean concept he invested it with verve and twisted it
around in his splendid head so that the thought came out pro-
foundly his.   Rarely does Merwin bring his conceptions off
that way.   My feeling is that he has chosen not to.   I will be
accused, possibly of saying that Merwin should be Stevens;
my comparison is speculative--and I have heard Merwin dis-
cussed as an important religious poet, quite aside from the
remarks by Richard Howard on the back cover.   If Merwin
is a religious poet, I expect him to be a good one; or, rath-
er, a superior one--not simply a good one.   When he chooses
the oracular role I want him to be as good as Moses, and I
don't mean Moses wearing bluejeans, expensive western boots,
and a frilly-lace shirt open at the throat, titillating girls at
fancy colleges.   I mean a Moses/Vates (as Carlyle called the
poet), one wearing a flannel nightgown, a truth-serum mystic
who can change lives forever.

One more example: "Words" is a poem so built
around the easy cliché.   It might better have been left out
of the book.   Technically, the poem is flawless.   But a poet
of Merwin's stature is capable of better.   To flex one's

stylistic muscles is fine, but the result should be seen as an
exercise and should either be kept for selling to the archives
at Buffalo or Texas, or consigned to the flames.   When the
world's pain speaks, the words seem to express joy.   Often
we are taken in and learn them by heart.   Just as often we
turn from these deceiving words "with hands of water."

Merwin's never-fail ingredient image: If the poets of this
country were to get together and have a bake-off, and a prize
were given to the author with the most dependable, never-
fail images and metaphors, I'm sure Merwin would receive
the sequined apron.   Here is what I mean.   His "Bread" is
a concoction of never-fail ingredients, his product a perfect
loaf for readers who think poems should be worked some be-
fore they're properly digested, but not worked too hard; the
crust, in other words should look hard, but once bitten should
yield easily.   Here are the ingredients:

> Each face in the street is a slice of bread
> wandering on
> searching.

This sounds clever and good.   Are these slices of bread look-
ing for a toaster? a butter-knife? some jam? an ocean to
jump into?   Are they craving to be Communion wafers?

Light is another never-fail image, a nice leavening for
any poem of mystical or religious purport.   True, light is
vague, because it may appear anywhere from the bowels of
the earth (as radium) to the sun.   This light is special,
since, Merwin says, it is "the true hunger" passing these
bread-folk by.   "They clutch"--what, we don't know--possibly
their own soft middles, or each other's soft middles.   An-
other never-fail image: caves.   Thanks, Plato.   A poet
won't go wrong, ever, with that archetype, and particularly
when he presents a choice of caves: first, the ones the
bread-people hide in, and second, the "pale" kind the bread-
people long for in their dreams.   Reality v. reality, folks.
Where is the scrim?   The home-cave is host to the foot-
prints left behind by the bread-people when they wander the
streets; the foot prints wait their return.   Also, these caves
are hung with "the hollow marks of their groping ... their
sleep ... and their hiding," an assortment of fish-nets and
Spanish moss.

At the end of the bread-people's street there is a

tunnel symbolizing "the heart of the bread"--it would seem
to be either pumpernickel or whole wheat since it is, Mer-
win suggests, "dark." The people quest for this bread-
heart; "step after step" they hear it ahead of them, as they
move through "ragged tunnels" coming at last "alone" (that
McKuenesque word!) facing a wheat field "raising its radiance
to the moon." So, the poem concludes on a nice up-beat.
Little old ladies from Woods Hole to Pasadena can be as-
sured that the verities of poetry are not dead. There is
hope, and that hope is W. S. Merwin.

Merwin's light at the end of the trail: We've just seen one
instance of this light, the illuminated wheat-field. Grail-
esque? The termination of struggle as peace/wisdom/light?
Again, the easy idea. And it appears frequently in Writings.

   "The Way Ahead" is a messianic-light poem. It be-
gins with paradox--a winter will come when small creatures
hibernate inside the bones of larger creatures, and "we will
be the largest of all / and the smallest." A Monday will
come when people will be shaken into spiritual awareness,
some broken, some stroked and blessed. An eye will come
revealing "what was never seen" and "beholding the end."
A voice charming nature will come. Toward this place
(wherever it is), feet--I assume they are ours--"are already
marching." Corn throw up their hands (why not their ears?)
weeds leap up from their ditches, eggs press on towards
"those ends" (omelettes?). "Those ends" are "terrible flow-
ers." These night-marish flowers--and Merwin is forceful
here--will usher in the apocalyptic "light ... to come."

   Technically, once again, "The Way Ahead" is brilliant.
The reading of its finely-wrought rhythms, their hesitancies,
advances, and withdrawals are superb, and lull one into sens-
ing greatness in the poem. The greatness is almost exclu-
sively in the technique and its power to arouse our emotion,
despite what is essentially a series of stale ideas. The Mer-
winesque recipe of parts (ingredients) leading towards a ce-
lestial dessert is tried and true. The Biblical tone, pro-
phetic, is masterfully handled. And the conclusion, spoiled
some by the funny image of eggs pressing on, is more vivid
than anything else in the poem.

Merwin's sound at the end of the trail: Sound, like light,
works mystically. Someone, something, calls us, weaving

its voice dimly through our wretched universe. If we could
only catch its (his?) words we would be saved and find the
true meaning of life and death. Unheard melodies are sweet-
er than heard melodies. A universe held together by a uni-
versal celestial Shelleyan chansoning! Carrying the idea to
its ultimate, the best of all poets would be deaf. And why
have there been no deaf poets of the stature of the blind
notables Homer and Milton? Silence is golden, as the popu-
lar song says, and I won't deny Merwin his golden idea.

        "When the Horizon is Gone" is one of Merwin's best
poems, since it handles the frayed motif of existential man
dropped into total absurdity with enough originality to bring
it off. The idea is that when the horizon disappears (a truly
freaky idea) man will lie down receiving comfort from the
horizontal earth. There'll be nothing to see out there where
the mirages form. His blood, since his veins, too, are
horizontal, will sink. Alas, though, the blood finds "no cen-
ter to sink toward." I do have problems at this point making
a connection between the absence of an horizon and the ab-
sence of a center. I can't measure it out, or see why an
horizonless world wouldn't have a center. Actually, there's
something attractive in lost horizons.

        But man's traumas aren't over. Whatever his hands
hold is also vertical, and since the hands can't feel "it,"
they let "it" go. The eyes, too, ordinarily see vertically,
and still do, since they project upwards from the supine
skull. They don't recognize "it." Merwin implies they
should. "It" is the sound, I guess, of the universe, also
vertical ... and since two parallel vertical lines never
meet ... they are deaf to what happens to be calling. "The
Silence Before Harvest" and "Beyond You" treat the same
theme. "A Door" (the last of the four poems in sequence
with the same title) is the most explicit of these voice-hear-
ing poems, and is the most uplifting: we are told that there
is a possibility of our being at home in the universe, "The
endless home." I am almost reassured.

Merwin's Ezy-Myth Mix Method: At times Merwin's facility
for making a poem sounds like an overly literal translation
from the ancient Ainu or Greek or Cherokee doesn't work.
It's apt to be too self-conscious an act. When these poems
do succeed, though, they carry a strange, wondrous authority;
poet appears as shaman--myth-wisdom of the ages is his
mantle; his events (cowrie shells) he sets in the mythic past

where our origins are.   He tells us how the gods began,
when fire came into being, and religion.   Writer as <u>vates</u>, a dif-
ficult role for a mid-twentieth century American <u>poet</u> to as-
sume.

"Division" is a frustrating example of Merwin's Ezy-
Myth-Mix method.   At the outset the loquacious story-teller
tone puts me off:

> People are divided
> because the finger god
> named One
> so he made for himself a brother like him ...

First, this is rhythmic prose of no particular distinction set
out to look like poetry.   Second, to say "familiar ground" is
not enough.   All myths about gods must begin somewhere,
and if god is creator he must create his selves from him-
self.   No news here.   Perhaps it's too easy.   Yes, it is too
easy.   Think of God's surprise had that Otherself leaped out
of his belly, or his balls, without any need for His will at
all.   Load on surprise, W. S. !   God's first responses to
his partner-twin are jealousy, fear, threat.

But why is he a "finger god?"   Why not a toe god?
an ear god? a pancreas god?   What was One doing with that
finger?   Did it smell good?

The appeal is easy.   Poets are supposed to sound
like this !   We earn our keep by being myth people; and if we
can sound like rewriters of <u>Genesis</u>, embellishing here and
there, readers in the great <u>cupcake</u> audience are happy.   For
these poems comfort us in our accedia.   We feel that we
aren't so far after all from our primitive roots.

Merwin's god drops big god-tears on the sand.   A
twin is not enough.   His pair of selves is still lonely.   So
he creates two more look-alikes--twins.   Fearing they'll
lose each other, Merwin's twins create hands to hold them
fast, and arms to connect the hands.   Their hearts, though,
fail to merge them into a single identity, against possible
loneliness.   This conclusion is fine, and I am caught in its
poignancy.   Too bad the Chingachgook opening isn't more orig-
inal.   As the Shakers knew, there are gifts for being simple,
and Merwin maintains a Biblical simplicity of diction and
tone.   In turning with the poem I feel Merwin's winsomeness.
And I do prefer his over-simplifications and his attempts to

come off vatic to much of the clever, self-conscious, solip-
sistic nose-picking poetry around today.   My carping is be-
cause Merwin's achievement is important.   A final note here:
his device of starting numerous lines with and, an easy de-
vice, suggests a primitive narrative style.   You might see
the ands as raisins in the plum pudding.   Generally, Merwin
knows when to restrain the device.   Technically, even when
he masquerades prose as poetry, he is nearly always right.

Merwin's totemism: Obviously, totemism smacks of the
primitive,   and I don't put it down--when it works.   Why not
set up certain objects in your poems as totems carrying
glyphs of the spiritual?   To charge some earthly, mundane
object with religious (quasi or complete) significance is a
positive act, and is the opposite of whimpering.

        "The Unwritten" is Merwin's rendition of the common
pencil as totem.   Poet as schreiber/scribe is implicit.
Words not yet written "crouch" inside the pencil, weissnicht-
wo.   These words are awake, hiding, and won't appear be-
cause the pencil-wielder wants them to.   None of his evoca-
tive magic will bring them forth: "not for love not for time
not for fire."   Secretive always, even if they were to drop
we wouldn't be able to decipher their language.   We'd need
a gift of tongues.   How many words are locked within?   Per-
haps only one, that ONE!   the word poets and philosophers
have sought for centuries!   If we could know it.   The impli-
cation is that any writer may release The Word.   But, like
Goethe's Faust, the poet may be writing so hard the Word
may drop without his being aware, and it will be lost.   As
writers, though, we continue to worship the pencil, ascribing
wonders to it, and by extension, of course to our wonderful
poetselves.   Merwin brings the whole idea off nicely.

        He is less effective with the first of "The Door"
poems; he is forced and clever, especially towards the end
where his paranoid self takes over, and they come to get
you:

                they need your ears
                you can't hear them

                they need your eyes
                but you can't look up
                now

> they need your feet oh
> they need your feet
> to go on
> they send out their dark birds for you

The vagueness fails to reach me, despite the interjectory
movement of the lines.   There is a surface beauty, but when
I look closely, the poem evaporates.   Merwin once again has
used his skillful voice to empty empty feelings.   I do not
quarrel with his theme--if indeed this is his theme--that we
are so lost and wandering in our colorless, endless, vapid,
horizonless landscape that we sense but can't define our per-
secutors.   You open your mouth and manna falls into it.   A
beautiful stew of undecipherable ingredients, well-seasoned
but short of sustaining value.

  His persons sound like brothers to Samuel Beckett's
persons: Beckett's characters might easily speak Merwin's
poems.   They seem depersonalized in the way that Beckett's
lines are depersonalized and chromed.   There is also a
spaced--in the sense of dope-spaced or stunned--quality be-
hind many of these poems (and I'm not accusing Merwin of
being a head--you can be of the devil's party without knowing
it).   The sense of persons wandering after some remote voice
or light, some of them with bandaged physiogs ... they sound
like partially lobotomized, dispirited Dicks and Janes seeking
for SPOT (an anagram for GOD).   Appropriate here is Mer-
win's "Dogs."   Note the "Happiness is a warm puppy" echoes.
"Loneliness," Merwin writes,

> ... is someone else's dog
> that you're keeping
> then when the dog disappears
> and the dog's absence
> you are alone at last ...
> but at last it may be
> that you are your own dog
> hungry on the way
> the one sound climbing a mountain
> higher than time

  If we are "the one sound" climbing the mountain (are
we also the one hand clapping?), our lives are miniscule
semi-existentialist acts.   Our strain is not quite that of
Sisyphus'; although climbing a mountain, packless, bookless,
can be wearing.   The need for struggle of some kind is im-
plicit.   Shelley's idea of Beauty, in its origins and combina-

tions is similar. Shelley took the image of a forest lake:
bubbles begin at the bottom and work their effervescent way
almost soundlessly to the surface. These bubbles escape,
combine with other bubbles emanating from other lakes, and
from all living matter, to form finally the Symphony of Life-
sounds in the Universe. In their highest ascension these
sounds reach the One, the All. Well, this may not be
good science, but it did make for a considerable art. And
it still does: I can think of no better way to conclude this
essay than to quote from the final stanza of the final poem
in Merwin's book. "Gift" moves from pure Shelleyan state-
ment to a prayer uttered by the speaker (Merwin?) in his
separateness. The Shelleyan symbols (and even the Shelley-
an language) reveal Merwin's sources, and his place in a
long and easy tradition. Here are the examples culled from
"Gift": "shadowless mountain" is the Romantic mountain seen
as the Ideal in full light; night; silence is the alembic for
Romantic mystical awareness; the Eternal--the mountain is
"no child of time"; the morning--Romantic symbol of refresh-
ment. These, Merwin says, are the "gifts." And from
whom do we receive them? In answer, Merwin supplies this
closing, surprisingly pure Shelleyan prayer:

> I call to it Nameless One O Invisible
> Untouchable Free
> I am nameless I am divided
> I am invisible I am untouchable
> and empty
> nomad live with me
> be my eyes
> my tongue and my hands
> my sleep and my rising
> out of chaos
> come and be given

I call this "writing" rather than poetry, and I call it "never-
fail writing." It's easy in its borrowings, and its leavenings
(chaos, nomad). It's a Can't-Fail Concoction.

INDEX